*The First Book of*

*The First Book of*

Q&A ®

**Sandra Eddy**

SAMS

*A Division of Macmillan Computer Publishing*

*11711 North College, Carmel, Indiana 46032 USA*

*For my family—from
the Atlantic to the Pacific.*

FIRST EDITION
FIRST PRINTING—1991

International Standard Book Number: 0-672-27311-X
Library of Congress Catalog Card Number: 91-61350

Publishing Manager: *Marie Butler-Knight*
Managing Editor: *Marjorie Hopper*
Acquisitions Editor: *Mary-Terese Cagnina*
Manuscript Editor: *Albright Communications, Incorporated*
Technical Editor: *Herb Feltner*
Cover Design: *Held and Diedrich Design*
Illustrator: *Tami Hughes*
Production Assistance: *Claudia Bell, Sandy Grieshop, Denny Hager, Bob LaRoche, Kim Leslie, Howard Peirce, Tad Ringo, Bruce Steed, Johnna VanHoose, Lisa A. Wilson*
Indexer: *Jeanne Clark*

*Printed in the United States of America*

# Contents

**viii**

## 7   *Q&A Write: Fundamentals, 183*

## 8   *Q&A Write: Advanced Operations, 207*

**xi**

**xii**

# Introduction

This book is for anyone who wants to start working with Q&A as quickly as possible. If you don't have much experience with either databases or computers, don't worry. Every chapter in the book provides you with background information, basic concepts, and step-by-step procedures.

## What Is Q&A?

Q&A is a database management system that also includes

- ▶ word processing
- ▶ report production
- ▶ artificial intelligence

Q&A allows you to create, organize, and change a database and the information within it.

Q&A is menu-driven, which means that it displays a menu on your computer screen and you choose what you want to do next. You don't have to decide what commands to enter—each menu offers you a choice.

Q&A Write is a powerful word processor with a spellchecker and thesaurus. Q&A Intelligent Assistant (IA) allows you to use English to get information from your databases, and you can train it to add more words to its vocabulary.

With Q&A, you can import and export data from other programs such as Microsoft Word, WordPerfect, Lotus 1-2-3, dBASE, and many more. You can use Q&A's programming language to customize many of its features, including its easy-to-use help screens.

## Conventions Used in This Book

This book contains special features that make it easier for you to learn Q&A. Each feature has an icon to identify it.

 **Quick Steps** summarize the sequence of tasks needed to perform a common function.

**xiv**

> ▶ **Tips** are shortcuts. **Notes** provide information about a function.

>  **Cautions** alert you to pitfalls.

New terms are printed in *italics* the first time they appear in the book. Output from Q&A or the computer is in `computer type`. Material that you type or enter is in a `second color`

## Acknowledgments

I would like to acknowledge the support and encouragement of all those who helped me "build" this book. Thank you one and all:

▶ My new colleagues at SAMS—especially Mary-Terese Cagnina, Marie Butler-Knight, Marj Hopper, and Amy Perry.

▶ Nancy Albright, who smoothed out all the rough spots in the text.

▶ Tami Hughes, who performed miracles on every one of the screen images.

▶ Herb Feltner, who caught my technical errors.

▶ My family and friends, who stood by me every step of the way.

▶ Especially my brother Andy, who made it possible for me to make these dreams come true.

# Trademark Acknowledgments

All terms mentioned in this book that are known to be trademarks or service marks are listed below. In addition, terms suspected of being trademarks or service marks have been appropriately capitalized. SAMS cannot attest to the accuracy of this information. Use of a term in this book should not be regarded as affecting the validity of any trademark or service mark.

Q&A is a registered trademark of Symantec Corporation.

3Plus is a registered trademark of 3COM Corporation.

dBASE, dBASE II, dBASE III, dBASE IV, and MultiMate are trademarks of Ashton-Tate Corporation.

DCA is a registered trademark of Digital Communications Associates, Inc.

Epson is a registered trademark of Epson America, Inc.

Gupta SQLBase is a registered trademark of Gupta Technologies, Inc.

HP and LaserJet are trademarks of Hewlett-Packard Corporation.

IBM is a registered trademark and IBM PC XT, IBM PC AT, PS/2, SQL, PC DOS, IBM Filing Assistant, IBM PC Network, and IBM Token Ring Lan are trademarks of International Business Machines Corporation.

Intel, CCAM Software, and Connection CoProcessor are registered trademarks of Intel Corporation.

Lotus 1-2-3 and Symphony are registered trademarks of Lotus Development Corporation.

# Getting Started with Q&A

## In This Chapter

▶ *Learning about your computer and DOS*

▶ *Starting and exiting Q&A*

▶ *Moving around Q&A screens*

▶ *Getting help*

## How Does Your Computer Work?

Your computer takes information, processes it, and then displays, prints, or stores the results of processing. For example, as you install Q&A, the computer gets input, or information, from the program disks and also from the commands that you type on the keyboard.

The computer processes information by using programs, such as Q&A, and DOS, its operating system (either MS-DOS or PC DOS). DOS is the group of small programs that tells your computer how to perform basic functions, such as copying files, deleting files, formatting disks, checking your disks for errors, and displaying today's date or the current time. Table 1.1 summarizes some common DOS commands.

*Table 1.1   Common DOS Commands*

| Command | Function |
| --- | --- |
| CD | Displays the name of the current directory (CD) or changes to a new one (CD \[directory name]) |
| CHKDSK | Checks for hard disk (CHKDSK) or floppy disk (CHKDSK A: or CHKDSK B:) errors |
| COPY | Copies a file within a directory, or from one, resulting in two copies of the same file with two different file names |
| DATE | Displays today's date |
| DEL | Deletes a file |
| DIR | Lists the contents of the current directory |
| FORMAT | Formats blank disks |
| MD or MKDIR | Makes a directory |
| PATH | Tells you what directories are linked together by your computer system (see your DOS reference guide for information about AUTOEXEC.BAT which determines the directories in your path) |
| RD or RMDIR | Removes a directory |
| TIME | Displays the current time |

To copy a file within a directory, type

```
COPY oldname.extnewname.ext
```

where oldname is the file that you want to copy, newname is the new file, and ext is the extension.

To copy a file from one directory to another, type

```
COPY \dir\oldname.ext \new\newname.ext
```

where dir is the old directory and new is the new directory.

> ⊘ **Caution:** Do not type the command FORMAT without adding a disk drive identifier to it. Type FORMAT A: to format the diskette that is in disk drive A:.

You will see more information about these and other DOS commands throughout this book. Refer to your DOS reference guide for information about DOS commands.

Your computer holds information in *files*, which are groups of related records—all of the data in a *database* or all of the statements in a computer program, for instance.

A database is a collection of information, such as your personal address book, a club membership list, or a company client list. You can compare a database to a folder in a file drawer. You learn how to plan and design a database in Chapter 2.

Each file has a *file name* and an *extension*. A file name identifies a file in a unique way. Give your files names that make it easy to remember the type of information that the files contain. For example, if the name of an inventory file is INVENT01, you won't have a problem remembering the type of file it is. A file extension, which is three characters long, is the file type. Some typical file extensions are .DOC, which represents a text (or document) file, .EXE, which is an executable (or program) file, and .DAT, which is a data file. Q&A has its own file extension types: .DTF, which is a database data file, and .IDX, which indicates an index file.

Files are stored in *directories* and *subdirectories*. Compare your computer's directory system to a tree. When you turn on your computer and your hard drive is the active drive, you always start in the *root directory*, the "trunk" from which all directories are formed.

When you install Q&A, the installation program creates a directory, which is a major branch off the root directory. This directory is only one of several branches, depending on the number of programs that are installed on your computer. At first, the Q&A directory holds just program files. You will probably create many databases and other Q&A-related files; as these files accumulate, consider creating subdirectories, which are smaller branches.

**3**

# A Quick Tour of Q&A

Q&A is made up of several separate modules:

- ▶ The File Module
- ▶ The Report Module
- ▶ The Write Module
- ▶ The Assistant Module
- ▶ The Utilities Module

## *The Q&A File Module*

4

The File module, which is a database management program, is the central part of Q&A. Use the File module to design and redesign databases, which hold information that File and the other modules use to produce reports, letters, mail labels, and other information.

You can redesign any type of database, even if you've been using it a long time and it contains many records. You can retrieve the forms that you want to see, and then sort, edit, update, or even delete the forms.

You can state whether a database field is a particular information type: text, numbers, money, hours, date, keyword, or Yes/No. You also can restrict and tailor the data that is entered in a form.

## *The Q&A Report Module*

The Report module has two built-in report formats: *columnar* and *cross tabs*. Columnar reports display your data in columns, used to calculate and summarize information. Cross tab reports summarize information from three database fields using rows and columns like a spreadsheet.

You can either design your own report format or use Q&A formats. You can use the Write module to add "fancy" formatting.

## The Q&A Write Module

The Write module is a full-featured word processing program that you can use not only to print Q&A database information and reports, but can also use to write documents that are not associated with any Q&A function.

Write has advanced search and replace, multiple columns, and headers and footers. You can also check your spelling or choice of words by using Write's spellcheck and thesaurus programs, and can use Write to import and export files from other programs, such as word processors and spreadsheets.

## The Q&A Assistant Module

Q&A provides the Query Guide and the Intelligent Assistant to ask a database questions that help you create reports, search and sort data, and even fill in forms.

The Query Guide is easy for a beginner to use. With it, you can build questions from text fragments that are displayed on the screen.

Instead of using Q&A menus, you can get information by asking the Intelligent Assistant (IA). IA is a natural language program; it answers questions that are either built in or that you have taught it to understand.

## The Q&A Utilities Module

Use the Utilities module to customize Q&A so that it works the way you want it to. For example, you can define up to five printers and change Q&A fonts so that you get the most out of your printer. You can also use some DOS functions without leaving Q&A, and you can start other programs or Q&A macros from the Q&A Main menu.

# Starting Q&A

When you start your computer, you may have to switch on one or two other computer *peripherals* (such as a printer and a surge protector). The small, blinking line or square (depending on whether you have a color, monochrome, or LCD monitor) next to the DOS prompt is the *cursor*. The cursor shows you the place on the screen where the next action will occur. A large cursor, which emphasizes a program option, is known as a *highlight*.

 **Starting Q&A**

1. Start your computer by turning on one or more switches.

   Wait until you see the DOS prompt (usually C:\) on the screen. This means that the starting routines have completed and the hard drive (in this case, C:) is active.

2. Change to the directory on which you installed Q&A. For example, if your Q&A directory is \QA, type CD\QA. Then press Enter.

   Your computer is now in the Q&A directory.

3. Type QA and press Enter.

   You will see the Q&A logo and a flashing message, Loading (Figure 1.1). After a short time, the Main menu appears (Figure 1.2).

4. Select one of the Q&A modules or choose an option by pressing one of the function keys displayed along the bottom of the screen.

   Q&A responds with the module or option you requested.

6

▶ **Note:** Depending on your computer's operating system, your prompt may look different than C:\. If you are running DOS 4.0 or 4.01 in DOS shell, you get to the DOS prompt by using a menu option. Press the Up or Down key until `Command Prompt` is highlighted; then press Enter. You'll see the DOS prompt.

▶ **Tip:** If your computer is equipped with Windows, move the cursor to the DOS Prompt icon on the Program Manager Main Group; then press the left mouse button twice. The standard DOS prompt will appear on the next screen.

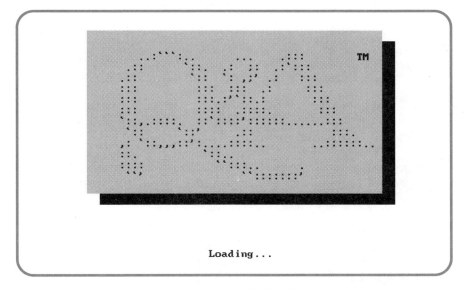

*Figure 1.1    The Q&A logo and the loading message*

## Customizing Q&A Startup

When you attempt to start Q&A the first time, there is a chance that the program won't start the way it has been explained here. For example, a message is "frozen" on your screen, or the screen image does not look the way you expect.

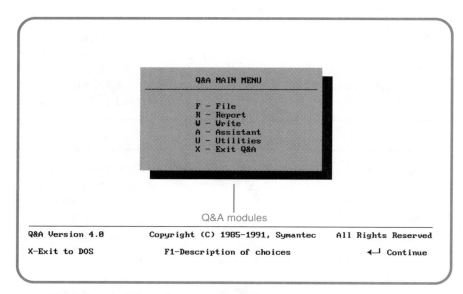

Q&A modules

**Figure 1.2    *From the Q&A Main menu, you can select any of the Q&A modules***

8

If you have one of these problems, you may have to modify your monitor setting one time only. Table 1.2 is arranged in order of the most common problem to the least likely problem. If you have to use one of these command combinations to start Q&A the first time, remember to type every character in the command, including hyphens (-) and spaces. After you enter the customized command, press Enter.

> ▶ **Tip:** If your screen image is too bright, adjust your monitor's brightness before you try any of the custom settings listed in Table 1.2.

From now on, you can start Q&A by typing QA and then pressing Enter.

> ▶ **Note:** If you install Q&A on another computer or have to reinstall Q&A on this computer, you may have to customize Q&A again.

*Table 1.2   Customizing Q&A Startup*

| Monitor | What To Type |
|---------|--------------|
| Color monitor | QA -SCC |
| Monochrome monitor | QA -SMC -A or QA -SMM |
| NEC Multispeed | QA -ST |
| IBM PS/2 with a monochrome monitor | QA -SMC -A |
| Toshiba 1100, 3100 | QA -SMC |
| Zenith laptops | QA -A |
| Compaq with a color monitor | QA -SCC |
| AT&T 6300 with a monochrome monitor | QA -SMC |
| Any computer with an LCD display | QA -A or QA -ST |

## Opening a File

9

After you have created Q&A databases, you can start the program and open a file at the same time.

### Starting Q&A and Opening a File at the Same Time

1. Change to the directory on which you installed Q&A. For example, type CD \QA. Then press Enter.

   Your computer is now in the Q&A directory.

2. Type QA filename and press Enter (where file-name is the name of the data file that you want to open).

   You will see the Q&A logo along with a flashing message, Loading. After a short time, the file on which you want to work appears.    □

# Navigating the Q&A Screens

Q&A is a menu-driven program. You use cursor movement keys or a mouse to move from option to option on a menu or to move from menu to menu—from one part of the program to another.

Because there are more Q&A functions than there are single keys on the keyboard, some functions are performed by *key combinations*, pressing two keys simultaneously. In this book, if you see the name of a key, a hyphen (-), and then the name of a second key, you are looking at a key combination. For example, if you see Ctrl-Left, you'll know that you first press and hold down the Ctrl key, and then press the Left key.

Table 1.3 lists the most commonly used cursor movement keys and key combinations.

*Table 1.3   Cursor Movement Keys*

| Key/Key Combination | Function |
| --- | --- |
| Left | Moves cursor to the next character to the left |
| Right | Moves cursor to the next character to the right |
| Ctrl-Left | Moves cursor to the next word to the left |
| Ctrl-Right | Moves cursor to the next word to the right |
| Up | Moves cursor up one line |
| Down | Moves cursor down one line |
| PgUp | Moves cursor to the first character on the prior screen or page |
| PgDn | Moves cursor to the first character on the next screen or page |
| Tab | Moves cursor to the next tab stop (to the right) or the next field |
| Shift-Tab | Moves cursor to the prior tab stop (to the left) or the prior field |
| Home | Moves cursor to the first character in this line or field |
| End | Moves cursor to the last character in this line or field |

> ▶ **Tip:** You can press the Home and End keys as many as four times to move the cursor four different ways, depending on where you are in Q&A: form design, data entry, or the Write module. You will find descriptions of the Home and End key combinations in Chapters 2 through 4 and 7 through 9.

For a complete list of Q&A keys and key combinations, see the inside back cover of this book.

To travel around Q&A, choose the module you want by moving the highlight over it or by typing its first letter; then press Enter. In Q&A, pressing Enter indicates that you have completed a function and want to start the next function. After you press Enter, you'll see a different menu.

> ▶**Tip:**  You don't have to press Enter after making a selection. For instructions on choosing options without pressing Enter, see "Set Global Options" in Chapter 11.

If you choose F or File, the next menu displayed after the Main menu is the File menu (Figure 1.3). Each Q&A menu is designed to offer you help and information. For example, there are several functions to choose on the File menu. Notice that at the bottom of each Q&A screen is a display of commonly used keys for this screen.

**11**

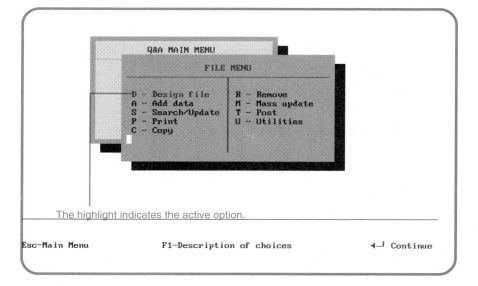

*Figure 1.3    The File menu is displayed in front of the Main menu so that you can see how you got to the current menu and how many layers back the Main menu is*

Notice that Design File is highlighted on the File menu, which means that if you press Enter, the next action is related to designing or redesigning a file (Figure 1.4).

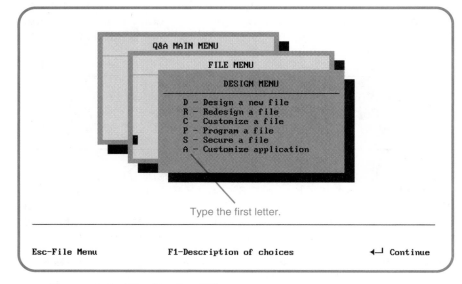

*Figure 1.4    The Design File menu*

Any time you want to go back to the Main menu, press Esc, which displays the previous screen. Keep pressing Esc to get back to the Main menu.

Q&A automatically recognizes whether you have a Microsoft (or compatible) mouse attached to your computer. You can use the mouse, along with—or instead of—pressing Left, Right, Up, or Down keys, to move around Q&A screens. You can also use the mouse to choose a function; this is the same as pressing F10 or Enter.

To use the mouse, the wire running between it and the computer should be at the far end of the mouse—pointing away from you. Place your hand lightly on top of the mouse. The mouse button that you push most often is the left one, so position a finger so that you can press, or *click*, that button when needed. Push the mouse around your desktop. Notice that for every movement of the mouse, there is a corresponding movement of the cursor on the screen. This takes a little getting used to, but after a short time, you'll find the mouse easy to use.

To use the mouse to choose a function or an item at the bottom of the screen, move the cursor over the function, and then quickly click the left mouse button. Sometimes you can perform two actions at once with a mouse by *double-clicking,* or quickly pressing and releasing the mouse button two times. If you seem to be "stuck" on a function, you can escape it by clicking outside the menu box.

> **Tip:** Q&A was designed for keyboard use. Although it recognizes the mouse, Q&A is easier to use with the keyboard.

Starting on the Main menu, highlight any letter on Assistant and click the mouse button to display the Assistant screen (Figure 1.5). Move the cursor over the word Continue at the bottom of the screen and click. See Figure 1.6 for a look at the What I Am screen. Click on PgDn - More to move through the screens as far as you want. Then click on Esc to travel back to the Assistant screen.

**13**

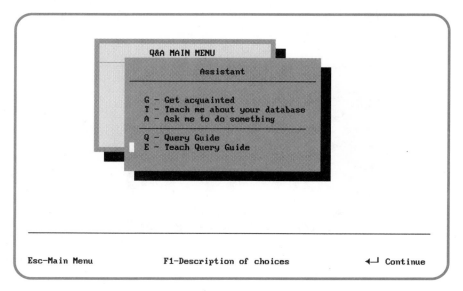

*Figure 1.5   On the Assistant screen, you can get information from a database*

If you don't remember the name of a file, Q&A helps you. Either press the Esc key or click on Esc to get back to the Main menu. Select File and from the File menu, select Add Data (Figure 1.7).

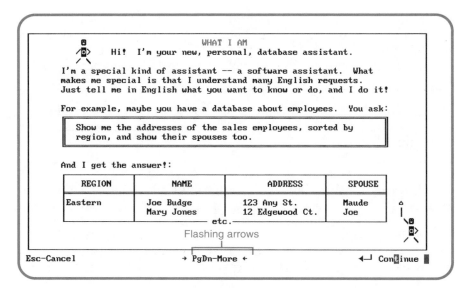

**Figure 1.6    The Assistant's What I Am screen displays flashing arrows that emphasize the PgDn choice**

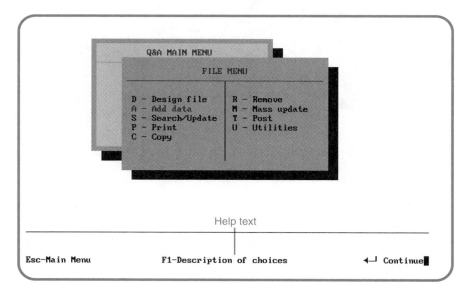

**Figure 1.7    Use the Add Data screen to add information to a database**

## **Q**Finding a File when You Can't Remember Its Name

1.  When Q&A asks you for a file name, press Enter.

    If you have worked on a file during this Q&A session, its name, its directory or subdirectory name, and the path name are displayed in a dialog box. If you have not worked on a file, the space for a file name is empty (Figure 1.8).

2.  If there is a name in the dialog box and it is the file that you want, select it by pressing Enter. If this is not the file you want, press Spacebar to remove the name.

    Q&A removes the file name from the prompt box, but keeps the directory and path names.

3.  If there is no name in the dialog box, press Enter to display a list of files in the current directory or subdirectory.

    Q&A displays the list of files.

4.  If you see the name of the file you want on the list, select it by moving the highlight to the name and pressing Enter or F10. You might also see a combined list of files and subdirectories. Select a subdirectory by moving the highlight to the name and pressing Enter or F10.

    Q&A displays the file or subdirectory you selected. (See Figure 1.9 for a short list with a subdirectory name \TUT.)

5.  Select the subdirectory by moving the highlight over it; then press Enter or F10.

    Q&A displays a new list of files from which you can choose. As you highlight a file name on the list, Q&A displays its file name, size, and date and time edited. Some files have a one-line description as well (Figure 1.10).

**15**

6. Move the selection bar to the file name that you want and press Enter or F10. If you are still searching for the missing file, you can blank out an entire path (all directories and subdirectories displayed in the dialog box) by pressing Shift-F4. Then type a new directory and/or subdirectory combination and press Enter or F10.

Q&A displays the file you selected.

□

**16**

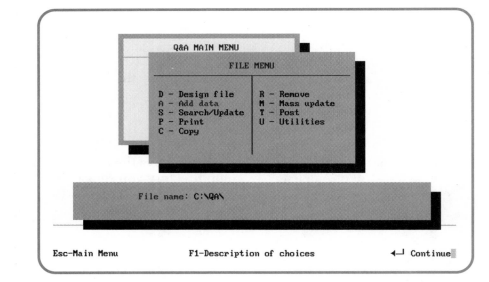

*Figure 1.8   The Add Data screen with an added dialog box in which you can type a file name*

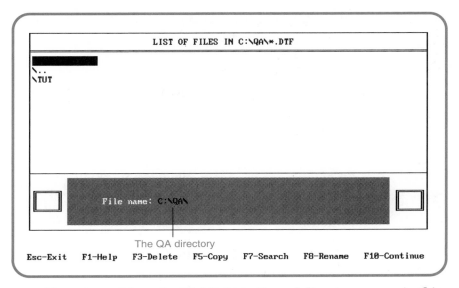

*Figure 1.9   Move the highlight to the subdirectory name in this
list and press Enter to display a list of files in that subdirectory*

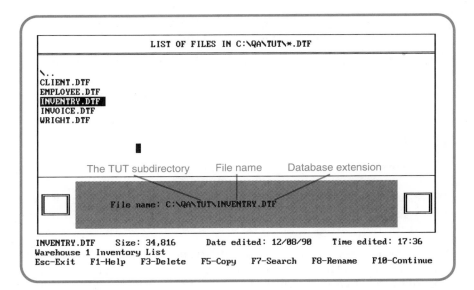

*Figure 1.10   Each file on this list is identified by file name, size,
and date and time edited*

You can add a description to a Q&A file by following these steps:

## *Q* Adding a Description to a Q&A file

1. Select a function from the File menu. When the dialog box is displayed, press Enter.

   Q&A displays a list of files.

2. Select a file name from a list by moving the highlight over the name of the file to which you want to add information. Press Enter or F10.

   When you highlight some file names, one line of information is displayed. If there is no description associated with the file you have selected, Q&A prompts you to add text (Figure 1.11).

3. Press F6 and then you can add up to 72 characters. You can change or remove a description by pressing either the Delete or Backspace key.

   If you press Delete, Q&A removes the character at the cursor location. If you press Backspace, Q&A removes the character to the left of the cursor.

4. Press F10 to save the comment.

   Q&A saves the comment. □

# Getting Help in Q&A

Wherever you are in Q&A, you can get help by pressing the F1 key. Press Esc to leave help and return to the screen from which you called for help.

If you press F1 at a menu, Q&A displays help related to that screen (Figure 1.12). At the bottom of any screen, Q&A tells you what sort of help is available for that screen. There may be more than one screen of help for a complex Q&A feature. Press F1 to reach the first screen.

18

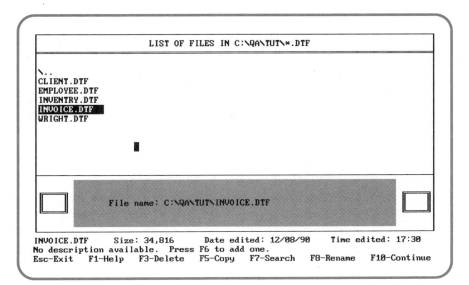

```
                  LIST OF FILES IN C:\QA\TUT\*.DTF

\..
CLIENT.DTF
EMPLOYEE.DTF
INVENTRY.DTF
INVOICE.DTF
WRIGHT.DTF

         ▌

                  File name: C:\QA\TUT\INVOICE.DTF

INVOICE.DTF    Size: 34,816      Date edited: 12/08/90    Time edited: 17:30
No description available.  Press F6 to add one.
Esc-Exit   F1-Help   F3-Delete   F5-Copy   F7-Search   F8-Rename   F10-Continue
```

*Figure 1.11    If there is no description associated with a file, you
are prompted to add one*

```
========================= USING A LIST ============= Appendix B =======
Type or select the name of the file, document, print spec, or report that you
want to use and press ◄──┘.  To select a name, type ↓ ↑ → ← or the SPACE BAR.
At a list of DOS files, you can subset the list.  NOTE: Specs (Print, Report,
Retrieve, Etc.) are not DOS files; they cannot be subsetted.

           HOW TO SUBSET A LIST OF DOS FILES

Type * or ? in various combinations followed by ◄──┘ to show a subset of the
files in a directory, just as you can with DOS.  For example:

*.doc  to show all the files in the directory with a "doc" extension.
p??.*  to show all files that have a 3-character name and begin with "p".

        HOW TO...                     HOW TO SEARCH FOR A NAME

Type or select a name, then press:   Type the first few unique letters of
                                     a name followed by two periods, then
  F3 - delete a file                 press F7 (SEARCH).  For example, type
  F5 - make a copy of a file         "m.." then F7 to find the first name
  F6 - add a description to a Q&A    in the list that begins with "m".
       document or database.
  F8 - rename a file

Esc-Exit
```

*Figure 1.12    The references on this sample help screen (F-15
or W-6) refer to the page number in the Q&A documentation*

If more help is available, you are prompted to press F1 to display the second level. Help works in the same way as other Q&A screens. If you want to go to the previous screen, press Esc.

You can create your own help screens. You can display custom help with or without pressing F1. For example, if you are working with a very complex database with obscure field names, you can program Q&A to automatically display custom help when you reach a specific field on a form, or if you enter invalid data.

If you incorporate custom help with Q&A help, the first time you press F1 displays the custom help screen, and the second time displays Q&A help.

# Exiting Q&A

You may be several menus into the program when you want to quit a Q&A session. Remember that Q&A is designed so that each time you press the Esc key, you move one menu back. Keep pressing the Esc key until you reach the Main menu.

Press X to leave Q&A and return to DOS. If you are offered the chance to back up your files, do so. There is more information about backing up your files in Chapter 3.

---

⊘ **Caution:** When you want to stop using any program, follow exit procedures for that program. Never turn off your computer to stop processing. Doing so causes you to lose or damage your data. If you lose your program because of a power failure, you may be able to recover your data files by choosing the Utilities modules from the Main menu.

---

# What You Have Learned

▶ Q&A is a menu-driven program.

▶ You can start Q&A and open a file at the same time.

▶ Q&A allows you to use both a mouse and the keyboard.

▶ You don't have to remember a file name; you can choose from a list of all files in a directory.

▶ You can create custom help screens that work along with Q&A help screens.

21

# Q&A File: Designing a New Database

## In This Chapter

▶ *Introduction to databases*
▶ *Planning and designing a database*
▶ *Using the Form Design screen*
▶ *Entering fields and their labels*
▶ *Defining field types*

## About Q&A File

File is the hub of the Q&A wheel. It gathers the information that other Q&A modules use to produce reports, letters, and mailing labels.

The Q&A File module enables you to organize information in database form. Use File to design forms to accept data in whatever order you want. You can tell Q&A what type and range of information goes into a database.

# A Quick Database Primer

A *database management system* is a program that allows you to gather information and then manipulate it—sort it, search for selected information, create reports about it, and then produce written output, such as letters and mailing labels.

A database is made up of individual *records*. In any given database, however, all records share a common structure. For example, a library database may contain a title and reference number for each book in the collection.

A *field* is the space into which information eventually is entered. For example, in a library database, a book title goes in one field and the catalog number goes in another field. If a letter in a file folder represents one record, the city and ZIP code on that letter are fields.

A *label* is the name that you give to a field; it helps the person entering data to identify what kind of information the field contains.

A *form* is a record layout that you design. Q&A presents you with a blank screen and you decide what fields and labels go on the form and where they appear. After you fill in the form, it represents what a record looks like when it is either displayed on the screen or printed. When you look at a completed form, you can see the size, content, and location of each field, and you also can plan reports and mailings. Figures 2.1 and 2.2 are examples of Q&A's tutorial forms. You can find these sample forms in the \TUT subdirectory.

# Planning Your Database

This book follows a very small catalog company through the planning, design, and redesign of its first Q&A database—a customer list. We also use this database to learn about the other Q&A modules and functions.

The first, and most important, part of database creation is the initial planning phase. For each database you design, take a piece of paper and write down the name of each field where you want it to appear on the screen. Think about how easy or difficult it will be to type information into the form that you have designed. Make sure that you allow enough space for the number of characters you need in each field.

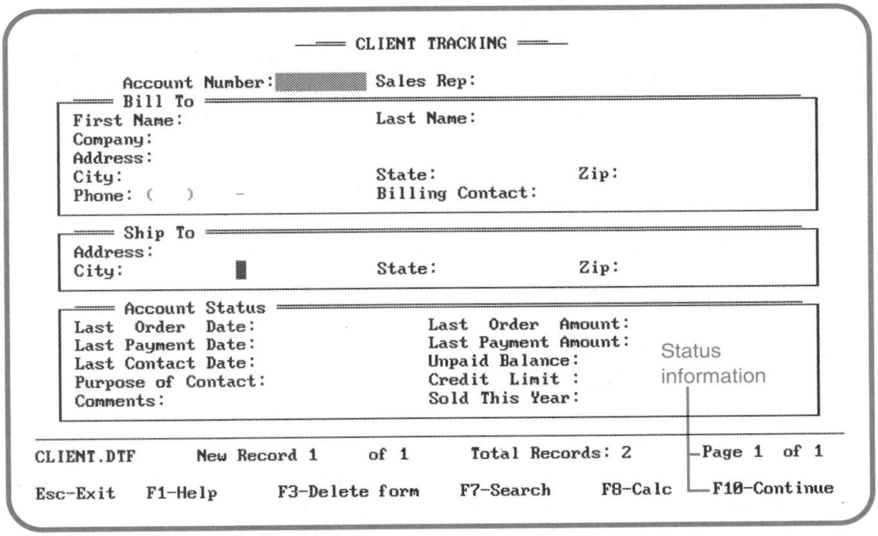

*Figure 2.1   The Q&A form, which collects information about customers for the CLIENT database*

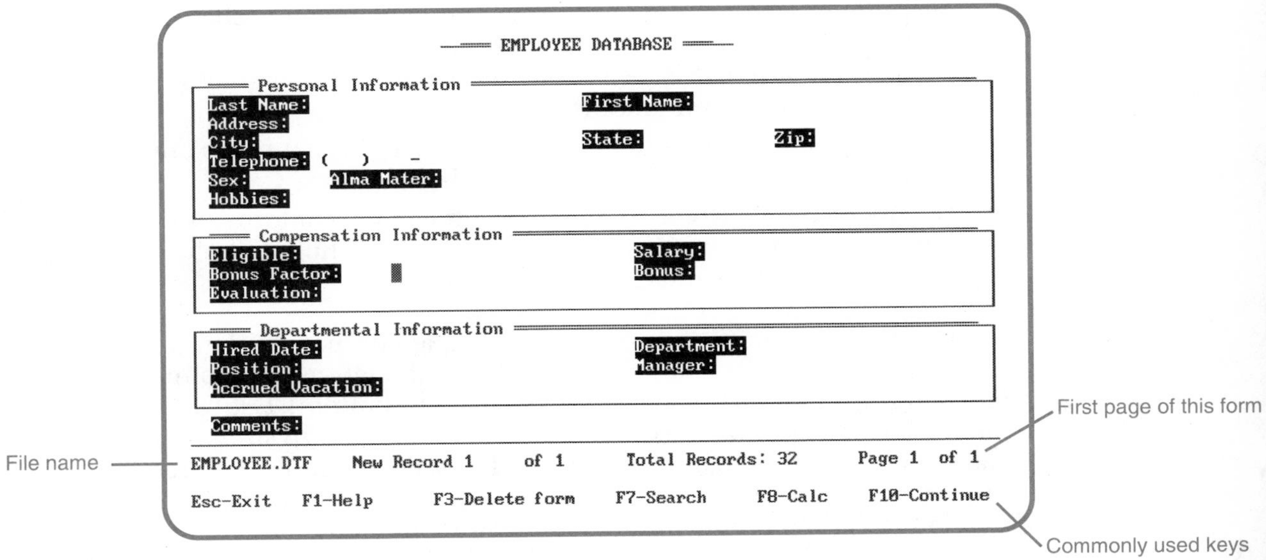

*Figure 2.2   The EMPLOYEE form records employee data*

Before you put pencil to paper, answer these questions for any database that you design:

▶ How are you going to use this database? For example, our catalog company could use a customer database to identify preferred customers, to produce mailing labels for all or some customers, and to track purchases to see what tools to reorder and what tools to reprice or to drop from inventory.

▶ What sort of reports do you want from this database? A catalog company could report on customers by ZIP code or by type of purchase, or produce a weekly inventory report.

▶ Can this database grow as the company grows? If we fill the form with superfluous information, will there be room for new fields?

▶ How easily can you modify your design? You are never finished redesigning a database, so if you squeeze several fields on one line, you can't put a new field on that line.

26

▶ Will data entry be easy, logical, and accurate? A customer list should group all name information and then all address information. You probably want to type name information in first name, middle initial, and last name order. You want to ensure that only appropriate values are entered in a field.

▶ In order to be complete, what fields does this database need? As you are planning a database on paper, try to think of every bit of information that you require today and probably will need six months from now. As our company grows, will we accept credit cards or be able to fax our customers? Will we want to target individuals for special mailings?

▶ What types of information go into each field? What fields are used for calculations? for sorting? for indexes?

▶ Do any of your current or future customers have addresses outside the United States? If so, plan to have a field to hold the name of the country.

In sketching out your own database design on paper, plan for easy data entry by spreading fields out (from the left margin to the right margin, and from the top of the screen to the bottom). Use *white space* (blank parts of the form), boxes, and lines to group similar or related fields and to separate dissimilar fields. For example, Figures 2.1 and 2.2 demonstrate good database design. Fields are laid out from left to right margin, and like fields are grouped.

Names of databases should be easy to understand. For example, if you have several databases on your computer, the name CLIENTLST is easier to remember than ABC-1190.

Don't make your first database too complicated. If you start with a small database, you are able to understand more about Q&A and are more comfortable when you design more complex databases later.

Make sure that each field is the smallest possible component. For example, instead of a Name field containing Mr. Thomas Smith, Jr., define Title (Mr.), First Name (Thomas), Last Name (Smith), and Suffix (Jr.).

Plan a field that holds a unique identifier for each record. For example, if a customer's last name is Smith and the first time the customer contacted you was September 10, 1984, the ID might be SMIT09101984. An ID field makes it more difficult for accidental duplicate records.

27

# Designing Your Database Form

Now we need to design a database form for the customer list. To design a new database form use the Form Design Screen.

## Q Creating a New Form

| | |
|---|---|
| 1. Start Q&A. | After title information is displayed, the Main menu appears. |
| 2. Choose File from the Main menu. | The File menu is displayed. |
| 3. Choose Design File. | The Design menu is displayed. Remember that each new menu is displayed in front of the previous menu. |
| 4. Choose Design a New File. | Q&A prompts you for a data file name by adding a dialog box to the Design menu screen (Figure 2.3). |

5. If you want to make sure that the name you want to enter is not already in use, press Enter. (If you have worked on a file during this session, Q&A displays that name in the dialog box. To erase that name from the dialog box, press Spacebar.)

Q&A displays a list of all files in this directory. If you are the first person to use Q&A on this computer, you will see the names of four database files.

6. Our sample database is called CUSTOMER, so type CUSTOMER and press Enter or F10.

Q&A automatically adds the .DTF file extension (Figure 2.4).

□

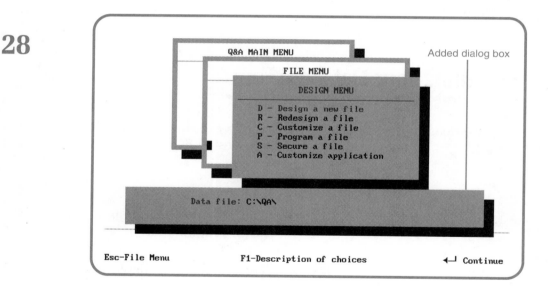

Q&A MAIN MENU                                                    Added dialog box

FILE MENU

DESIGN MENU

D – Design a new file
R – Redesign a file
C – Customize a file
P – Program a file
S – Secure a file
A – Customize application

Data file: C:\QA\

Esc-File Menu          F1-Description of choices          ↵ Continue

*Figure 2.3    The dialog box is added to the Design menu*

▶ **Tip:** If you happen to type a data file name that already exists, Q&A tells you. If this happens, press Esc to return to the Design menu and then repeat steps 3 and 4 in the Quick Steps, Creating a New Form.

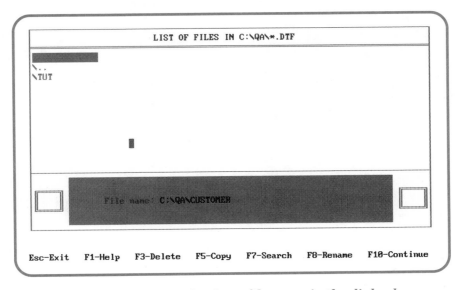

LIST OF FILES IN C:\QA\*.DTF

\. .
\TUT

File name: C:\QA\CUSTOMER

Esc-Exit    F1-Help    F3-Delete    F5-Copy    F7-Search    F8-Rename    F10-Continue

*Figure 2.4    Your new database file name in the dialog box*

**29**

If Q&A accepts the data file name, it flashes the word Working in the lower left corner of the screen. This indicates that Q&A is creating the database (Figure 2.5). When database creation is completed, you see the empty design form on the Design Screen (Figure 2.6).

The ruler line shows you where the cursor is located along the left to right margin. You can see that tabs are already set; look for the T to see the tab positions. If you press the Tab key, the cursor jumps to the next tab location. Press Shift-Tab to move to the prior tab location.

The status line shows you several pieces of information:

▶ The name of the file on which you are working

▶ Indicators that tell you the settings of some keys: Num (the NumLock key is active), Ins (you are in Insert mode), and Cap (all alphabetic keys are entered in uppercase)

▶ The percentage of file-filled *RAM* (random access memory, which is used by your computer to run programs faster and more efficiently)

▶ The line on which the cursor is now located, as well as the page number and the total number of pages in this form

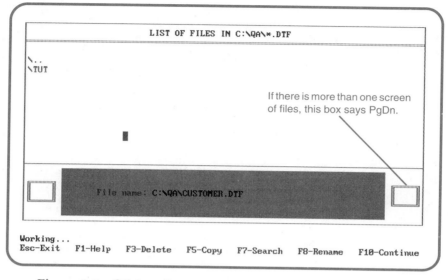

**30**

*Figure 2.5    Q&A as it creates a new database*

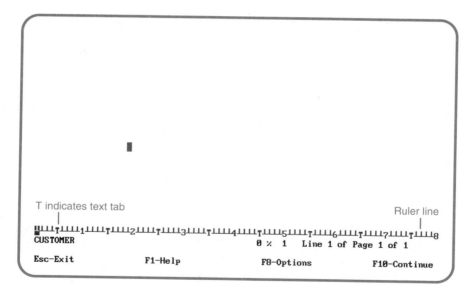

*Figure 2.6    This blank Form Design screen is ready to be used*

When the Ins indicator is not displayed on the status line, Q&A is in overtype mode—anything that you type goes into the next position on the line, regardless of the presence of other characters or spaces. A character or space is erased every time you type a new character or space. When the Ins indicator is displayed on the status line, Q&A is in insert mode—every time you type a character or space, it pushes the spaces and characters ahead of it and nothing is erased from the line. (All the indicator keys are *toggle* keys, which means that you press the same key to turn an action on or off.)

The message and key assignment lines tell you what function keys are available from this screen. In addition, Q&A displays any messages in this area.

Table 2.1 lists the important maximum limits for Q&A File. With the exception of pages per form, you probably don't have to worry about reaching any of these limits.

*Table 2.1   Q&A File Limits*

| Item | Maximum Limit |
| --- | --- |
| Pages per form (record) | 10 |
| Fields per record | 2,045 |
| Fields per page | 248 |
| Characters per record | 65,536 |
| Characters per field | 32,768 |
| Number of records per file | 34,288 |
| File size (in megabytes) | 1,024M |

## Entering Fields

Most of the commands and features of the Write module can be used to create attractive forms. Begin typing fields anywhere on the screen, in whatever order you want. One field can extend over several lines or you may put more than one field on the same line. If you wish, you may put one or more blank lines between fields.

Each field of a record should have a label to prompt you about the contents of a field, for example, Last Name. A label should also clearly indicate the meaning of a field. For example, a label called ADDRESS2 is much more understandable than one called A2.

There are rare occasions when you do not assign a label to a field. For example, certain accounting forms, such as invoices, may contain fields without labels. When you do not assign a label to a field, Q&A creates an invisible label so that it has some way of keeping track of each field. For an example of an invoice form, see Figure 2.7.

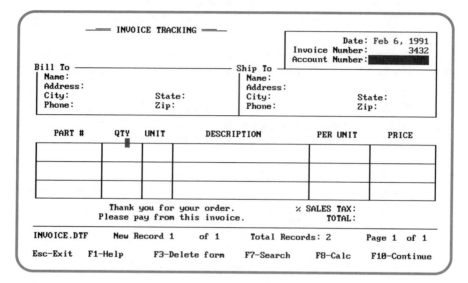

*Figure 2.7    The top of the Q&A INVOICE form is labeled, but the bottom is not*

A field ends when it reaches

▶ The right side of the screen
▶ The end of the screen
▶ The start of another field
▶ A line character
▶ The > character

Your customer list database contains 16 fields. Your first database will probably be larger than our example. You might want to put the design for this database on paper before you start filling in the Form Design screen. When you add the State entry, add this comment below it: (If the customer lives outside the U. S., type a country name here.). When you add the Comment entry, remember that it is a multiple-line field. (For information about multiple-line entries, see the next section.) Table 2.2 contains all the necessary information about the customer list database.

## Table 2.2 Customer List Fields

| Label | Field Length | Field Type | Description |
|---|---|---|---|
| ID Number | 10 | T | Unique identifier, consisting of part of last name and date of first contact |
| First Name | 15 | T | Customer's first name |
| Last Name | 20 | T | Customer's last name |
| Street1 | 65 | T | Number and name of street or post office box |
| Street2 | 65 | T | Apartment number or other street data[1] |
| City | 20 | T | Customer's city |
| State | 15 | T | State or name of country[2] |
| ZIP Code | 10 | T | Long ZIP code (formatted nnnnn-nnnn)[3] |
| Day Telephone | 18 | T | Telephone number (formatted nnn-nnn-nnnn xnnnn) |
| Night Telephone | 18 | T | Telephone number (formatted nnn-nnn-nnnn xnnnn) |
| Original Date | 10 | D | Date of first customer contact (any format) |
| Favored Customer | 1 | Y/N | Has this customer met longevity and good payment standards? |
| Catalog Numbers | 10 | K | Catalog numbers of every item ordered |
| Last Order | 7 | M | Dollar amount of last order |
| Order | 9 | M | Dollar amount of all orders |
| Comments | * | T | A multiple-line field |

[1]Street1 and Street2 should be about one line long, but if you plan on printing mailing labels, factor in the width of a label, typically about 30 characters.

[2]If you are sure that you will have only one country represented in this field, choose a two-character state field. If you ever have to enter the name of a country, 15 characters is an appropriate size.

[3]Plan on using the 10-digit (including the hyphen) ZIP code field. When you send out a mass mailing, mail that is presorted by the longer ZIP code results in discounted postal rates.

> ⊘ **Caution:** Before you go to step 6 in the next Quick Steps series, Laying Out a Form, carefully look at the form you have designed. If you see anything that you want to correct, do so then. If you press F10 before you are satisfied with the form layout, you have to use Redesign a File to correct it.

## 𝒬 Laying Out a Form

1. Press any combination of cursor movement keys to move the cursor to the place on the screen where you want to type the label.

   Q&A moves the cursor to the spot you designate.

2. Type the field label, then either a colon (:) or less than symbol (<) to indicate the beginning of the field's data entry area. Optionally, place the cursor where you want the field to end; then type a greater than symbol (>). Make sure that the length of the field is at least the size you planned. If you are close to the end of a line, don't try to squeeze a field in.

   If you don't type a : or <, Q&A processes the database as though this were a comment, not a field.

3. Repeat steps 1 and 2 until you have finished laying out the fields you want in your form.

   Q&A lays out the fields as you specify them.

4. When you have finished laying out the form (Figure 2.8), press F10. (Figure 2.9).

   Q&A saves your form and database design, and displays the Format Spec, which prompts you to enter information types for each field. □

```
ID Number:              >                                                    ▮

First Name:              >   Last Name:                  >
Street1:
Street2:
City:                >    State:              >   Zip Code:          >

Day Telephone:                 >   Night Telephone:              >

Original Date:        >
Favored Customer: >

Catalog Numbers:          >
Last Order:       >
Order:        >

Comments<

                                                                      >

‖‖‖‖T‖‖‖1‖‖‖T‖‖‖2‖‖‖T‖‖‖3‖‖‖T‖‖‖4‖‖‖T‖‖‖5‖‖‖T‖‖‖6‖‖‖T‖‖‖7‖‖‖T‖‖‖3
CUSTOMER                             2 %  80  Line 21 of Page 1 of 1

Esc-Exit          F1-Help         F8-Options          F10-Continue
```

*Figure 2.8   A form at the end of the design process*

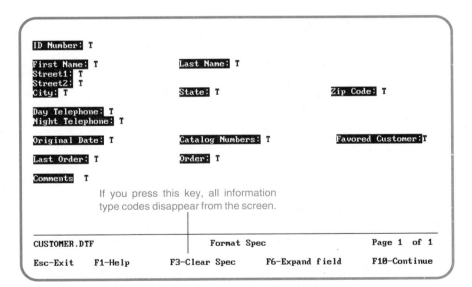

*Figure 2.9   One possible completed form design for the catalog company database*

## Multiple-Line Fields

A multiple-line field starts with a colon (:) or less than (<) symbol and must end with the greater than (>) symbol. If you start a multiple-line field with : , Q&A begins succeeding lines of the field at the left margin of the screen. If you start a multiple-line field with <, Q&A aligns succeeding lines wherever the < was typed. The > indicates the right margin of every line of a multiple-line field.

You cannot put a multiple-line field inside a box.

Two multiple-line fields cannot start on the same line. Only the last line of a multiple-line field can contain another field (including the start of another multiple-line field).

# Editing and Formatting the Form Design

As you enter fields on a form, you will probably have to edit. For example, after you have completed the design, you may see a crowded line. In this case, you might want to move text from that line to another. You might see a field that should be highlighted to show its importance. Your form might have a label that is difficult to associate with the field or is too long for its line. In all these cases, you should edit or reformat your design.

## Inserting Text

If you need to move a field to a new position or want to insert a new field on the line, consider using Insert mode. Press the Ins key and the Ins indicator should appear on the status line. You can press Home (or End) to move the cursor to the beginning (or end) of the line, or you can use any cursor movement key to move to the appropriate location on the line. Remember that when you are in insert mode, every time you type a character or space, the characters after the cursor are pushed along the line.

> ⊘ **Caution:** When you are filling in a new form, you should be in overtype mode. If you are in insert mode, the fields that you have already laid out might be moved inadvertently.

## Deleting Text

To delete text, you have some choices. You can press the Backspace key to delete the character to the left of the cursor, or you can press the Del key to delete the character on which the cursor is located. If you press either key repeatedly, you can quickly delete words and sentences.

There is a faster way to delete blocks of text. You can press F8 to display the Options menu (Figure 2.10). Select Block Operations, then press Right (or Tab) and highlight Delete, and press Enter (or just press F3). Q&A prompts you to mark the area that you want to delete (Figure 2.11). When you have marked the area, press F10.

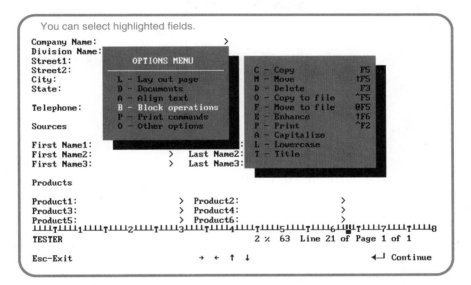

*Figure 2.10   The Options menu with Block Operations, which are available in both the File and Write modules*

▶ **Note:** When you try to select a function that seems to be displayed more dimly than the others on a menu, the cursor skips over that selection. If a function on a list is displayed in text that looks paler than other functions, it is not available. You may have to perform another function before this one is usable.

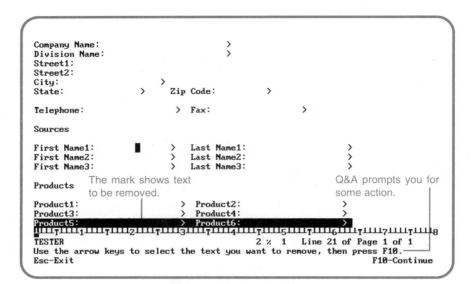

Figure 2.11   *Q&A prompts you to mark an area for deletion*

## Moving Text

To move text from one location on the screen to another, place the cursor at the beginning of the block you want to move. Press F8 to display the Options menu. Select Block Operations, then press Right and highlight Move, and press Enter (or just press F3). Q&A prompts you to mark the area that you want to move. Then move the cursor to the location on the screen where you want the text and press F10. When you have marked the area, press F10. For examples of the two prompts related to the Move function, see Figures 2.12 and 2.13.

## Copying Text

To copy text to another location on the screen, place the cursor at the beginning of the block you want to copy. Press F8 to display the Options menu. Select Block Operations, then press Right and highlight Copy, and press Enter (or just press F5). Q&A prompts you to mark the area that you want to copy. Then move the cursor to the location on the screen where you want the text and press F10. When you look at the screen, you will see two copies of the same text.

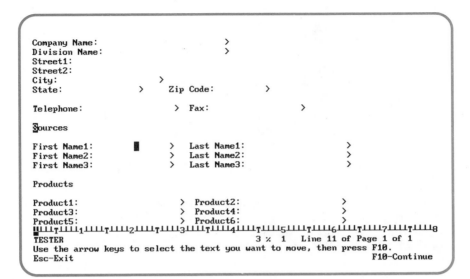

*Figure 2.12    When you use the Block Operation's Move option, first you are prompted to mark the text to be moved*

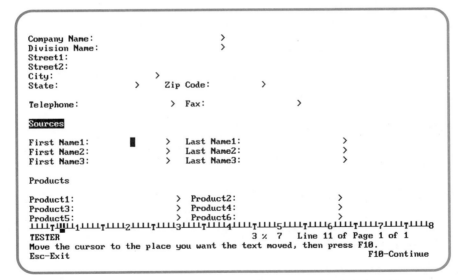

*Figure 2.13    Q&A prompts you to mark the new text location on the form*

## Setting Tabs

You can set tabs to align fields over more than one line. Because there are default tab stops already set, you may want to delete them or simply add new tab settings to the default settings. You can set text tabs, which align to the left side of the field, or decimal tabs, which align to the right side of the field. For more information about aligning fields, see "Choosing Data Display Format Options" later in this chapter.

To set tabs, press F8 to display the Options menu. Choose Lay Out Page, then press Right and highlight Set Tabs, and press Enter. Q&A displays a ruler line, and a highlight represents the cursor location (Figure 2.14). Move the cursor to the position on the ruler line where you want to set a new tab. Type ⊤ (or ⅅ) to indicate text (or decimal) tab. After you finish setting tabs, press F10. When you save the file, the new tab settings are saved. Any tabs set within the File module are also good for the Write module. See Table 2.3 for tab cursor movement keys.

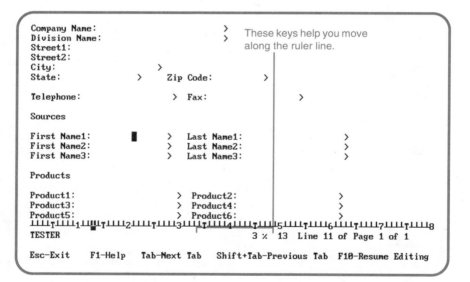

*Figure 2.14    To set tabs, Q&A displays a ruler line with a highlighted current cursor location*

*Table 2.3    Tab Cursor Movement Keys*

| Left Movement Key | Function | Right Movement Key |
|---|---|---|
| Home | Moves to the end of the line | End |
| Ctrl-Left | Moves five spaces from cursor | Ctrl-Right |
| Shift-Tab | Moves to next tab marker | Tab |
| Left | Moves one character over | Right |

## Centering Lines

If you want to give a form a centered title, place the cursor some-where on the line that you want to center and press F8 to display the Options menu. Choose Align Text, then press Right and highlight Center, and press Enter. All the text on the line is centered. If you want to align text against either the left (or right) margin, select Left (or Right) instead.

## Drawing Lines

Q&A allows you to draw lines and boxes around all fields but multiple-line fields.

> **Caution:** You cannot draw boxes around multiple-line fields because when Q&A detects a nonblank character (a line character), it ends the field automatically.

You'll notice that your computer's keyboard looks like a com-bination of typewriter and adding machine keys. The adding ma-chine arrangement of keys is known as the numeric keypad. Many new computers have two sets of arrow keys—one is between the typewriter keys and the numeric keypad, and the other set is in the numeric keypad. To draw lines with Up, Down, Left, and Right, use

**41**

the keys on the numeric keypad. Be sure that you are in overtype mode. See Table 2.4 for the keys used to draw lines and boxes. Note that Clock refers to the hour-hand position; sometimes the hour hand points between numbers. For an example of a screen with single and double lines and boxes, see Figure 2.15.

*Table 2.4   Line and Box Drawing Keys*

| Key | Type of Line | Direction | Clock |
|---|---|---|---|
| Up | Single | Vertical | 12 |
| 8 | Single | Vertical | 12 |
| Shift-Up* | Double | Vertical | 12 |
| Shift-8* | Double | Vertical | 12 |
| Down | Single | Vertical | 6 |
| 2 | Single | Vertical | 6 |
| Shift-Down* | Double | Vertical | 6 |
| Shift-2* | Double | Vertical | 6 |
| Left | Single | Horizontal | 9 |
| 4 | Single | Horizontal | 9 |
| Shift-Left* | Double | Horizontal | 9 |
| Shift-4* | Double | Horizontal | 9 |
| Right | Single | Horizontal | 3 |
| 6 | Single | Horizontal | 3 |
| Shift-Right* | Double | Horizontal | 3 |
| Shift-6* | Double | Horizontal | 3 |
| Home | Single | Diagonal | 10-11 |
| 7 | Single | Diagonal | 10-11 |
| PgUp | Single | Diagonal | 1-2 |
| 9 | Single | Diagonal | 1-2 |
| End | Single | Diagonal | 7-8 |
| 1 | Single | Diagonal | 7-8 |
| PgDn | Single | Diagonal | 4-5 |
| 3 | Single | Diagonal | 4-5 |

*Or press Numlock.

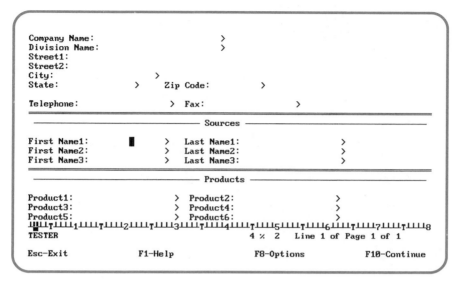

```
Company Name:                      >
Division Name:                     >
Street1:
Street2:
City:                  >
State:                 >    Zip Code:          >

Telephone:                  >  Fax:                >
─────────────────────────── Sources ───────────────────────────

First Name1:      █        >  Last Name1:                  >
First Name2:               >  Last Name2:                  >
First Name3:               >  Last Name3:                  >
─────────────────────────── Products ──────────────────────────

Product1:             >  Product2:                >
Product3:             >  Product4:                >
Product5:             >  Product6:                >
⊥⊥⊥⊥⊥⊤⊥⊥⊥⊥1⊥⊥⊥⊥⊤⊥⊥⊥2⊥⊥⊥⊤⊥⊥⊥3⊥⊥⊥⊤⊥⊥⊥4⊥⊥⊥⊤⊥⊥⊥5⊥⊥⊥⊤⊥⊥6⊥⊥⊥⊤⊥⊥⊥7⊥⊥⊥⊤⊥⊥⊥8
TESTER                                  4 % 2   Line 1 of Page 1 of 1

Esc-Exit              F1-Help              F8-Options       F10-Continue
```

*Figure 2.15    A form with single and double lines*

**43**

---

▶ **Note:** If you want to draw and then print boxes and lines
that look like boxes and lines, your printer must be
compatible with IBM box graphics characters. Otherwise, Q&A
draws boxes and lines using dashes, pluses, and other symbols
from the keyboard.

---

## Ⓠ Drawing Lines and Boxes

1. Use any combination of
cursor movement keys to
place the cursor where
you want to start the line
or box. Then press the
F8 key.

The Options menu appears.

2. Select Lay Out Page.

A submenu is displayed.

3. Press the Right key to
move the selection
highlight into the
submenu and choose
Draw. Press Enter.

Q&A displays drawing
information on the status
line.

| | |
|---|---|
| 4. Use the appropriate keys to draw single or double lines (refer to Table 2.4). | Q&A draws the line or box. |
| 5. To move the cursor without creating a line, press F6. | You will see a message that the pen is up. |
| 6. If you want to start drawing again, press F6 again. | Q&A returns to drawing. |
| 7. To erase a line, press F8. If you want to start drawing again, press F8 again. | Q&A erases the line and returns to drawing. |
| 8. Press F10. | Q&A returns you to editing your form.                   □ |

# Using the Format Spec Screen

After you press F10 to complete the form layout, the Form Spec is displayed. Here you tell Q&A the kind of data to be entered into each field, and you also have the option to define the way it is displayed on the form.

Notice that the appearance of the Form screen has changed. All fields are highlighted (comments, which are not fields, are not highlighted). When you move the cursor to a field, a T suddenly appears. All fields are assigned the T (for Text) information type; which is the *default*. A default is a value that is automatically assigned by the program. Q&A assumes that this information type is the most commonly used for any field in any database. For a complete list of all Q&A information types, see Table 2.5.

When you define a Q&A database, you also designate an information type for each field. As you enter data, it is checked to make sure it's the right type. Q&A field types are: text (T), number (N), money (M), keyword (K), date (D), hours (H), or yes/no (Y/N). You can calculate number, money, date, and hours fields. Fields that accept only numbers—specifically, only numbers that you want to calculate in some way—are *numeric* fields. All other fields contain *alphanumeric* characters (that is, letters of the alphabet, numbers that won't be calculated, punctuation, and other symbols).

*Table 2.5    Q&A Information Types*

| Code | Type | Information in This Field |
|------|------|--------------------------|
| T | Text | Alphanumeric data, such as names, addresses, comments |
| N | Number | Numeric data, such as quantities, numbers for calculations |
| M | Money | Numeric data, for dollars and cents formatting |
| D | Date | Dates only |
| H | Hours | Times only |
| K | Keyword | Alphanumeric data (lists of words, which identify all or part of a database) |
| Y | Yes/No | Answers to Yes/No, True/False, or On/Off |

## Text Fields

A text (T) field accepts any combination of characters: alphabetic, numeric, punctuation, or special symbols. Use this field type for any data that you do not use for calculations. Example of text fields are last name, address, city, state, telephone number or ZIP code.

## Number Fields

Use the number (N) information type for generic numeric fields on which you perform calculations or numeric sorts. If you make a field numeric, Q&A does not allow you to enter anything but a number in that field.

## Money Fields

Use the money (M) information type to ensure that only money information is entered into this field. When you type numeric data into a money field, Q&A automatically converts the numbers into a money format, starting with a currency symbol (like $) and adding commas or periods where needed.

The Q&A default money format contains the comma (,) and period (.), and the default currency symbol is the dollar sign ($). For example, if you enter 5555555 in a money field that also is formatted to accept cents, Q&A makes the conversion to $55,555.55.

You can change the default dollar format and currency symbol by using the Global Format Options menu. For more information, see "Global Format Options" later in this chapter.

## Date Fields

Use the date (D) information type to make sure that only date information is entered in this field. When you type numeric data into a date field, Q&A automatically converts the numbers into a date format.

**46**

A date field must be at least ten characters wide. You can enter dates in a variety of ways. For example, you can enter July 29, 1991, 7/29/91, or 7-29-91. In all these cases, Q&A is preset to reformat and display the entry as July 29, 1991 when the cursor leaves the field.

You can calculate date fields. For example, you can compute how long a customer has been your customer or how long since the last order.

You can change the default date information by using the Global Format Options menu. For more information, see "Global Format Options" later in this chapter.

## Hours Fields

Use the hours (H) information type to make sure that hours (time) information is entered in this field. When you type hour data into an hour field, Q&A automatically converts the numbers into an hour format (hh:mm am/pm, where hh indicates hours, mm indicates minutes, and am/pm indicates before or after noon, respectively).

You can change the default hours format (either 12-hour, the default setting, or 24-hour format) by using the Global Format Options menu. For more information, see "Global Format Options" later in this chapter.

You can calculate hours fields. For example, you can compute how many hours an employee has been entering data today.

## *Keyword Fields*

The keyword (K) field allows you to have more than one entry in a single field. Two examples of keyword fields are

► Lists of all the items that customers ever bought from you
► Names of the carving tools included in a carving tool kit (under one part number)

Use a keyword field to specifically search for one component in a field. For example, if a customer wants to order a 12mm chisel, you could search for 12mm chisels and find that they are sold not only individually but within a ten-piece kit. You can also create a keyword list by using the Custom Help feature, described in Chapter 3.

## *Yes/No Fields*

47

A Yes/No field is for situations in which there are just two choices: Yes or No, On or Off, True or False. Use Yes/No fields, which are always one character long, to answer questions, such as `Credit card customer?` (with an answer of either Y or N). The Yes/No information type is not *case-sensitive*, which means that you can enter any combination of upper- and lowercase letters.

Use a question mark (?) after Y/N fields to prompt people entering data that this is a Y/N field.

### *Q* **Assigning an Information Type**

1. Move the cursor to the field that you want to change.

   The cursor should be on top of the code for the field. Right now, the code is T.

2. Type the letter code for the information type for that field (T, N, M, D, H, K, or Y). If the code is already T and you want to keep it, don't change it. (If you change your mind about an information type, simply move the cursor over the letter code you want and press Enter.) Press F10.

   Q&A displays the Global Format Options screen.

□

> ▶ **Tip:** If a field is too small to enter the formatting informa-
> tion you want, press F6. The Expand Field area appears at
> the bottom of the screen where you can enter up to 240
> characters of formatting information. Press Shift-F4 to clear the
> contents of the line that the cursor is on.

## Choosing Data Display Format Options

When you assign information types, you can also add formatting
codes. For example, Q&A aligns text from the left side of the field
(that is, left justified), but you may want to align text against the right
side of the field. First, type T in the field. Then type , or a space,
followed by the code JR.

If you want to set the number of decimal digits for a number
field, type N in the field. Then type a comma or a space, followed by
a number from 0 to 7. You can combine codes in a field if each code
is valid for that information type.

Table 2.6 is a list of formatting options, and valid information
types and functions for each. In the second column, the letters refer
to the information types given in Table 2.5: T=text, K=keyword,
Y=yes/no, N=number, M=money, D=date, H=hours.

## Global Format Options

You can change defaults for the date, hours, number, or money
information types from the Global Format Options screen (Figure
2.16). Use any combination of cursor movement keys to select from
the choices on this screen. Press F10 and the changes that you
selected are saved.

**48**

*Table 2.6   Data Display Format Options*

| Code | Valid Types | Function |
|------|-------------|----------|
| JR | TKYNMDH | Aligns the information in the field at the right margin |
| JC | TKYNMDH | Aligns the information in the field from the center of the line |
| JL | TKYNMDH | Aligns the information in the field at the left margin |
| U | TKY | Converts all text in the field to upper-case |
| L | TKY | Converts all text in the field to lower-case |
| I | TKY | Makes the first letter of every word in the field uppercase |
| 0-7 | N | Indicates the number of digits to the right of a decimal point |
| C | NM | Automatically inserts commas to format numbers |

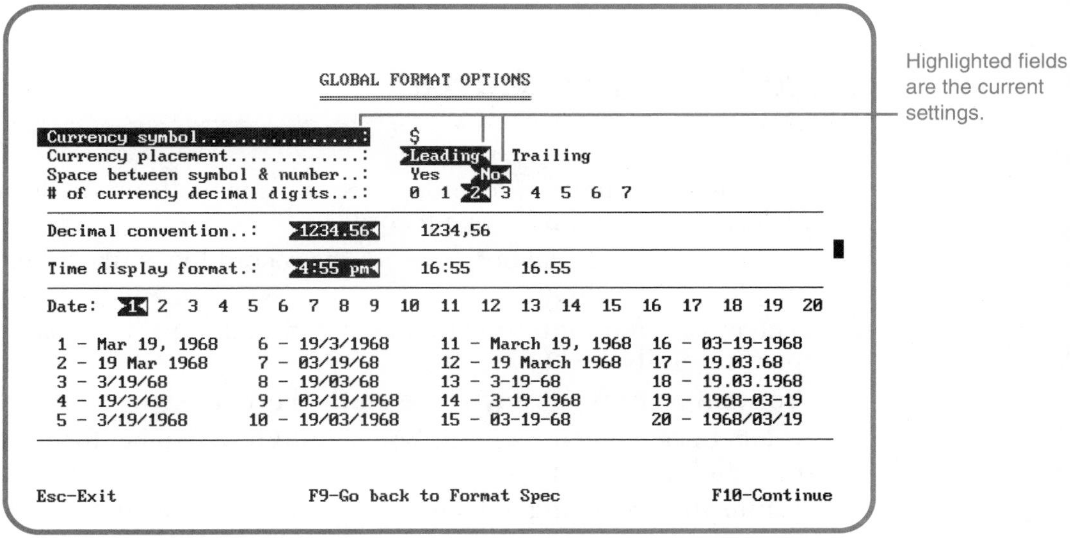

**49**

Highlighted fields are the current settings.

```
                        GLOBAL FORMAT OPTIONS

  Currency symbol.................:      $
  Currency placement..............:   Leading   Trailing
  Space between symbol & number..:    Yes    No
  # of currency decimal digits...:    0  1  2  3  4  5  6  7

  Decimal convention..:    1234.56     1234,56

  Time display format.:    4:55 pm     16:55       16.55

  Date:    1  2  3  4  5  6  7  8  9  10  11  12  13  14  15  16  17  18  19  20

  1 - Mar 19, 1968      6 - 19/3/1968     11 - March 19, 1968   16 - 03-19-1968
  2 - 19 Mar 1968       7 - 03/19/68      12 - 19 March 1968    17 - 19.03.68
  3 - 3/19/68           8 - 19/03/68      13 - 3-19-68          18 - 19.03.1968
  4 - 19/3/68           9 - 03/19/1968    14 - 3-19-1968        19 - 1968-03-19
  5 - 3/19/1968        10 - 19/03/1968    15 - 03-19-68         20 - 1968/03/19


  Esc-Exit              F9-Go back to Format Spec             F10-Continue
```

*Figure 2.16   The Global Format Options screen*

## *Q* Changing Global Format Options

| | |
|---|---|
| 1. Press Tab or Enter to move the cursor down the screen to an item that you want to change. | Defaults are highlighted. |
| 2. Press Left or Right. | Q&A moves the cursor to the choice that you want to select. |
| 3. After selection, press Enter to move to the next item that you want to change. | Q&A moves the cursor to your next choice. |
| 4. After you have finished making all changes, press F10. | Q&A returns to the File menu. |
| 5. If you want to finish this Q&A session, press Esc. | Q&A returns to the Main menu. |
| 6. Press X. | You exit Q&A. ☐ |

**50**

# What You Have Learned

▶ A database is made of records; a record is made from fields; a field is one component in a record.

▶ A form is a record layout, or what the record looks like when displayed or printed.

▶ The most important thing to do when designing a database is plan carefully.

▶ You can place fields anywhere on the Form Design screen.

▶ A label is a name for a field. You should have a label for each field, with very few exceptions.

▶ While you are laying out a form, you can edit the layout.

▶ Q&A information types are text, number, money, date, hours, keyword, and yes/no.

▶ You can calculate number, money, date, and hours fields.

▶ Unless you are going to calculate a numeric field, it is better to define it as a text type.

51

# Redesigning and Customizing a Database

## In This Chapter

▶ *Managing your database files*
▶ *Copying database designs and records*
▶ *Adding, deleting, copying, and moving fields*
▶ *Changing information types and field formats*
▶ *Customizing a database*

## Managing Your Database Files

Managing a database consists of more operations than adding new records and changing information on existing ones. For example, it may be your job to design and distribute a new database form to other departments in your company. Or you may have to distribute regularly a database with some records to other branch offices. You may want to post specific data from the databases of branch offices into one central database, or remove duplicate or outdated records.

When there's a change that affects many or all the records in a database (for example, an office moves or your company acquires another business), you need to update the database.

You can handle all these management tasks from the File module.

## Deleting a Database

If you want to eliminate a database and all its records, use the DOS DEL command. Exit from Q&A and return to DOS. With the DOS prompt on the screen, type

```
DEL filename.*
```

**54**

where filename is the data file name and the asterisk (*) is a *wildcard* representing both the .DTF and .IDX extensions. Then press Enter.

> ⊘ **Caution:** When you use the DEL command, there is no way (other than restoring from either a Q&A or DOS backup) to bring back the file or its contents. When you delete a file, it is gone forever unless you have a backup copy.

## Copying a Database

When you copy a database file, first you have to copy its design and then copy the file. After you have finished making a copy, the result is two copies of the database—the original and the new one.

**Q Copying a Database**

1. From the Main menu, select File.

   Q&A displays the File menu (Figure 3.1).

2. Select Copy.

   Q&A adds a dialog box, which prompts you for the name of the database file to copy (Figure 3.2).

3. You either can enter the name of the database or press Enter to have Q&A display a list of files from which you can select. After you have selected a file, press Enter. (If you have been working on a database during this session, Q&A automatically displays that name in a dialog box. To erase that name from the box, press Spacebar and then Enter.)

The Copy menu is displayed.

4. Select Copy Design Only to copy the design, and either enter a unique database name or press Enter to display a list of databases from which you can choose.

Q&A copies the design to the new database and tells you that your design is being copied. If the design is complex, this process may take a while to complete. Q&A then returns you to the Copy menu. Note that it automatically adds a .DTF extension to the new name.

**55**

5. Select Copy Selected Records, and press Enter to display the new database name.

The Retrieve Spec screen for the original database is displayed. This screen shows the specifications or attributes of this screen, or everything about the screen before data is entered. If you get the message No records were found that meet your retrieve request, you have selected an empty database to copy.

6. Press F10 to copy the information from all the fields of the original database to the new database.

You see the Merge Spec screen, which looks the same as the Retrieve Spec screen.

7. Press F10 again.

Working flashes at the bottom left of the screen. Q&A tells you what record is being copied. Then Copying flashes at the bottom left (Figure 3.3). After the process completes, you are returned to the File menu. □

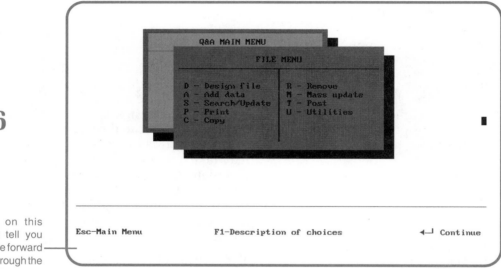

The keys on this status line tell you how to move forward and back through the program.

*Figure 3.1    The Q&A File menu*

▶ **Note:** When you copy a database, the new version is smaller than the old one because the copy process omits some of the spaces built into the original over time.

## Renaming a Database

Occasionally, you want to rename a database. For example, if you think that a particular name is easier to remember than the name you originally used, rename it. After you have renamed a database, only one copy—the one with the new name—remains. (If you copy a database, two copies remain.) To rename a database, first exit from Q&A. With the DOS prompt on the screen, type

```
REN oldfile.* newfile.*
```

where oldfile is the original data file name, newfile is the name that you wish to give to the file, and the asterisk (*) is a wildcard representing any number of characters. In this case, it represents any extension, .DTF and .IDX among them. Then press Enter.

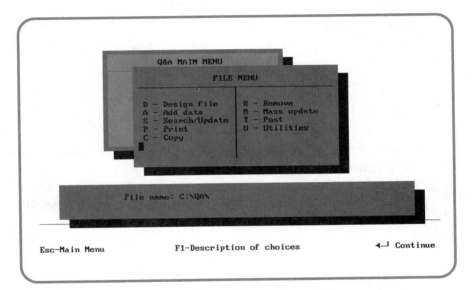

*Figure 3.2   The dialog box asks you for a file name to copy*

## Backing Up Database Files

You should back up your database often by making a copy of one or more files. Then copy it to floppy disk and store that disk in a safe place—preferably in a building that is away from the one in which you work. If you work on Q&A every day, consider backing up once or even twice a day.

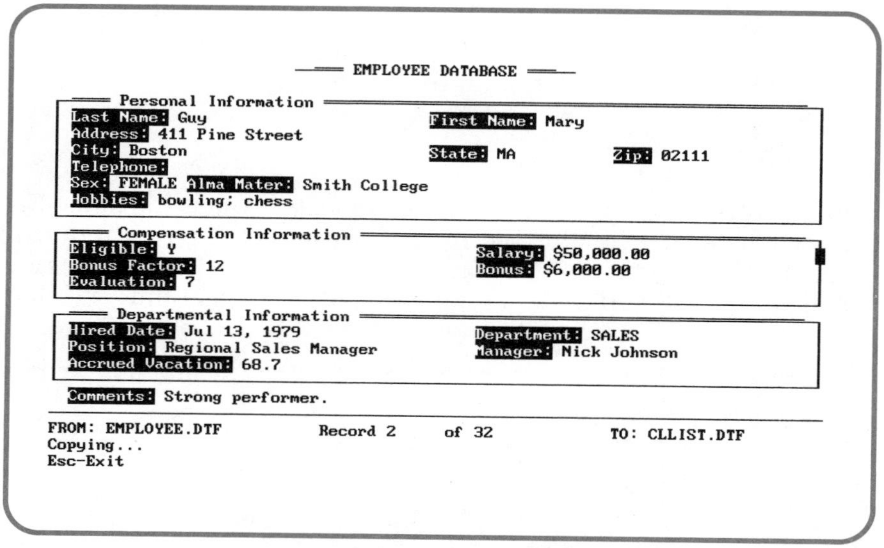

```
                    ═══ EMPLOYEE DATABASE ═══

      ═══ Personal Information ═══
   Last Name: Guy                     First Name: Mary
   Address: 411 Pine Street
   City: Boston                       State: MA              Zip: 02111
   Telephone:
   Sex: FEMALE  Alma Mater: Smith College
   Hobbies: bowling; chess

      ═══ Compensation Information ═══
   Eligible: Y                        Salary: $50,000.00
   Bonus Factor: 12                   Bonus: $6,000.00
   Evaluation: 7

      ═══ Departmental Information ═══
   Hired Date: Jul 13, 1979           Department: SALES
   Position: Regional Sales Manager   Manager: Nick Johnson
   Accrued Vacation: 68.7

   Comments: Strong performer.

   FROM: EMPLOYEE.DTF        Record 2    of 32        TO: CLLIST.DTF
   Copying...
   Esc-Exit
```

*Figure 3.3   The Merge Spec screen with the copying message*

**Caution:** Whenever you plan to make any design change to your database, back up your data file. Then, if you lose your electricity or if something goes wrong with the change in design, you'll have a good file to go back to.

## Backing Up Files

1. Choose File from the Main menu.

   Q&A displays the File menu.

2. Choose Utilities.

   Q&A displays the File Utilities menu.

3. Choose Backup Database.

   Q&A adds a dialog box to the screen and asks for the name of the database you wish to back up (Figure 3.4). If you have been working with a database, Q&A proposes that name.

4. Type in the name of the database (or press Enter to accept the proposed name); then press Enter. If you can't remember the name of the file to be backed up, and if no file name is proposed, press Enter or F10 to display the list of database files in this directory; then select a file by highlighting a name and pressing Enter or F10.

In the dialog box, Q&A asks for the name that you want to give the backup database.

5. If you want to back up to the hard drive, simply type the name of the backup database; then press Enter or F10.

Q&A places the backup files in the same directory that has your original files. Q&A makes a copy of both the data file (.DTF) and the index file (.IDX), so if you have a problem with your hard drive, you may lose both.

**59**

6. To back up to floppy disk, press the Backspace key to erase the default path (C:\QA). Then type A:and the file name and press Enter (Figure 3.5).

Q&A makes a copy of both the data file (.DTF) and the index file (.IDX). If your file is too big to fit on one floppy disk, Q&A tells you `Not enough disk space.`

7. To back up to multiple floppy disks, use the DOS BACKUP facility. Exit from Q&A. Put a blank disk in the floppy disk drive and, with the DOS prompt on your screen, type: `BACKUP C:\QA\filename.DTF A:,` `BACKUP C:\QA\filename.IDX A:`and press Enter.

If additional disks are needed, DOS prompts you every time it is ready for each new one.

□

To restore files backed up this way, use the DOS RESTORE command.

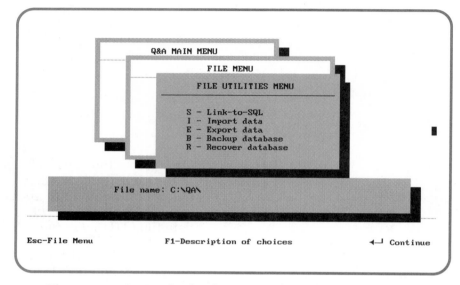

*Figure 3.4    Q&A asks for the name of the file to be backed up*

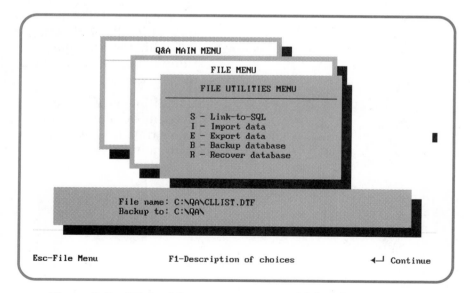

*Figure 3.5    Q&A adds a new prompt, which asks you for the name of the backup file, to the dialog box*

## Recovering Database Files

If your database files have been damaged for some reason, you may have to try to recover the data by using the Recover Database option. Q&A cannot guarantee that this process is totally successful, but it is worth a try.

Before you start this procedure, make sure that you have one backup of your database.

**Q Recovering Files**

1. Choose File from the Main menu.

   Q&A displays the File menu.

2. Choose Utilities.

   Q&A displays the File Utilities menu.

3. Choose Recover Database.

   Q&A adds a dialog box to the screen and asks for the name of the database to be recovered. If you have been working with a database, Q&A proposes that name.

4. Type in the name of the database (or press Enter to accept the proposed name); then press Enter. If you can't remember the name of the file to be restored, and if no file name is proposed, press Enter or F10 to display the list of database files in this directory; then select a file by highlighting a name and pressing Enter.

   Q&A displays a warning screen.

61

5. Either press Esc to cancel the operation or press F10 to start the recovery.

Q&A displays a warning screen, then a status screen (Figure 3.6), which shows you how the operation is progressing. When the operation has completed, Q&A returns to the File Utilities menu and displays a message about the success of the recovery process.  □

The horizontal bar fills in as the file is recovered.

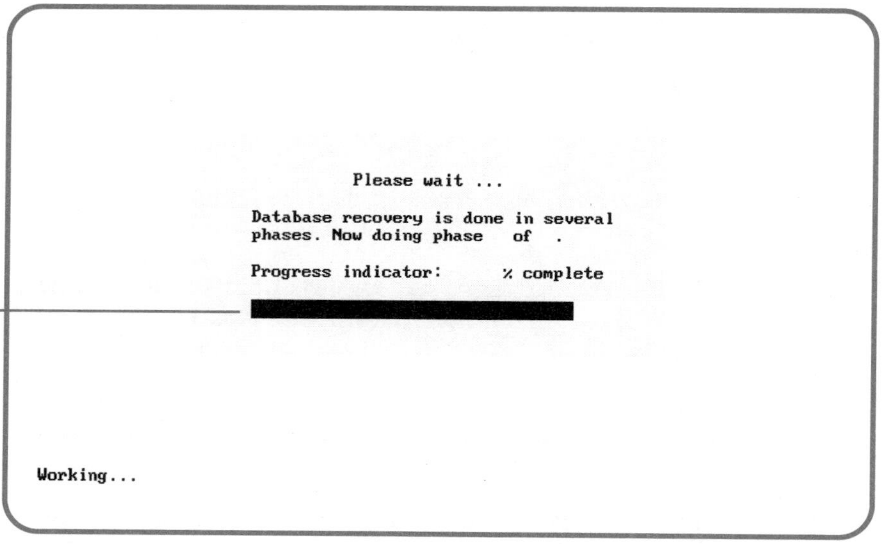

```
                        Please wait ...

            Database recovery is done in several
            phases. Now doing phase    of  .

            Progress indicator:        % complete

            ████████████████████████████████


   Working...
```

*Figure 3.6    During the recovery process, Q&A informs you of its progress*

## Redesigning a Database

Q&A makes it easy for you to change a database design. You can use Q&A to

▶  Change a label by typing over the original name

▶  Insert text within the label by pressing Ins

► Delete text within the label by pressing Del

► Change a field length by inserting or deleting spaces within it

► Indicate the new field length by typing > at the end of the field, moving the cursor to the old end of the field, and pressing Del

► Delete a field by moving the cursor over that field and pressing the Spacebar until you have erased the name

► Move a field by retyping the field in its new location, then deleting the field in its original location

► Add a field by typing the new field label and either : or <

► Insert a new line by moving the cursor to the beginning of the line above the location of the new line and pressing Ins

► Delete a line by moving the cursor to any location on the line that you want to delete and pressing Shift-F4

> **Caution:** If you move a field, make sure that you are not in Insert mode; otherwise, you may push fields off the right margin of the screen and onto the next line.

You also can use the Options menu to change the form layout, to perform block operations, and for other options. Press F8 to display the Options menu.

Q&A labels each field with a two-letter code: AA, AB, etc. As you redesign your form, remember the following about this two-letter code:

► If you delete a field, also delete the two-letter code.

► If you move a field, also move the two-letter code.

► If you add a field, Q&A automatically adds a two-letter code when it updates the form.

► Never change a two-letter label.

You can redesign forms any time you want, even if they already contain data. If a database contains data, don't drastically redesign it. As a matter of fact, before you change one field, back up your data.

After you back up your database, the next step in changing a database design is to identify the data file on which you want to work. Then retrieve the data file from the Q&A directory in which it is stored.

## **Q Changing the Design of a Database**

1. Choose File from the Main menu.

   Q&A displays the File menu.

2. Choose Design File.

   Q&A displays the Design menu.

3. Choose Redesign a File.

   Q&A adds a dialog box, which asks for a file name, to the Design menu (Figure 3.7).

4. If you have worked on a database file during this session, Q&A proposes that name. You can accept that name by pressing Enter. If you can't remember the name of the file that you want to redesign, remove any proposed file name from the dialog box; then press Enter. If you know the name of the file to be redesigned, type the name in the dialog box and press Enter.

   Q&A displays the database form, but each field is now labeled with the two-letter Q&A code. See Figure 3.8 for a sample database form.

5. Change the layout of the form. You can change the form by deleting, moving, or adding fields. You can also draw lines and boxes. (Refer to Chapter 2 for information about form design.)

   Q&A makes the changes you specify.

6. When you have finished changing the layout of the form, either press Esc to undo your changes or press F10 to continue with the new form.

   If you press Esc, you will see the original form without the changes that you just made. If you press F10, Q&A gives you the opportunity to redefine information types for the form (Figure 3.9).  ☐

> **Note:** If you have deleted any fields on your form, Q&A warns you that some of your data may be lost.

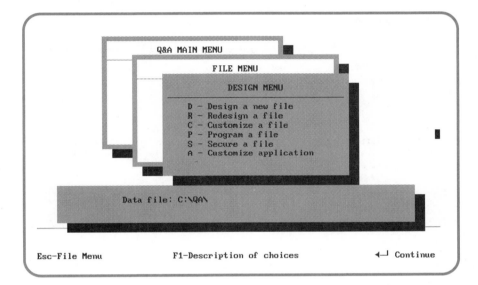

*Figure 3.7   Q&A adds a dialog box into which you type a file name*

# Changing Field Types

The next step in redesigning a database is to change its information types, if needed. For example, if you have added a new field requiring a Yes or No answer, you should define its information type as Y. If you have added new fields to stamp the date, those fields should be identified as D. If you saw that you defined a money field as a number information type rather than money, you should redefine the type as M. For a detailed description of each information type, see Chapter 2.

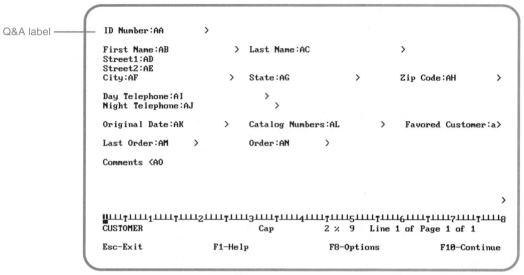

Q&A label

*Figure 3.8    A sample database form has fields that are labeled by Q&A*

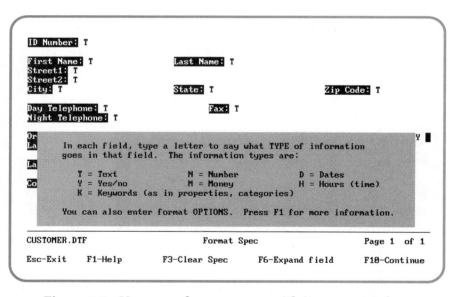

*Figure 3.9    Now your form appears with its current information types along with a display of Q&A information types*

## *Q* Changing Existing Information Types

1. Move the highlight to the field by pressing any combination of Tab, Shift-Tab, Up, and Down. Remember to change from the default T type for all new fields, if needed. Type over the code to enter the appropriate information type. You can update as many fields as you want.

   The prompt box on the screen provides you with the names and codes of each Q&A information type.

2. Remember that you can also use format options here. After you add or change information types, type ., then enter format options (all separated by commas). You can justify right, left, or center; you can convert text to all uppercase, all lowercase, or initial caps; you can insert commas in money fields; and you can define the number of decimal places for number fields. (For more information, see Chapter 2.) Press F10.

   Q&A displays the Global Format Options screen if your data file has money, number, date, or hours fields. These settings are those that you set for the original form design.

3. Edit the Global Format Options, if needed, and then press F10.

   Q&A returns to the File menu.

   □

---

**Caution:** If you want to change the information type for an existing field, ensure that the new type is compatible with the old. If you are not careful about this, Q&A will be unable to calculate, sort in a different way, or treat programming commands in an appropriate manner.

Q&A assigns field names as you create a database. Most of the time these field names are identical to the labels that you gave to fields. However, if Q&A finds label duplication, it makes a field name unique. In our CUSTOMER database, if you decide to name both address field labels Address, Q&A calls one field Address and the other Address1.

You can modify or expand a field name. For example, in the CUSTOMER database, the Favored Customer field is not thoroughly explained. You can describe a field in greater depth by either creating a custom help screen or by expanding the field name.

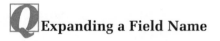

## Expanding a Field Name

1. If you want to put more information in a Q&A field name than there is space on the screen, move the cursor to that field and press F6.

   The cursor moves to a prompt at the bottom of the Field Spec screen.

2. Type a longer (and more informative) field name or explanation. Press F6.

   The cursor moves back to the field. If a field name is longer than its screen display, there is a small right arrow at the beginning and/or end of that field that shows you where you can find more text.

3. To display an expanded field (and to move the cursor to the Expand field: prompt), press F6. Press F10.

   Q&A finishes the form redesign.

   □

Figure 3.10 shows you the new look of the CUSTOMER database form.

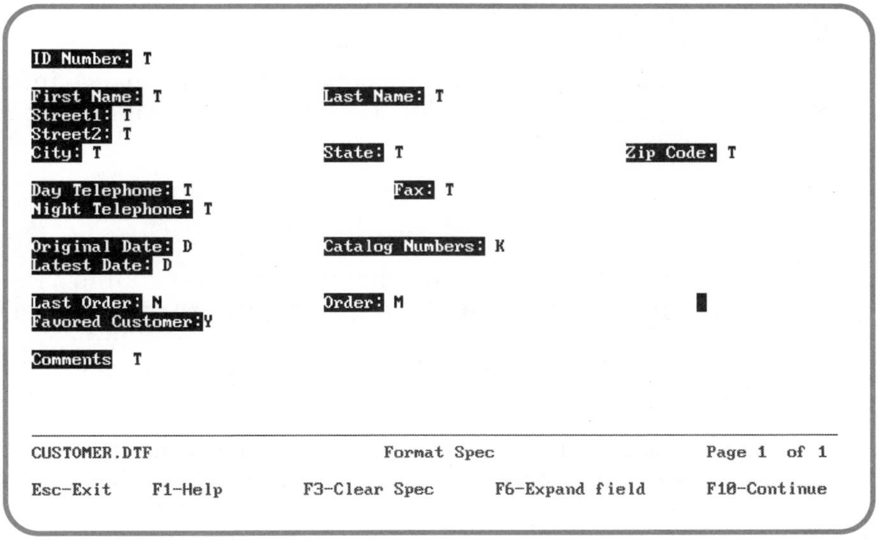

*Figure 3.10   The CUSTOMER database form with new format, added lines, and changed fields and information types*

**69**

# Customizing a Database

After you have a completed your database form design, you can ensure that the database is easier for you to use. Q&A provides the opportunity to

► Change information types and enter field formatting options

► Restrict the values that can be entered in a field

► Add a field template to ensure that certain types of characters are typed into a field

► Automatically put the most regularly entered value in a field

► Speed up searching by defining certain fields as commonly used search fields

► Provide custom help for a field

► Change the palette, or color scheme, for the record

## Format Values

The Format Values option gives you another chance to change information types and add or change formatting options (see Chapter 2).

## Restrict Values

The Restrict Values option ensures that the data entered into a field is valid. You can also request or require that any or restricted data is entered so that this field is not blank. For example, if only 1, 2, or 3 are valid, you should not allow 0 or 99. As a matter of fact, you should make sure that only 1, 2, or 3 are entered.

You can also use this option to ensure that a value in a field is less than, equal to, or greater than a specific number, or that it starts with a particular character, and so on.

**70**

### *Q* Setting Restrictions

| | |
|---|---|
| 1. From the Main menu, choose File. | Q&A displays the File menu. |
| 2. Choose Design File. | Q&A displays the Design menu. |
| 3. Choose Customize a File (not Customize Application). | Q&A adds a dialog box to the screen and asks for the name of a file to customize. If you worked on a file during this session, it appears in the dialog box. |
| 4. Type the name of the file that you want to customize or accept the name that Q&A has proposed. Press Enter. | Q&A displays the Customize menu (Figure 3.11). |
| 5. Choose Restrict Values. | Q&A displays the Restrict Spec screen. |

6. Use cursor movement keys, Tab, Shift-Tab, or Enter to highlight the field whose input you want to restrict. Type a restrict expression into the field (Figure 3.12). If you need help, press F1.When you have finished typing restrict expressions, press F10.

Q&A returns you to the Customize menu.

□

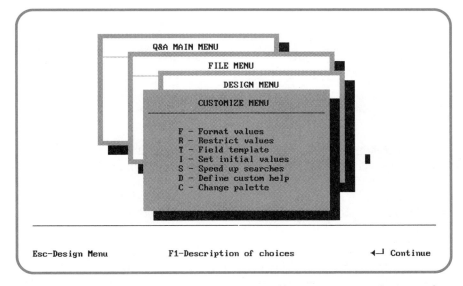

*Figure 3.11    The Customize menu offers you seven choices of database customization*

▶ **Tip:** You can also customize a database by using the @MSG (message) or @HELP programming commands to display a message or custom help to the user. For information about Q&A programming commands, see Chapter 12.

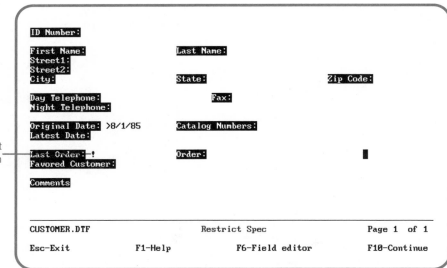

This arrow indicates that there is information in this field.

*Figure 3.12    This Restrict Spec screen limits the values that you can enter in some fields*

Tables 3.1, 3.2, and 3.3 list field restriction expressions by categories. These restrictions apply to both numeric and alphanumeric characters. Use these tables by replacing the characters in the left column (for example, X, Y, Z) with the restriction expression that you want to enter in a field. For example, if you enter the first value in Table 3.1 in a field, data entry is restricted to either leaving the field blank or typing 123; any other value in this field is invalid.

Table 3.1 lists the field restriction expressions that are either exact matches or ranges within which one or more values must fall. The number of characters in a field is only limited to the valid value.

*Table 3.1    Match- or Range-Related Field Restriction Expressions*

| Typing | Means that the Value of the Field Is |
| --- | --- |
| X | X |
| =X | Empty or X |
| /X | Any value but X |
| = | Empty |
| X;Y;Z | X or Y or Z, but nothing else |

| Typing | Means that the Value of the Field Is |
|--------|--------------------------------------|
| >X | Greater than X |
| <X | Less than X |
| >=X | Greater than or equal to X |
| <=X | Less than or equal to X |
| >X..<Y | From greater than X to less than Y |
| >X..<=Y | From greater than X to less than or equal to Y |
| <X;>=Y | Less than X or greater than or equal to Y |

Table 3.2 lists the field restriction expressions that restrict the actual characters or number of characters in a field.

*Table 3.2  Character-Related Field Restriction Expressions*

**73**

| Typing | Means that the Value of the Field Is |
|--------|--------------------------------------|
| ? | Any single character, but no more than a single character |
| ?? | Any two characters, but no more than two characters |
| ????t | Any five-letter value that ends with t |
| .. | Any group of alphabetic characters |
| K.. | Any value that begins with K |
| ..K | Any value that ends with K |
| s..d | Any value that begins with s and ends with d |
| ..K.. | Any value that contains K anywhere |
| ..T..E..D | Any value that contains T, E, and D in that order |

Table 3.3 lists the two remaining restrictions. If you use either of these restrictions, Q&A displays an appropriate message.

*Table 3.3  Required and Requested Field Restriction Expressions*

| Typing | Means |
|--------|-------|
| /= | An entry in this field is requested, but not required |
| ! | An entry in this field is required; you cannot leave this field until you fill it in |

> ▶ **Tip:** When you restrict a field and then need to enter "inappropriate" data, Q&A displays an error message. If you press Enter or Tab twice, you can force Q&A to ignore the restriction. There is one exception to this: you cannot override a required field.

You can combine restriction expressions by using the logical characters in Table 3.4. Using these characters produces the following examples:

X..Y means X and Y or X through Y

X;Y means X or Y

/X means not X

*Table 3.4   Field Restriction Expressions Combination Characters*

| Typing | Means that the Value of the Field Is |
| --- | --- |
| .. | The first expression and the second expression, (or the first expression through the second expression) |
| ; | The first expression or the second expression (but not both) |
| / | Any value but the expression |

> ⊘ **Caution:** Requested and required restrictions should not be combined with any other restrictions.

## Field Templates

Field templates make it easier for information to be typed the way you want it. Use them both to restrict and format contents of text fields only. Remember that a field can be all numbers (such as ZIP code or telephone number) and still be defined as text information type. For example, if you format a telephone number field by entering (###)###-####, a user entering data in this field sees a template that already contains the parentheses and dash. All a user can do is type ten numbers; they are formatted automatically.

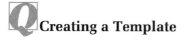

## Creating a Template

1.  From the Main menu, choose File.

    Q&A displays the File menu.

2.  Choose Design File.

    Q&A displays the Design menu.

3.  Choose Customize a File.

    Q&A adds a dialog box to the screen and asks for the name of a file to customize. If you worked on a file during this session, it appears in the dialog box.

4.  Type the name of the file that you want to customize or accept the name that Q&A has proposed. Press Enter.

    Q&A displays the Customize menu.

5.  Choose Field Template.

    Q&A displays the Field Template Spec.

6.  Use cursor movement keys, Tab, Shift-Tab, or Enter to highlight the field to which you want to apply the template. Type a template into the field (Figure 3.13). (Refer to Table 3.5 for valid field templates.) When you have finished typing field templates, press F10.

    Q&A returns you to the Customize menu.

    □

**75**

*Table 3.5  Valid Field Templates*

| Typing | Means |
| --- | --- |
| # or 9 | To assign a single alphanumeric number (0 through 9) |
| @ | To assign a single alphabetic character (A through Z or a through z) |
| $ | To assign a typed character, which can be any character that you can type from the keyboard |
| \ | To assign an escape character, telling Q&A to take the following character as a literal |

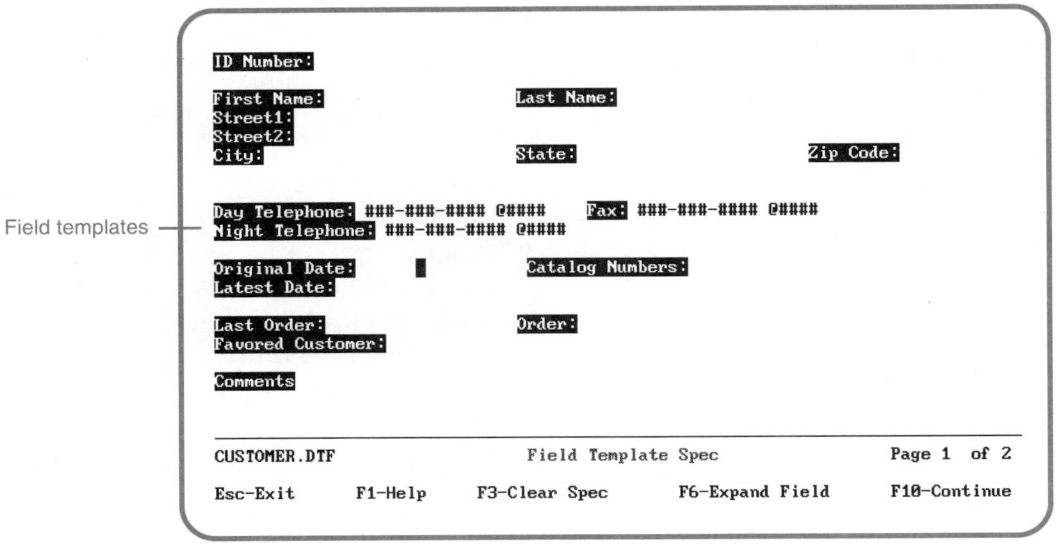

Field templates —

Figure 3.13    The Field Template Spec with telephone and ZIP code field templates

To include # in the template, for example, type \#. Typing #####-#### ensures that five alphanumeric numbers are entered, followed by a dash and four more numbers. If you want to include the possibility of an extension with a telephone number, type (###) ###-#### @####. The at symbol (@) ensures that a character is entered in that position. To separate one part of the template text from another, use a space or any of the following printable characters: !#$%'()*+,-./:;<=>?@[]^{}.

> **Tip:** When you search for values that have been formatted, enter the raw data. For example, if you want to find a formatted telephone number, such as (212) 555-1212, enter the data as the program sees it—2125551212.

## Set Initial Values

The Set Initial Values option sets a default value for a field. For example, if our catalog company sells a mix of 30% screwdrivers and 70% all other tools, consider setting a default value of "screwdriver" for the Type field. Then, if a value for a particular record is not screwdriver, erase it and type the appropriate value.

## Q Setting Initial Values

| | |
|---|---|
| 1. From the Main menu, choose File. | Q&A displays the File menu. |
| 2. Choose Design File. | Q&A displays the Design menu. |
| 3. Choose Customize a File. | Q&A adds a dialog box to the screen and asks for the name of a file to customize. If you worked on a file during this session, it appears in the dialog box. |
| 4. Type the name of the file that you want to customize or accept the name that Q&A has proposed. Press Enter. | Q&A displays the Customize menu. |
| 5. Choose Set initial Values. | Q&A displays the Initial Values Spec. |
| 6. Use cursor movement keys, Tab, Shift-Tab, or Enter to highlight the field to which you want to apply the value. Type the initial value into the field (Figure 3.14). The initial value must conform to the information type of the field. When you have finished setting initial values, press F10. | Q&A returns you to the Customize menu. |

□

Enter NY in the State field of the CUSTOMER database if most of your customers live in New York. Enter @DATE in the Last Contact Field in another database if you apply a datestamp when a customer calls.

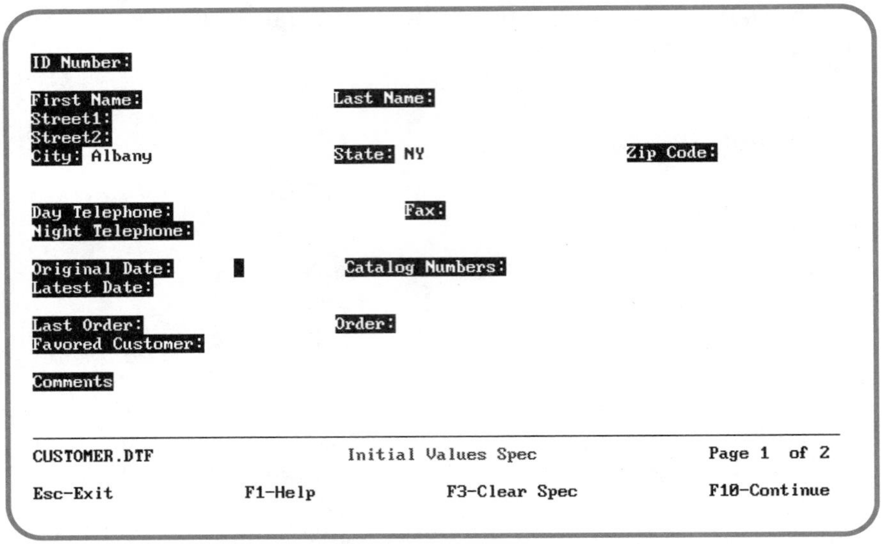

```
 ID Number:

 First Name:              Last Name:
 Street1:
 Street2:
 City: Albany             State: NY              Zip Code:


 Day Telephone:                 Fax:
 Night Telephone:

 Original Date:       ▌       Catalog Numbers:
 Latest Date:

 Last Order:              Order:
 Favored Customer:

 Comments

 ─────────────────────────────────────────────────────────────
 CUSTOMER.DTF            Initial Values Spec      Page 1  of 2

 Esc-Exit        F1-Help          F3-Clear Spec        F10-Continue
```

78

*Figure 3.14   The Initial Values Spec with state and date initial values*

> ▶ **Tip:** You can set the current date using the @DATE function, the current time using the @TIME function, and obtain a unique number by using the @NUMBER function. For more information about Q&A programming commands, see Chapter 12.

## Speed Up Searches

The Speed Up Searches option speeds up Q&A searches and retrievals for a few specified fields. When you define "speedy fields," Q&A creates a small database that only contains indexes. For example, if you often want to retrieve records within a certain ZIP code range, make the ZIP code field a speedy field.

However, each time you add a new record, Q&A must find the right location for the new index in the minidatabase. This means that the program processes each new record a little more slowly.

> ▶ **Tip:** If you plan to use the XLOOKUP function in programming, you must apply Speed Up Searches to certain fields. For more information about Q&A programming commands, see Chapter 12.

## *Q*Defining Speedy Fields

1. From the Main menu, choose File.

   Q&A displays the File menu.

2. Choose Design File.

   Q&A displays the Design menu.

3. Choose Customize a File.

   Q&A adds a dialog box to the screen and asks for the name of a file to customize. If you worked on a file during this session, it appears in the dialog box.

4. Type the name of the file that you want to customize or accept the name that Q&A has proposed. Press Enter.

   Q&A displays the Customize menu.

5. Choose Speed Up Searches.

   Q&A displays the Speed Up Spec.

6. Use cursor movement keys, Tab, Shift-Tab, or Enter to highlight the field that you want to make speedy. Type a speedy value. Type S in a field that you regularly use for searching. Type SU to require a unique value in that field. Type SE to require a nonunique value in that field. Press F10.

   When you enter a new value in that field and press F10, Q&A tells you that the value has never been entered before and prompts you to verify the value.

7. If the value is valid, press
F10 again. The initial
value must conform to the
information type of the
field. When you have
finished defining speedy
fields, press F10. See
Figure 3.15 for an example
of a filled-in Speed Up
Spec screen.

Q&A returns you to the
Customize menu.

□

**80**

Speed this field,
which has a unique
value.

```
ID Number: SU

First Name:              Last Name:
Street1:
Street2:
City:                    State:              Zip Code:


Day Telephone:                  Fax:
Night Telephone:

Original Date:      █       Catalog Numbers:
Latest Date:

Last Order:             Order:
Favored Customer:

Comments
_____

CUSTOMER.DTF              Speed-up Spec              Page 1  of 2

Esc-Exit        F1-Help           F3-Clear Spec        F10-Continue
```

*Figure 3.15    This Speed Up Spec is filled in*

## Define Custom Help

The Define Custom Help option allows you to explain to those who
enter data for your company the meaning of—or something else
about—a field.

 **Entering Custom Help for a Field**

1. From the Main menu,
choose File.

Q&A displays the File
menu.

2. Choose Design File.

Q&A displays the Design menu.

3. Choose Customize a File.

Q&A adds a dialog box to the screen and asks for the name of a file to customize. If you worked on a file during this session, it appears in the dialog box.

4. Type the name of the file that you want to customize or accept the name that Q&A has proposed. Press Enter.

Q&A displays the Customize menu.

5. Choose Define Custom Help.

Q&A displays the Help Spec, which is superimposed on your database record. The first field on the screen is highlighted.

**81**

6. Press F8 (or F6) to move to the next (or previous) field for which you want to add custom help. Enter up to eight lines of text.

The cursor is positioned on the Help Spec.

7. When you have finished entering the message for one field, press F8 to move the highlight to the next field in the form (or press F6 to move to the previous field).

Unless you have previously typed custom help text, the Help Spec is blank.

8. When you have finished entering all help messages for your form, press F10 to return to the Customize menu. For an example of a form with the Help Spec displayed, see Figure 3.16.

Q&A returns you to the Customize menu.

□

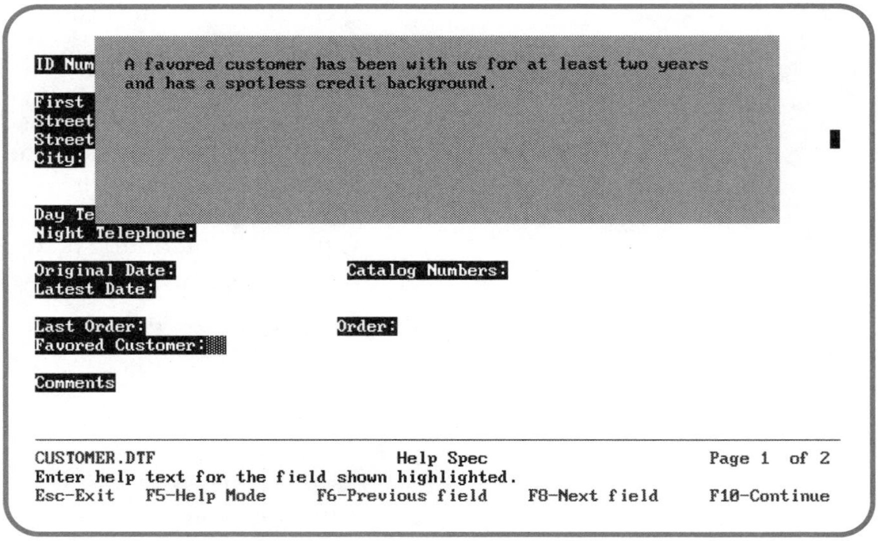

```
ID Num    A favored customer has been with us for at least two years
          and has a spotless credit background.
First
Street
Street
City:

Day Te
Night Telephone:

Original Date:              Catalog Numbers:
Latest Date:

Last Order:                 Order:
Favored Customer:

Comments

_____
CUSTOMER.DTF                    Help Spec                  Page 1  of 2
Enter help text for the field shown highlighted.
Esc-Exit    F5-Help Mode    F6-Previous field    F8-Next field    F10-Continue
```

82

Figure 3.16    The Help Spec is displayed on top of your database record

> ▶ **Tip:** To erase custom help messages, display the Help Spec and select the field that has the help message you want to delete. Press Backspace to delete the message, or press Shift-F4 to delete individual lines.

## Change Palette

The Change Palette option uses colors, shading, and underlining to highlight all or part of the current database form's background and foreground. This does not affect the palette for other Q&A databases. You might want to experiment to see which of Q&A's color combinations are easier for you to look at if you spend a great deal of time staring at the screen.

Your computer's monitor determines the level of palette change available. A color monitor allows you the greatest choices of palettes; a laptop LCD allows the least.

## *Q* Changing the Palette

| | | |
|---|---|---|
| 1. | From the Main menu, choose File. | Q&A displays the File menu. |
| 2. | Choose Design File. | Q&A displays the Design menu. |
| 3. | Choose Customize a File. | Q&A adds a dialog box to the screen and asks for the name of a file to customize. If you worked on a file during this session, it appears in the dialog box. |
| 4. | Type the name of the file that you want to customize or accept the name that Q&A has proposed. Press Enter. | Q&A displays the Customize menu. |
| 5. | Choose Change Palette. | Q&A displays the form with the name of the current palette displayed near the bottom of the screen. |
| 6. | Press F8 (or F6). | Q&A moves to the next (or previous) palette. |
| 7. | When you have found the palette of your choice, press F10. | Q&A returns you to the Customize menu. |

83

# What You Have Learned

▶ Use the Redesign a File option to make many types of changes to a database form.

▶ Back up your files often.

▶ Use the Customize a File option to make many types of changes to fields on a database form.

▶ Q&A provides several options that ensure the validity of information entered into a database.

► Define fields that you use regularly for searches as "speedy" fields so that your search is faster.

► Custom help messages associated with particular fields make data entry easier and more accurate.

**84**

# Q&A File: Advanced Operations

## In This Chapter

▶ *Adding data to a database*
▶ *Entering data into different field types*
▶ *Copying data from one form to another*
▶ *Deleting words, fields, lines, and forms*
▶ *Displaying information about screens and fields*
▶ *Printing and saving forms*
▶ *Sorting and retrieving records*
▶ *Viewing forms in Table View*

You can add new information to a database form or search for information already in the database in order to change it in some way. In Q&A, these two functions are Add Data and Search/Update.

The data entry screen for your database is similar to the form that you designed, but there is no ruler line at the bottom of the screen and more function keys are displayed. In addition, the top status line displays how many records are now in your database and keeps a running count of the new records you have added in this data entry session.

# Adding Data to a Database

When you designed a form, File allowed you to move anywhere on the screen. Now as you enter data, you can move only among the fields.

## *Q* Adding Data

| | |
|---|---|
| 1. From the Main menu, select File. | Q&A displays the File menu. |
| 2. Select Add data. | Q&A adds a dialog box to the bottom of the screen. |
| 3. Accept the file name in the dialog box or type another file name; then press Enter. | Q&A displays a blank form (Figure 4.1). The highlight indicates the length of the field. |
| 4. Type a value into the first field. | If you have customized the form, you will see some evidence of your work, such as an initial value or a format. |
| 5. Press Tab or Enter. If you are at the end of the field, press Right. | Q&A moves to the next field. |
| 6. Press the Up (or Down) key. | Q&A moves you up (or down) the form. |
| 7. Press Shift-Tab. | Q&A moves you to the prior field. ☐ |

# Entering Data into Different Field Types

As you enter data, File gently prompts you (or even ignores the entry) if a value is invalid. If a database administrator has applied Q&A security features to any field or the entire database, a user may not have the right to enter data or even to look at the information previously placed there. Refer to Appendix B for information about database and field security.

If you have defined a field template (such as a telephone number), you'll see some of the characters that help you enter appropriate data. The cursor skips to the next appropriate position every time you type a character.

Because you also can indicate the places that are restricted to numbers or alphabetic characters, if you try to enter something other than the character defined for that place in the field, File ignores your entry. In this way, if you define a telephone number as text, you can still restrict the entry to all numbers by defining a field template. See Chapter 3, "Redesigning and Customizing a Database," for more information about field templates.

If you have set an initial value for a field, the field contains that value (see Chapter 3). If you want to enter a different value, type the information you want in the field over the initial value.

When you have reached the last field (see Figure 4.2), press F10 and the next blank form appears.

**87**

```
ID Number:

First Name:                    Last Name:
Street1:
Street2:
City: Albany                   State: NY              Zip Code:       -

Day Telephone:      -   -         Fax:     -    -
Night Telephone:      -    -

Original Date:              Catalog Numbers:
Latest Date:

Last Order:                 Order:
Favored Customer:

Comments

_____

CUSTOMER.DTF    New Record 1     of 1     Total Records: 2     Page 1  of  2

Esc-Exit    F1-Help       F3-Delete form    F7-Search    F8-Calc    F10-Continue
```

*Figure 4.1    The Data Entry screen is the first in a new database*

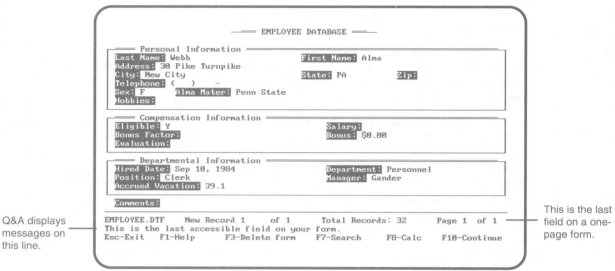

Q&A displays messages on this line.

This is the last field on a one-page form.

Figure 4.2   Q&A issues this message when you have reached the last field on a form

**88**

# Using Data Entry Shortcuts

You can use keys and key combinations to save yourself time as you enter information. Table 4.1 lists the data entry shortcut keys and key combinations.

Table 4.1   Data Entry Shortcut Keys

| Key | Function |
| --- | --- |
| F1 | Displays custom help |
| F2 | Prints the current form |
| Shift-F2 | Displays the Macro menu |
| Ctrl-F2 | Prints all the forms entered in the current session |
| F3 | Deletes the current form |
| F4 | Deletes the first word after the cursor position |
| Shift-F4 | Deletes either the current line or the contents of the current field, whichever is shorter |

| Key | Function |
| --- | --- |
| Ctrl-F4 | Deletes all characters after the cursor position to the end of the field |
| F5 | Copies the field information from the previous form into the current form |
| Shift-F5 | Copies the entire contents of the previous form into the current one |
| Ctrl-F5 | Places the current date in the current field |
| Alt-F5 | Places the current time in the current field |
| F6 | Opens the Long Value Edit box into which to type more information than the current field is defined to hold or perform some other functions |
| Shift-F6 | Defines Table View during an update |
| Ctrl-F6 | Adds forms during an update |
| Alt-F6 | Displays forms in a table format during an update |
| F7 | Searches for forms |
| Shift-F7 | Deletes the last change and returns to the previous value during an update |
| Alt-F7 | Displays any field restrictions for the current field |
| F8 | Recalculates the values in fields that contain formulas |
| Shift-F8 | Sets the Calculation mode |
| Ctrl-F8 | Sets the @Number function to the value by which the value in a field is increased over the previous form's value |
| F9 | Saves the current form and returns to the previous one |
| Shift-F9 | Adds the Custom Specs box to the bottom of the screen |
| F10 | Saves the current form and gets the next one |
| Shift-F10 | Saves the current form and exits the current data entry session |
| Alt-F10 | Enables entering a literal character |

**89**

> ▶ **Tip:** A function key does not have to be printed on the status line of a form or document for you to use it. If you want to perform a function, try pressing the key even if it doesn't appear on the bottom of the screen—it might work!

# Copying Data from One Form to Another

You can copy the entire contents of the previous form into the current form or copy field information from the previous form into this form.

If you want to keep separate records for key executives of the same corporation, for instance, you might find it easier to fill in the fields of one form, and then copy that form for each executive, editing such data as telephone extensions and titles as you go. Or, if you are typing a series of customer forms from a town in which you just opened a branch store, rather than retyping the town, state, and ZIP code on each form, press F5 to copy that information as you move to the appropriate fields.

**90**

 **Copying the Previous Form to the Current Form**

1. Add at least one form to your database and press F10.

   Q&A displays a new, empty form.

2. Press Shift-F5.

   File fills out the current form with all the field information from the previous form.

3. Edit the current form and press F10.

   Q&A saves the current form and File displays a new blank form. ☐

# Deleting Words, Fields, Lines, and Forms

As you are adding data, you can delete all or parts of fields, lines, and forms:

1. To delete the first word after the current cursor position, press F4.
2. To delete either the current line or the contents of the current field, whichever is shorter, press Shift-F4.

3. To delete all characters after the current cursor position to the end of the field, press Ctrl-F4.

4. To delete the current form, press F3.

---

**Caution:** When you press F4, Shift-F4, or Ctrl-F4, Q&A does not issue a warning message before making the deletion. File displays a warning message before deleting the form (Figure 4.3).

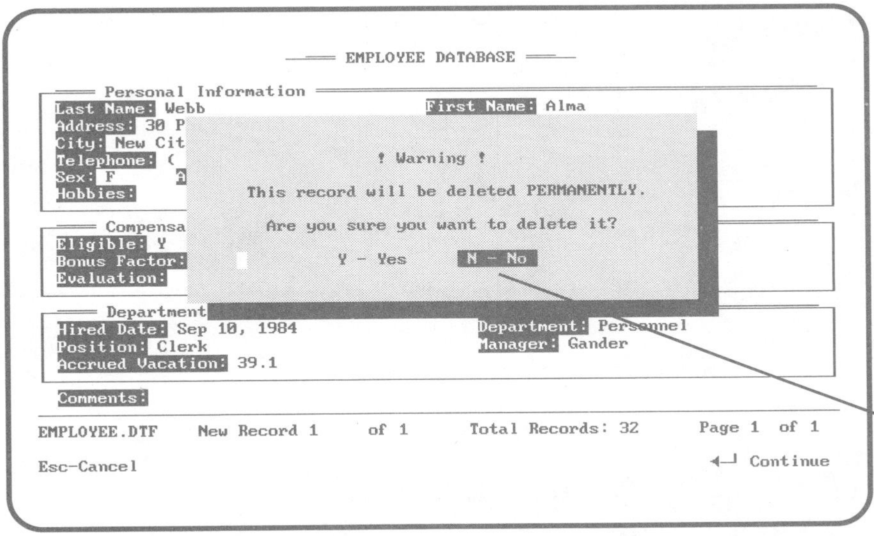

---

Figure 4.3 is referenced with a callout note:

Q&A always ensures that the the least destructive message is highlighted.

*Figure 4.3    File warns you before you can delete the current form*

# Displaying Custom Help Screens

As you add information, you may find that you need a reminder about what to type in a particular field. If you have defined custom help for a field, you can press F1 to display the custom help message (see Figure 4.4). If there is no custom help for a field, press F1 again to display the Q&A standard help screen. Press Esc to leave the standard help screen and Esc again to leave custom help.

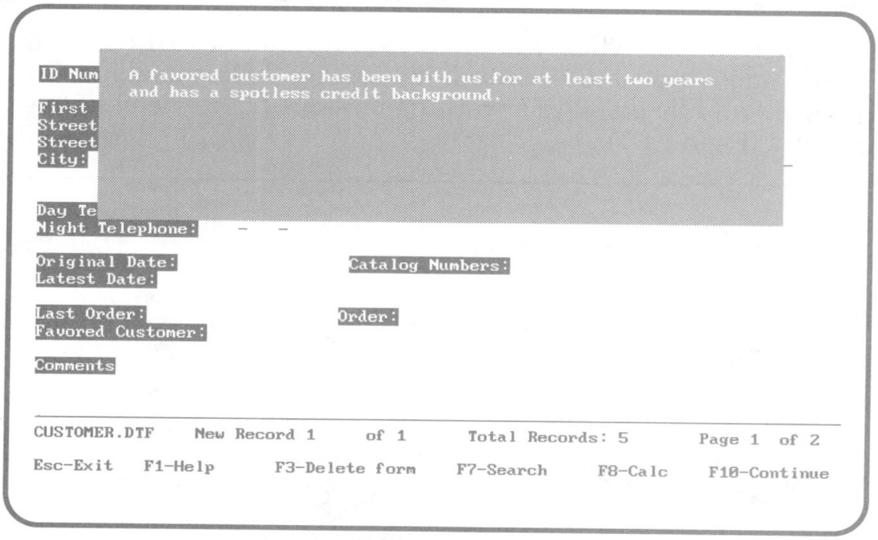

*Figure 4.4    This is a sample custom help screen*

# Printing Forms during a Data Entry Session

As you enter information into the current form, you may want a printed copy of it to use as a guide for entering data in the next forms, or you may want a copy of all the forms you entered during this session.

Press F2 to print the current form or Ctrl-F2 to print all the forms you entered during this session. After you press either F2 or Ctrl-F2, File displays the File Print Options screen (see Figure 4.5).

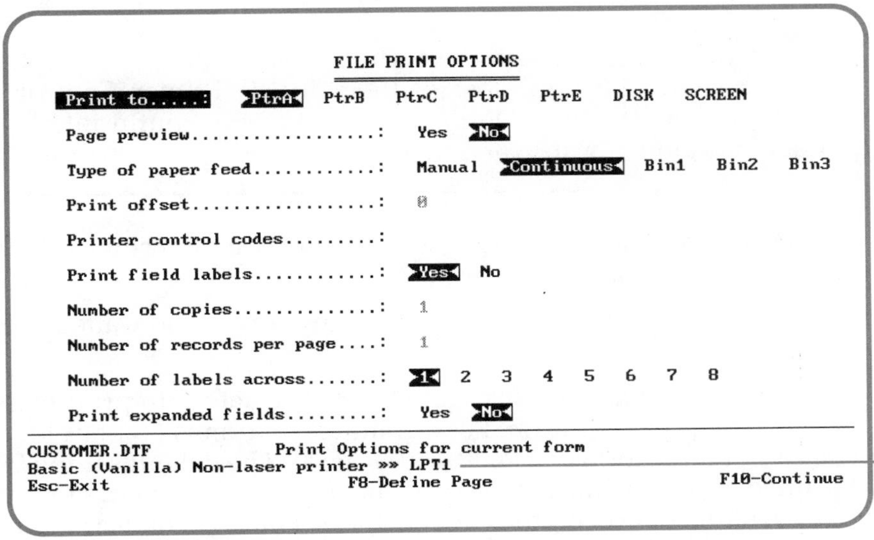

```
                    FILE PRINT OPTIONS
                    ‾‾‾‾‾‾‾‾‾‾‾‾‾‾‾‾‾‾
  Print to.....:   ►PtrA◄  PtrB   PtrC   PtrD   PtrE   DISK   SCREEN

  Page preview.................:   Yes  ►No◄

  Type of paper feed...........:   Manual  ►Continuous◄  Bin1   Bin2   Bin3

  Print offset.................:   0

  Printer control codes........:

  Print field labels...........:  ►Yes◄  No

  Number of copies.............:   1

  Number of records per page...:   1

  Number of labels across......:  ►1◄  2   3   4   5   6   7   8

  Print expanded fields........:   Yes  ►No◄

CUSTOMER.DTF          Print Options for current form
Basic (Vanilla) Non-laser printer »» LPT1
Esc-Exit                       F8-Define Page              F10-Continue
```

Q&A reminds you that you have not installed your printer and its special attributes.

Figure 4.5   *The File Print Options screen allows you to determine what your printed output will look like*

Some of the fields on this screen are highlighted; those are the defaults.

*Print to* is the printer to which you want to send this print job. Most times you'll select PtrA, your default printer.

*Page preview* indicates whether you want to see what the form looks like before you print. Select Yes for page preview or no to print the form. If your printer does not have a graphics card or monitor, this feature does not work.

*Type of paper feed* is the way your printer handles paper. Select Continuous if your printer provides a continuous flow of paper— either pin-fed or from one bin.

*Print offset* leaves a wider margin on the left side of the page. Use this for pin-fed printers.

*Printer control codes* offer special printing effects. For information about these, refer to your printer's reference manual.

> ▶ **Tip:** If you have a PostScript printer, you can store PostScript program files and specify them in the Printer Control Codes field of the Print Options screen. Refer to your printer's reference guide for instructions.

*Print field labels* tells Q&A whether you want to print the field labels. Select Yes or No.

*Number of copies* tells Q&A how many copies you want of this form.

*Number of records per page* tells Q&A whether to print more than one page of your form. For example, if a form is 20 lines long, you can fit three forms on an 8$^1/_2$" x 11" page. The default setting for a printed page is 66 lines until you change it using the Change Define Page Defaults option on the Global Options menu. You learn more about printing in Chapter 5, "Q&A File: Printing and Retrieving Forms."

*Number of labels across* indicates that you want to print the record on labels. The default (1) tells Q&A that you plan on printing the record from the left to the right margin.

*Print expanded fields* indicates whether you want Q&A to print the entire contents of an expanded field or the short version of this field.

After making whatever changes you want to the File Print Options screen, press F10 to print.

# Using the Long Value Edit Box

Q&A allows you to type more information into a field than it can display on the screen. For example, you might want to document the history of a customer who has a long string of complaints about your service. If you define a field called Complaint and press F6, you can type up to 32,000 characters.

## Q Using the Long Value Edit Box

| | |
|---|---|
| 1. With the cursor in the form that you want to expand, press F6. | Q&A opens the Long Value Edit box. |
| 2. Enter whatever information you want in the box with function keys and key combinations (see Table 4.2). | Q&A displays a small arrow indicating that this field holds more information than you can view immediately. |
| 3. Press F6 again. | Q&A displays the contents of this field. |
| 4. Press F10. | Q&A closes the Long Value Edit box. □ |

*Table 4.2   Long Value Edit Box Function Keys*

| Key | Normal | With Shift | With Ctrl | With Alt |
|---|---|---|---|---|
| F1 | Help | Spellcheck field | Spellcheck word | Thesaurus |
| F2 | Print field | Macros | Print text block | |
| F3 | Delete block | | Field statistics | |
| F4 | Delete word | Delete line | Delete from cursor to end of line | |
| F5 | Copy block | Move block | Copy block to file | Move block to file |
| F6 | Exit field editor | | | |
| F7 | Search and replace | Restore deleted text | Go to page/line | |
| F9 | Scroll up | Scroll down | | Calculate |
| F10 | Continue | | | Enter literal character |

Because many of these functions are used to process the words in the Long Value Edit box, you are actually using Write functions. For information about Write, and particularly the Options menu from which many of these functions come, see Chapters 7, "Q&A Write: Fundamentals" and 8, "Q&A Write: Advanced Operations."

## Displaying Field Restrictions

If you have restricted the value for a field to a single value or a range of values, you can press Alt-F7 to add a box stating the restrictions that have been applied (see Figure 4.6).

```
ID Number: 33343

First Name: Webb (also lis→    Last Name: Alma
Street1: 1 Seagull Boulevard                          ┌─────────────────┐
Street2:                                              │   FIELD VALUES  │
City: Wherever                  State: PA             │                 │
                                                      │ N               │
Day Telephone:     -   -        Fax:      -   -       │ Y               │
Night Telephone:   -   -                              │                 │
                                                      │                 │
Original Date:                  Catalog Numbers:      │                 │
Latest Date:                                          │                 │
                                                      │                 │
Last Order:                     Order:                │                 │
Favored Customer:                                     │                 │
                                                      └─────────────────┘
Comments


CUSTOMER.DTF   New Record 1      of 1      Total Records: 5        Page 1  of 2

Esc-Exit           A-Z   ↑  ↓  PgUp  PgDn  Home  End          ◄─┘ Continue
```

*Figure 4.6    Press Alt-F7 to see the current field restrictions, if any*

## Accessing Customize Options

As you are adding information to a database, Q&A provides you with the chance to select a customizing or programming spec in order to either display or edit the form in some way. For example, you can change an initial value or further restrict the value that can be entered. You also can just look at a spec to see how a field is formatted or what the initial value is. Press Shift-F9 to add the Custom Specs box to the bottom of the screen and then select the appropriate option. Table 4.3 lists Custom Spec options and what they display.

*Table 4.3    Custom Specs*

| Option | Display |
|--------|---------|
| F-Frmt | Format Spec |
| R-Rstrct | Restrict Spec |
| I-Initl | Initial Values Spec |
| M-Masks | Field Template Spec |
| P-Prgrm | Program Spec |
| L-Lkup | Lookup Table |
| H-Help | Help Spec |
| N-Nav Prog | Navigation Spec |

**97**

# Saving Forms

File provides two save functions to use when adding data to your database. Press F9 to save the current form and return to the previous form. Press F10 to save the current form and go to the next form to continue adding data.

Rather then pressing F10 to save and display the next form, press Shift-F10 to save the current form and return to the File menu.

# Retrieving Forms with the Retrieve Spec Screen

In order to modify records in your database, you must search for records that you have previously added. To do this, use the Search/Update option.

Before you start a search, you can have Q&A sort records so that they can be retrieved in a certain order. For example, if you want to select only those records from the city of Albany, and it is important that they be retrieved alphabetically by last name, first sort by last name from A to Z. Then retrieve Albany records.

### Q Sorting and Retrieving Records

| | |
|---|---|
| 1. From the Main menu, select File. | Q&A displays the File menu. |
| 2. Select Search/Update. | Q&A adds a dialog box to the bottom of the screen, which prompts you for the name of the file in which you want the search to take place. |
| 3. Enter the name of the file or press Enter for a list of files. After selecting a file, press Enter. | File displays the Retrieve Spec, an empty form. |
| 4. Press F8. | File displays the Sort Spec. |
| 5. Move the cursor to the field by which you want to sort and type 1. Add a space and then type AS (ascending order) or DS (descending order). | If you enter an incorrect or incomplete sort value, Q&A issues an error message (Figure 4.7). |
| 6. To retrieve all forms arranged in the order that you specified, press F10. | Q&A sorts all the forms in the database and then retrieves them all. |
| 7. To retrieve selected forms arranged in the order that you specified, press F9. | Q&A displays the Retrieve Spec again. |
| 8. Enter a value for which you want to search in one of the fields on the Retrieve Spec. Press F10. | Q&A retrieves all the forms that meet the criteria in the order in which Q&A sorted them. □ |

> ▶ **Tip:** If you want to add more fields to the sort, add secondary sort fields. For example, enter 3 AS or 3 DS, 4 AS or 4 DS, and so on, in other fields.

```
┌─────────────────────────────────────────────────────────────────────┐
│                                                                       │
│  ID Number:                                                           │
│                                                                       │      Sorting codes
│  First Name:                    Last Name: 1 xs ──────────────────────│──── are AS and DS.
│       Not a valid Sort Spec.  Press F1 for help, or see pg. F-63 of your manual. │
│                                                                       │
│                                                                       │
│  Day Telephone:                 Fax:                                  │
│  Night Telephone:                                                  ▪  │
│                                                                       │
│  Original Date:          Catalog Numbers:                             │
│  Latest Date:                                                         │
│                                                                       │
│  Last Order:             Order:                                       │
│  Favored Customer:                                                    │
│                                                                       │
│  Comments                                                             │
│                                                                       │
│  ─────────────────────────────────────────────────────────────────  │
│  CUSTOMER.DTF                   Sort Spec              Page 1  of 2    │
│                                                                       │
│  Esc-Exit  F1-Help  F6-Expand  Alt+F8-List  ↑F8-Save  F9-Retrieve  F10-Continue │
│                                                                       │
└─────────────────────────────────────────────────────────────────────┘
```

*Figure 4.7   If you type an incomplete or inaccurate sort specification, Q&A issues this message*

You also can retrieve records without sorting them first.

## **Q** Retrieving Records without Sorting First

| | |
|---|---|
| 1. From the Main menu, select File. | Q&A displays the File menu. |
| 2. Select Search/Update. | Q&A adds a dialog box to the bottom of the screen, which prompts you for the name of the file in which you want the search to take place. |
| 3. Enter the name of the file or press Enter to display a list of files. After selecting a file, press Enter. | File displays the Retrieve Spec, an empty form. |

99

4. Enter a value for which you want to search in one of the fields on the Retrieve Spec. Press F10.

If File does not find any records that match your request, it prompts you to either check or change your request (Figure 4.8).

5. Select Yes to check or change your request.

File returns you to the Retrieve Spec from which you can make another selection.

6. Select No if you don't want to check or change your request.

File returns you to the File menu. If File finds records that match your request, it displays any records that fit the information and restrictions that you have entered. Q&A displays Retrieved form 1 of — to indicate that it has retrieved the first form.

**100**

7. Press Ctrl-End from this screen.

Q&A displays all the records.

8. To select certain forms from those that you just selected, press F7 again.

Q&A displays the forms you select.

☐

▶ **Tip:** If you want to update all the records in the database, do not enter any value in the Retrieve Spec. Then press F10.

After you have retrieved forms, you can either enter new data to empty fields or change existing data. Enter the information exactly as you did when you added data to new forms. If you have finished updating forms and want to take a shortcut back to adding data, press Ctrl-F6. File displays a blank form for you to fill in.

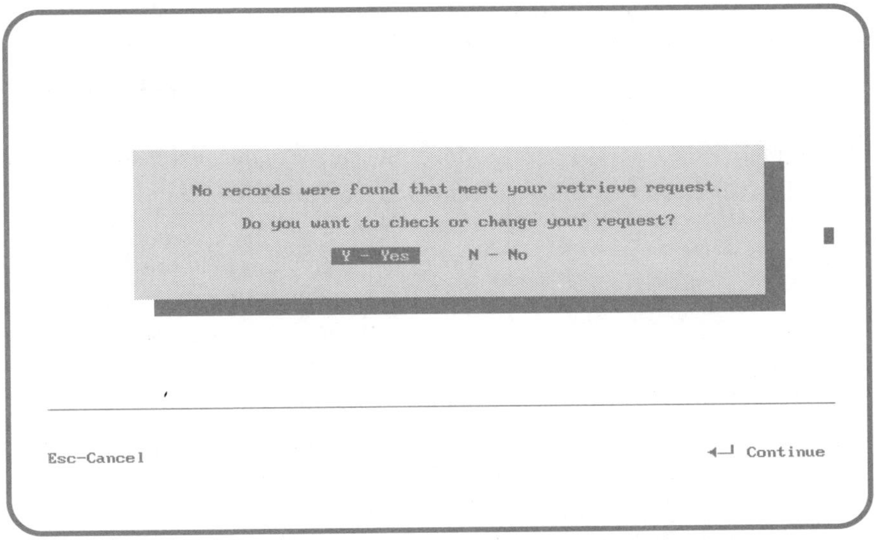

*Figures 4.8    If File does not find any matching records, it gives
you the opportunity to change your request or stop the search*

**101**

# Viewing Forms in Table View

Ordinarily, after you retrieve forms, you can view them one at a time
by pressing F10 to move forward through the forms or F9 to move
back through the previous forms. This is known as Form View. Q&A
also allows you to browse (look at) or edit records in a table format.
Table View allows you to see up to five fields of your choice and 17
records at a time. For a list of keys and key combinations that you can
use while in Table View, see Table 4.4.

Either on the first retrieved form or from the Table View, press
Shift-F6 to display the Table View Spec (see Figure 4.9). The number
next to a field indicates where the field appears in the table.

*Table 4.4   Table View Keys*

| Key/Key Combination | Function |
|---|---|
| Esc | Returns to the File menu |
| Enter | Moves the cursor to the next field |
| Tab | Moves to the next field or scrolls toward the right side of the table |
| Shift-Tab | Moves to the previous field or scrolls toward the left side of the table |
| Right | Moves to the next field or scrolls toward the right side of the table |
| Ctrl-Right | Scrolls five columns to the right |
| Left | Moves to the previous field or scrolls toward the left side of the table |
| Ctrl-Left | Scrolls five columns to the left |
| Up | Moves to the same field of the previous record or scrolls toward the top of the table |
| Down | Moves to the same field of the next record or scrolls toward the bottom of the table |
| Home | Jumps to the top of the screen |
| Ctrl-Home | Jumps to the first form in the table |
| End | Jumps to the bottom of the screen |
| Ctrl-End | Jumps to the last form in the table |
| PgUp | Moves to the top of the previous page |
| PgDn | Moves to the top of the next page |
| F1 | Q&A help |
| F2 | Prints the current form |
| Shift-F2 | Displays the Macro menu |
| Ctrl-F2 | Prints all the forms from the current cursor to the end of the table |
| F3 | Deletes the current record |
| F4 | Deletes the first word after the cursor position |
| Shift-F4 | Deletes the current line |
| Ctrl-F4 | Deletes the current line |
| F5 | Enters Edit mode |
| Ctrl-F5 | Places the current date in the current field |
| Alt-F5 | Places the current time in the current field |
| F6 | Enters the Field Editor |

| Key/Key Combination | Function |
| --- | --- |
| Shift-F6 | Defines the Table View Spec |
| Ctrl-F6 | Returns to Form View to add records |
| Alt-F6 | Returns to Form View |
| F7 | Displays the Retrieve Spec |
| Shift-F7 | Deletes the last change and returns to the previous value |
| F9 | Moves the cursor to the same field of the previous record |
| Shift-F9 | Go to Customize Specs |
| F10 | Displays the selected form in Form View |
| Shift-F10 | Exit |

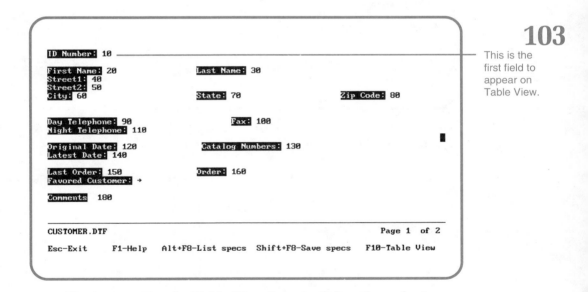

This is the first field to appear on Table View.

*Figure 4.9    Use the Table View Spec to define the order in which you want the fields displayed*

You can define a special spec for a file. For example, you can display the last five fields in reverse order. Simply blank out any numbers next to fields that you don't want to display; then type numbers that start high (with the field in the first column) and end low (with the field in the last column). Press Shift-F8 to save the new spec. Q&A displays a box in which you enter a description of the spec (see Figure 4.10). Then press Enter to save the new spec. If you want to see a list of all the specs related to this file, press Alt-F8. To move on to Table View, press F10 from the Table View Spec (see Figure 4.11).

You can define a Table View format and then save it for later.

ID Number:

First Name: 50          Last Name: 40
Street1: 30
Street2:
City

Save spec as:   sample

Day
Night

Original Date:          Catalog Numbers:
Latest Date:

Last Order:             Order:
Favored Customer:

Comments

CUSTOMER.DTF                                    Page 1  of 2

Esc-Exit                                        ◄┘ Continue

**104**

*Figure 4.10    When you define a special Table View Spec, Q&A asks you to describe it in this dialog box*

The arrow indicates more text than could be displayed in this space.

| State | City | Street1 | Last Name | First Name |
|-------|------|---------|-----------|------------|
| NY | Albany | 120 Hatteras B→ | James | Smith |
| NY | Albany | | | |
| NY | Albany | 123 Cypress Co→ | Smith | John |
| MA | Boston | 1001 President→ | Quincy | Adams |
| NY | Anywhere | 5 Fifth Gate | Miller | Milton |
| PA | Wherever | 1 Seagull Boul→ | Alma | Webb (also li→ |
| NY | Albany | 135 Customs La→ | Frizzele | Fritz |
| NY | Albany | 5 Clarrow Apar→ | Notritz | Adam |
| NY | Albany | 123 Any Street | Weblock | Jim |

CUSTOMER.DTF      Retrieved record 1      of 9          Total records: 9

Esc-Exit  F1-Help   { ↓ ↑ → ← Home End PgUp PgDn }-Navigate      F10-Show form

*Figure 4.11    Table View displays your records in a tabular format*

To get to Table View from a retrieved form without going through the Table View Spec, press Alt-F6.

> ▶ **Note:** You can only access Table View from the Search/ Update option; you cannot add new records in this mode. Edit the fields in Table View by simply typing into the fields.

## Removing a Group of Records

You have already learned how to use the delete operations to delete anything from a single character to a form.

**105**

You can use the Remove command to delete a group of records at one time. You can remove selected records or duplicate records, or remove duplicate records and then export them to an American Standard Code for Information Interchange (ASCII) file.

### *Q* Removing Selected Records

| | |
|---|---|
| 1. From the Main menu, select File. | Q&A displays the File menu. |
| 2. From the File menu, select Remove. | Q&A adds a dialog box to the File menu and asks you for the file from which you want to remove records. |
| 3. Enter the name of the file, or press Enter for a list of files. After selecting a file, press Enter. | Q&A displays the Remove menu (Figure 4.12). |
| 4. Select Selected Records. | Q&A displays the Retrieve Spec. |

5. Fill in the Retrieve Spec. Optionally, press F8 to enter sorting information in a Sort Spec; then press F10.

Q&A retrieves records that match the information you type. Before it removes any records, it warns you that it is about to remove the records permanently.

6. If you are sure you want to continue, select Yes. If you have changed your mind, select No.

Regardless of your choice, Q&A returns you to the Remove menu.

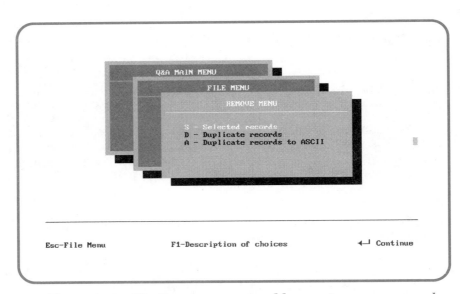

*Figure 4.12   The Remove menu enables you to remove records in one of three ways*

**Caution:** If you do not specify records on the Retrieve Spec, Q&A assumes that you want to remove all the records.

It is easy to enter information into a database twice. For example, if you ask customers whether this is their first contact with your company, they may forget that they ever ordered from you before. As a result, you might add these customers again to your database. From time to time, it is a good idea to check for duplicate records.

Q&A gives you two choices of removing duplicate records by identifying the fields to check for duplication. The first choice allows you to simply remove duplicate records; the second choice allows you to write the removed records to an ASCII file. This choice is a form of backing up. You can always double-check and move the records back into the database if you made a mistake.

### Ⓠ Removing Duplicate Records from Your Database:

| | |
|---|---|
| 1. From the Main menu, select File. | Q&A displays the File menu. |
| 2. From the File menu, select Remove. | Q&A adds a dialog box to the File menu and asks you for the file from which you want to remove records. |
| 3. Enter the name of the file or press Enter for a list of files. After selecting a file, press Enter. | Q&A displays the Remove menu. |
| 4. Select Duplicate Records. | Q&A displays the Duplicate Spec (Figure 4.13). |
| 5. Type D in the fields in which you want Q&A to check for duplicate entries, regardless of case. Type DS in the fields in which you want Q&A to check for duplicate entries that exactly match by case. Press F10. | Q&A finds what it considers to be duplicate records and warns you that it will remove these records (Figure 4.14). It asks if you want to confirm each removal or allow the removal without confirmation. |
| 6. Press Shift-F10 to delete this record, Ctrl-F10 to delete the rest of the records that it selected, or F10 to keep this record in the database. You also can press Esc to stop the removal. | Q&A returns you to the Remove menu. |

**107**

□

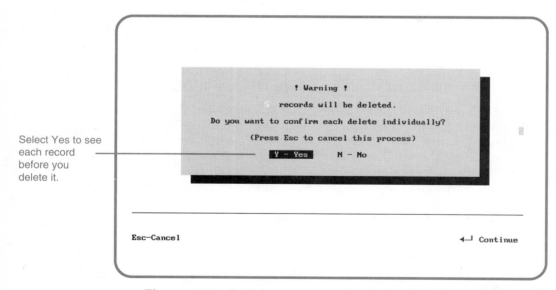

*Figure 4.13    The Duplicate Spec enables you to select fields that you want Q&A to check for duplication*

**108**

```
ID Number:

First Name:                    Last Name:
Street1:
Street2:
City:                          State:              Zip Code:

Day Telephone:                 Fax:
Night Telephone:

Ori    Type D in the fields on which you want Q&A to do case insensitive
Lat    duplicate checks, or DS for case sensitive duplicate checks.  Q&A
       checks the records for identical data in the specified fields.  If
Las    duplicates are found Q&A saves the first and deletes the rest.  It
Fav    is best to specify many fields to reduce chance of losing data.
       NOTE:  Blank field values count as duplicates.
Com
       SUGGESTION: It is faster if the selected fields are speedy fields.


CUSTOMER.DTF                  Duplicate Spec              Page 1  of 2

Esc-Exit      F3-Clear      F6-Expand      Alt+F8-List      ↑F8-Save      F10-Continue
```

Select Yes to see
each record
before you
delete it.

```
                        ! Warning !

                  5  records will be deleted.

         Do you want to confirm each delete individually?

               (Press Esc to cancel this process)

                     Y - Yes      N - No




Esc-Cancel                                              ←┘ Continue
```

*Figure 4.14    Q&A issues a warning before it deletes duplicate records*

When Q&A removes duplicate records, it always keeps the first record it has found and then offers you the choice to remove some or all of the other duplicate records. As a safeguard, remove duplicate records to ASCII.

## Removing Duplicate Records to an ASCII File

1. From the Main menu, select File.

   Q&A displays the File menu.

2. From the File menu, select Remove.

   Q&A adds a dialog box to the File menu and asks you for the file from which you want to remove records.

3. Enter the name of the file or press Enter for a list of files. After selecting a file, press Enter.

   Q&A displays the Remove menu.

**109**

4. Select Duplicate Records to ASCII.

   Q&A adds a dialog box asking for a new, unique file name to give to the ASCII file that will hold the deleted records.

5. Enter the ASCII file name and press Enter.

   Q&A displays the Duplicate Spec.

6. Type D in the fields in which you want Q&A to check for duplicate entries, regardless of case. Type DS in the fields in which you want Q&A to check for duplicate entries that exactly match by case. Press F10.

   Q&A finds what it considers to be duplicate records and warns you that it will remove these records. It asks if you want to confirm each removal or allow the removal without confirmation.

7. Press Shift-F10 to delete this record, Ctrl-F10 to delete the rest of the records that it selected, or F10 to keep this record in the database You also can press Esc to stop the removal.

   Q&A removes the records you specify and returns you to the Remove menu.

□

# What You Have Learned

▶ When you design a form, File allows you to move anywhere on the screen. When you add data, File allows you to move only among the fields.

▶ Q&A allows you to press keys and key combinations to save time as you enter information.

▶ You can enter all or select information from the previous form into the current form.

▶ As you add information, you can delete, display custom help, or print forms.

▶ You can save the current form and return to the previous form or the next form.

▶ Q&A allows you to retrieve data that is either sorted or unsorted.

**110**

# Q&A File: Retrieving and Printing Forms

## In This Chapter

111

- ► *Searching for ranges or exact matches*
- ► *Changing File's search logic*
- ► *Printing from the Print menu*
- ► *Updating an entire database*
- ► *Sending data from one database to another*
- ► *Importing and exporting data*

In Chapter 4, you learned how to conduct a simple search. Q&A also offers advanced, but still easy-to-use, methods to search for records.

### Q Searching for Ranges or Exact Matches

1. From the Main menu, select File.

   Q&A displays the File menu.

2. Select Search/Update.

   Q&A adds a dialog box to the bottom of the screen, which prompts you for the name of the file in which you want the search to take place.

3. Enter the name of the file or press Enter for a list of files. After selecting a file, press Enter.

File displays the Retrieve Spec.

4. Enter a value in the field in which you want to search. Press Ctrl-F7.

Q&A displays the Search Option box.

5. After entering all the search information, including restrictions and sort instructions, press F10.

File starts displaying any records that fit the information and restrictions that you have entered. If File does not find any records that match your request, it prompts you to either check or change your request.

6. If you want to check or change your request, select Yes.

File returns you to the Retrieve Spec from which you can make another selection.

7. If you don't want to check or change your request, select No.

File returns you to the File menu. □

You can restrict your search by entering combinations of alphabetic, numeric, and special characters. Table 5.1 contains examples of ways to match specific field entries or a range of entries. For example, you can use these types of values to search for a field that

Is equal to Tennis
Starts with a character less than Z
Is greater than 2 but less than 9

Table 5.1   *Searches for Values*

| Typing | Means Find Fields that Are |
|---|---|
| A | Equal to A |
| =A | Equal to A |
| /A | Equal to any value but A |
| = | Empty |
| /= | Full (contains any value) |
| A;B;C | A or B or C, but nothing else |
| &A;B;C | A and B and C (for keyword fields) |
| /A;B | Not A or B |
| /A..B | Not beginning with A and not ending with B |
| >X | Greater than X |
| >3 | Greater than 3 |
| <X | Less than X |
| <5 | Less than 5 |
| >=C | Greater than or equal to C |
| C.. | Greater than or equal to C |
| <=C | Less than or equal to C |
| ..C | Less than or equal to C |
| ..D.. | Made up of any values that include a D |
| B..D | Within the range from B through D |
| >A..<D | From greater than A to less than D |
| >A..<=D | From greater than A to less than or equal to D |
| <A;>=D | Less than A or greater than or equal to D |
| MAXn | The number of (n) highest values |
| MINn | The number of (n) lowest values |
| ]None | Not usually valid for this field |

**113**

If you type a backslash (\), you indicate that the next value is literal. For example, if you type \;, you are looking for a semicolon (;) in this field.

You also can use two backslashes in a field. For example, if you enter \?\?, you are looking for two question marks. (This does not indicate two ? wildcard characters.)

If you use a sounds-like search, you may have strange results. For example, `~Cartr` sounds like Carter, and retrieves Carter. If you enter `~Johns`, you may get Jones but not Johnson.

> ▶ **Note:** There can be only one MAXn or MINn in a Retrieve Spec. You cannot use MAXn or MINn with keywords.

Table 5.2 lists and demonstrates the use of wildcards to search for specific values or ranges of values.

*Table 5.2  Searches with Wildcards*

| Typing | Means Find Fields that Are |
|---|---|
| ? | Any single character, but no more |
| \? | A question mark in the field |
| ?? | Any two characters, but no more |
| ????t | Any five-letter value that ends with t |
| .. | Any group of alphabetic characters |
| K.. | Any value that begins with K |
| ..K | Any value that ends with K |
| s..d | Any value that begins with s and ends with d |
| ..K.. | Any value that contains K anywhere |
| ..T..E..D | Any value that contains T, E, and D (in that order) |

# Changing Q&A File's Search Logic

When you use the Search Options box, you tell File to search for various combinations of restrictions. Let's say that your database contains two fields—Last Name and City—and has a grand total of four records—Carter living in Albany, Carter living in Rochester, Smith living in Albany, and Smith living in Rochester.

If you search for records that DO meet ANY of the restrictions, you get the records that contain Carter OR Albany. File selects three of the four records; it does not select Smith living in Rochester.

If you search for records that DO meet ALL of the restrictions, you get the records that contain Carter AND Albany. File selects one of the records—Carter living in Albany.

If you search for records that DO NOT meet ANY of the restrictions, you get the records that do not contain Carter OR Albany. File selects one of the records—Smith living in Rochester.

If you select the records that DO NOT meet ALL of the restrictions, you get the records that do not contain Carter AND Albany. File selects three of the records—all but Carter living in Albany.

# Searching by Information Type

Most of the search restrictions in Tables 5.1 and 5.2 as well as Search Options logic apply to all information types. The following sections discuss how to handle different types of searches, including those for specific information types.

## *All Types*

You can search for only one MINn or MAXn in just one field per Retrieve Spec. Q&A refers to the last MINn or MAXn in the form; it ignores all others.

Do not combine MINn or MAXn with any other restrictions in a single field. If you use MINn or MAXn with other restrictions in other fields, Q&A retrieves the minimum values or maximum values of records that first meet all the other restrictions you have entered; Q&A processes all MINn and MAXn after all other restrictions.

## *Nonstandard Values*

If you enter a value that does not meet the usual criteria for a particular field, you have to force Q&A to accept it. For example, if you enter None in a money field (to indicate that there is no need to enter a money value in this field in this particular record) and press F10, you have to press F10 again to verify that this is the entry you want in the field.

To search for a value that does not meet the usual criteria for a field, use the right bracket (]) to start the search value (for example, ]None). The ] must be the first character in the search value.

## Entering Multiple Restrictions within One Field

Use a semicolon (;) to separate each restriction entered in a field. You have seen this already for entries such as A;B;C and <A;>=D.

> ▶ **Note:** Q&A evaluates multiple restrictions from left to right. For example, the entry >A;=B;C..D means greater than A or equal to B or between C and D.

**116**

### *Text*

Enter A..;..D.. in a field to retrieve all values starting with A or including D.

## Number, Money, Date, and Hours

For any fields that you can calculate, you can enter a calculation to retrieve certain values. To enter a programming expression, enclose the expression in braces ({ }). You can enter any of the many valid Q&A programming functions except @NUMBER, @TOTAL, @AVERAGE, @COUNT, @MAXIMUM, @MINIMUM, @CVAR, @CSTD, @MSG, @HELP, and @DITTO.

For example, if you want to retrieve a group of customers whose last order equaled the total of all orders (that is, to get a list of one-time or very new customers), enter Last order: = {Order}.

If you enter an invalid expression, Q&A warns you and places the cursor where you have made the mistake. Press Esc to return to the Retrieve Spec and change the expression.

If you enter <8/6/70 in a date field, you are searching for any date that is earlier than 8/6/70; if you enter >8/6/70, you are searching for any date that is later than 8/6/70.

If you are searching for a nonstandard value in a date field, enter ]YYYY/MM/DD; this is the format that Q&A uses for dates.

Midnight (12:00 m) is the beginning of the day. The end of the day is represented by 11:59 p.m. If you enter `<8:45 am`, you are searching for any time that is between midnight through 8:45 in the morning.

## Keyword

If you use the search value `tennis;golf;swimming`, you are searching for any of these values in a keyword field.

If you use the search value `&tennis;golf;swimming`, you are searching for all of these values in a keyword field. If one of the records has golf and tennis, but not swimming, Q&A does not retrieve that record.

Enter `&tennis;]/..;golf..` to select tennis but exclude golf. If you want to exclude all tennis keywords, enter the search value `tennis` and then press Ctrl-F7 to display the Search Options box. Set the values to DO NOT and ALL to retrieve every record that does not have tennis as a keyword. You also can enter `/tennis;=` to not search for tennis.

Enter `g..;..i..` in a field to retrieve all values starting with g (such as golf) or including i (such as tennis and swimming).

## Yes/No

If you try to use search logic to search for all records with a Yes OR No, you get all records. For exact retrieval, you can't use `=X`; just use `X`.

You can use `=` to find all forms with empty keyword fields, or `/=` to find fields that are not empty.

## Special Retrievals

Enter `..` if you want to search for standard Q&A-approved values for a specific information type. For example, if you want to search for a valid date, enter `..` in a date field. Q&A retrieves any record that includes any date in any valid format, but does not retrieve a record that includes a date in a nonstandard format.

117

Enter / .. if you want to search for nonstandard formats. For example, enter / .. to search for any nonstandard date field format (such as NONE, February first, or Bart). This is particularly useful if you want to bring all the fields in a database into standard format or if you have imported data, which is unlikely to have all valid formats, into your database.

# Printing Forms in a Database

In Chapter 4, you learned how to press F2 to print a single form or Ctrl-F2 to print all the records that you have just added to your database. You also have the option of using the Print menu to print all or selected records in several formats—as parts of mail merge operations or as formal or informal reports.

**118**

### ***Q*** Printing from the Print Menu

1. From the Main menu, select File.

   Q&A displays the File menu.

2. Select Print.

   Q&A adds a dialog box to the bottom of the screen and asks you for the name of the file from which you want to print.

3. Enter the name of the file or press Enter for a list of files. After selecting a file, press Enter.

   Q&A displays the Print menu (Figure 5.1).

   ☐

The first choice on the Print menu is Design/Redesign a Print Spec. Use this option to specify the records and defaults that define the content of the print job and how you want a page to look.

> ▶ **Tip:** If you want to change either the File Print Options or Define Page Defaults for a new Print Spec, do so before you start the design. Q&A incorporates the latest defaults into new Print Specs. Existing Print Specs are not changed.

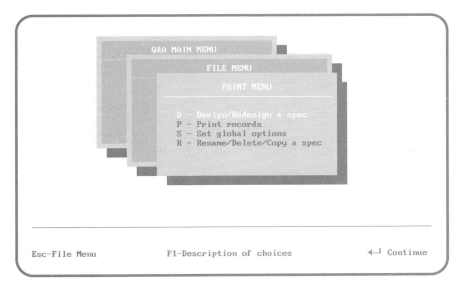

*Figure 5.1    The Print menu offers you four choices of printing-related options.*

The only difference between designing and redesigning is that if a Print Spec already exists, you're redesigning it; if you are designing a Print Spec, you're starting from scratch. After you design a Print Spec, you can not access it from DOS. Q&A links it to the database where it resides.

### Designing or Redesigning a Print Spec

1. Select Design/Redesign a Spec from the Print menu.

   Q&A displays the List of Print Specs in Database screen.

2. To redesign a Print Spec, either move the highlight to the name of a Print Spec or type a name (up to 30 characters) in the Enter Name field. To design a new Print Spec, type a new, unique name in the Enter Name field (Figure 5.2).

   Q&A displays a Retrieve Spec that is connected automatically to this Print Spec (Figure 5.3).

3. Fill out the Retrieve Spec with search criteria. If you are redesigning this Print Spec, change the search criteria as you wish.

   Q&A processes your search criteria.

4. If you want to sort records, press F8.

   Q&A displays a Sort Spec that is connected automatically to this database.

5. When you have completed the Retrieve Spec and, optionally, the Sort Spec, press F10.

   Q&A displays the Fields Spec (Figure 5.4).

6. Type codes on the Fields Spec and press F10.

   Q&A displays the File Print Options screen (Figure 5.5).

7. After making any changes to the File Print Options screen, press F10.

   Q&A saves the Print Spec and asks you whether you want to print the forms now.

8. Respond to the prompt with Yes or No.

   If you select Yes, the printing starts, accompanied by a prompt giving you the choice between quitting or editing the File Print Options (Figure 5.6). If you select No, Q&A returns you to the Print menu.  □

---

> **Tip:** Press Shift-F7 to get the most recently created Retrieve Spec for the current database in the current session. This does not work if you are operating Q&A via a network.

---

If you do not enter any restrictions in the Retrieve Spec, all forms will be printed.

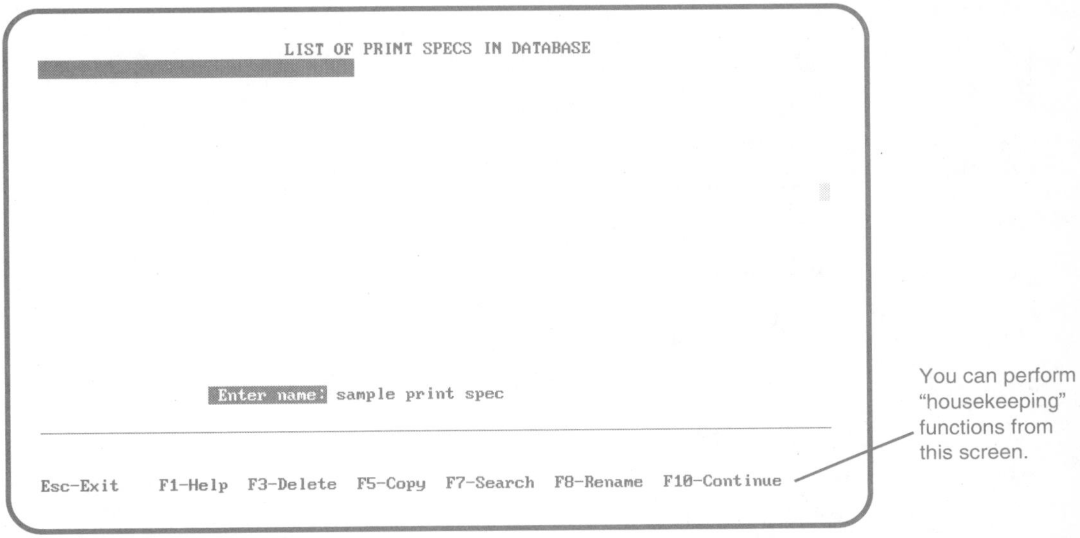

```
                    LIST OF PRINT SPECS IN DATABASE
██████████████████████████



                        Enter name: sample print spec
_____

Esc-Exit    F1-Help  F3-Delete  F5-Copy  F7-Search  F8-Rename  F10-Continue
```

You can perform "housekeeping" functions from this screen.

**121**

*Figure 5.2   The List of Print Specs in Database screen after we entered a name and right before we pressed F10*

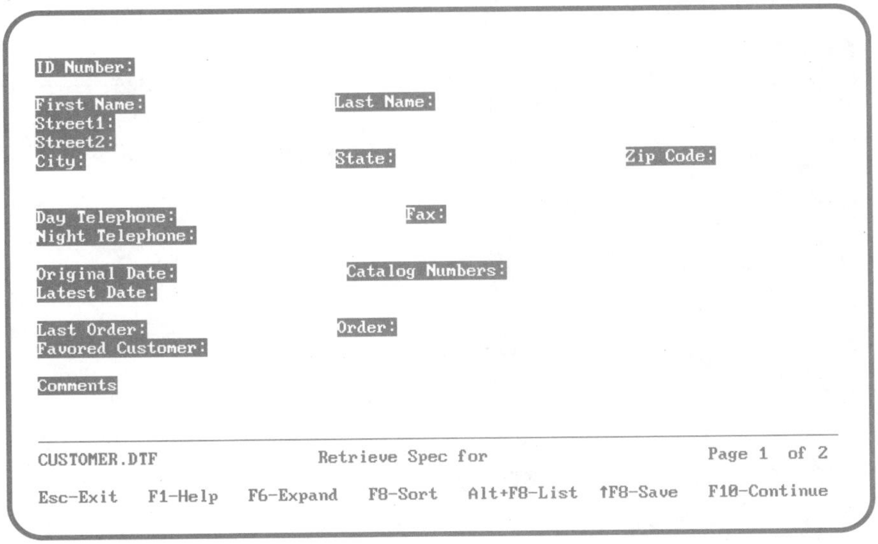

```
ID Number:

First Name:              Last Name:
Street1:
Street2:
City:                    State:              Zip Code:


Day Telephone:           Fax:
Night Telephone:

Original Date:           Catalog Numbers:
Latest Date:

Last Order:              Order:
Favored Customer:

Comments
_____

CUSTOMER.DTF           Retrieve Spec for            Page 1  of 2

Esc-Exit   F1-Help   F6-Expand   F8-Sort   Alt+F8-List  ↑F8-Save   F10-Continue
```

*Figure 5.3   This Retrieve Spec looks like any other until you look at the first status line, which clearly identifies it as belonging to the Print Spec that we are designing*

The next field prints on the same line if the code is +.

The next field prints on the next line if the code is x.

```
ID Number:

First Name: 1+                    Last Name: 2X ──────────────
Street1: 3X
Street2: 4X
City: 5+                          State: 6+,2          Zip Code: 7X,3

Day Telephone:                    Fax:
Night Telephone:

Original Date:                    Catalog Numbers:
Latest Date:

Last Order:                       Order:
Favored Customer:

Comments
─────────────────────────────────────────────────────────────────
CUSTOMER.DTF                 Fields Spec for              Page 1  of 2

Esc-Exit  F1-Help  F6-Expand field  Shift+F6-Enhance  F9-Go back  F10-Continue
```

**122**

*Figure 5.4    Fill in a Fields Spec to control where and how fields are printed on a form*

```
                          FILE PRINT OPTIONS
   Print to......:    ▶PtrA◀  PtrB   PtrC   PtrD   PtrE   DISK   SCREEN ──

   Page preview.................:     Yes  ▶No◀

   Type of paper feed...........:   Manual  ▶Continuous◀  Bin1   Bin2   Bin3

   Print offset.................:     0

   Printer control codes........:

   Print field labels...........:     Yes  ▶No◀

   Number of copies.............:     1

   Number of records per page....:    1

   Number of labels across.......:   ▶1◀  2   3   4   5   6   7   8

   Print expanded fields.........:     Yes  ▶No◀
─────────────────────────────────────────────────────────────────────
CUSTOMER.DTF              Print Options for sample print spec
Basic (Vanilla) Non-laser printer »» LPT1
Esc-Exit           F8-Define Page          F9-Go back          F10-Continue
```

You can print to your computer screen.

You can print to a disk file now and print using your printer later.

*Figure 5.5    Keep the present defaults or change the defaults on the File Print Options screen*

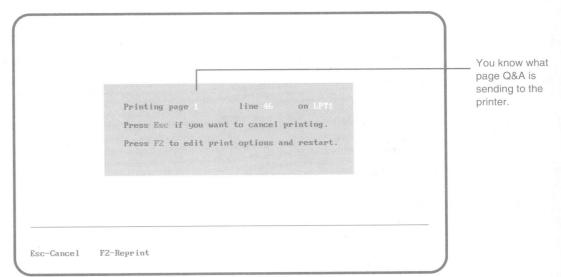

Printing page 1          line 46          on LPT1

Press Esc if you want to cancel printing.

Press F2 to edit print options and restart.

Esc-Cancel     F2-Reprint

You know what
page Q&A is
sending to the
printer.

*Figure 5.6   After your job starts printing, Q&A gives you the*
*opportunity to quit printing or to edit the File Print Options*

**123**

## Filling In the Fields Spec

The Fields Spec controls the way the retrieved forms look as printed
output. To print a form the way it looks on the screen, don't fill in the
Fields Spec. Just make sure that you don't select Print Expanded
Fields from the Print Options screen; otherwise, the format could
change, resulting in strange-looking output.

If you want to customize your printed output, you must make
some choices. If you take a look at a blank Fields Spec, you'll notice
that it is another version of the form that you originally designed.
The way you fill it out is unique, however.

## Free-Form Style

Use free-form style for mailing labels or reports, or whenever you are
not printing on preprinted forms. The way you fill out the Fields
Spec tells Q&A whether you are using free-form style or coordinate
printing. You can't combine codes for both. See Figure 5.7 for an
example of a Field Spec for free-form printing.

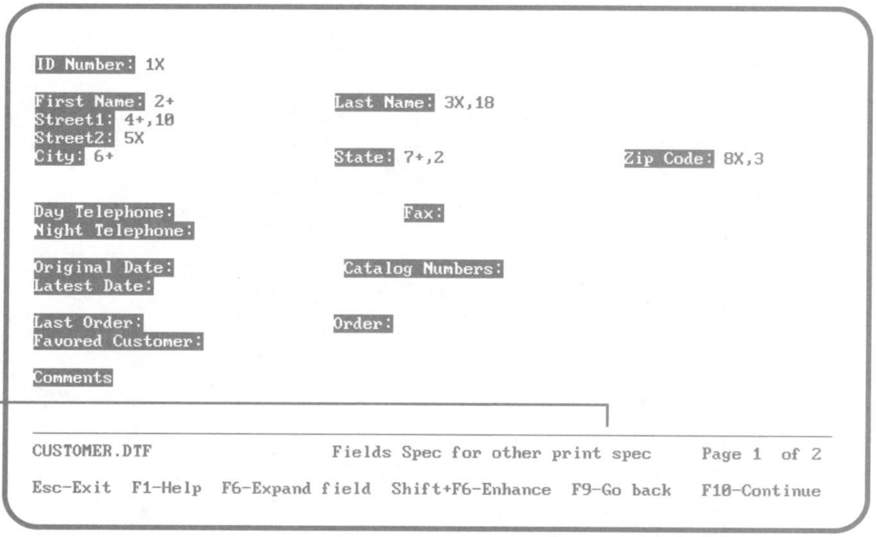

```
┌──────────────────────────────────────────────────────────────────┐
│                                                                    │
│   ID Number:  1X                                                   │
│                                                                    │
│   First Name:  2+              Last Name:  3X,18                    │
│   Street1:  4+,10                                                  │
│   Street2:  5X                                                     │
│   City:  6+                    State:  7+,2         Zip Code:  8X,3 │
│                                                                    │
│                                                                    │
│   Day Telephone:               Fax:                                │
│   Night Telephone:                                                 │
│                                                                    │
│   Original Date:               Catalog Numbers:                    │
│   Latest Date:                                                     │
│                                                                    │
│   Last Order:                  Order:                              │
│   Favored Customer:                                                │
│                                                                    │
│   Comments                                                         │
│   ─────────────────────────────────────────────────┐              │
│   ─────────────────────────────────────────────────┘              │
│   CUSTOMER.DTF            Fields Spec for other print spec   Page 1  of 2 │
│                                                                    │
│   Esc-Exit  F1-Help  F6-Expand field  Shift+F6-Enhance  F9-Go back  F10-Continue │
└──────────────────────────────────────────────────────────────────┘
```

This Print Spec contains codes that could be used to print labels.

*Figure 5.7    A Field Spec for a free-format style printout*

## Q Filling In the Fields Spec: Free-Form Printing

1. Type a number 1 through 999 in each field to be printed. After each number, type either an x (print the next field on the next line) or a + (print the next field on this line after a space). After you have filled in this form, press F10.

   Q&A displays the File Print Options screen.

2. Indicate the number of labels (1 through 8). Add enhancements such as boldface and italics, if desired. Press F10.

   Q&A saves the Print Spec and asks you whether you want to print the forms now.

3.  Respond to the prompt
    with Yes or No.

If you select Yes, the printing starts, accompanied by a prompt giving you the choice between quitting (press Esc) or editing the File Print Options (press F2). If you select No, Q&A returns you to the Print menu. □

---

▶ **Tip:** When you are printing mailing labels for the first time, keep in mind that only a certain number of characters fit on the width of a label (typically 30). Set up a small database to test your format.

---

Table 5.3 lists examples of codes for free-form style printing and their meanings.

**125**

*Table 5.3    Free-Form Codes*

| Code | Meaning |
|------|---------|
| 6x | This is the sixth field to be printed. Print the next field on the next line. |
| 3+ | This is the third field to be printed. Follow with a space and then print the next field on this line. |
| 3+,3 | This is the third field to be printed. Follow with three spaces and then print the next field on this line. |
| 6x,2 | This is the sixth field to be printed. Skip two lines and then print the next field on the next line. |
| 3+,3,15 | This is the third field to be printed. Follow with three spaces and then print the first 15 characters of the next field on this line. |
| 6x,2,10 | This is the sixth field to be printed. Skip two lines and then print the first 10 characters of the next field on the next line. |
| 2xE | This is the second field to be printed. Print all data in this field, even though it is extended data. Then move to the beginning of the next line to print the next field. |

*(continued)*

*Table 5.3*    *(continued)*

| Code | Meaning |
|------|---------|
| 2+E | This is the second field to be printed. Print all data in this field, even though it is extended data. Follow with a space and then print the next field on this line. |
| 5x,5,5,L | This is the fifth field to be printed. Before printing this field, print its label. Skip five lines and then print the first five characters of the next field on the next line. |
| 5+,5,5,L | This is the fifth field to be printed. Before printing this field, print its label. Skip five spaces and then print the first five characters of the next field. |
| 5x,5,5,L(Name) | This is the fifth field to be printed. Before printing this field, substitute Name for its label. Skip five lines and then print the first five characters of the next field on the next line. |

You can add more room for typing codes into a field by pressing F6.

## Coordinate Style

To print forms on preprinted forms, use Q&A's coordinate printing format (see Figure 5.8). When you use coordinate printing, you can print at a specific location on a form.

You can specify row and column page coordinates either based on characters per line and row (the default) or by measuring in inches or centimeters, which is ideal when you use proportional fonts. The coordinates that you enter are the starting position of each field (or label, if you select that option).

Decide what fields go in what locations. Then find the coordinates of those locations. If you are using characters per line as the measurement, remember that Q&A generally has 66 lines per page and there are six lines to the inch. These measurements are based on the defaults, which you can modify on the Define Page screen (select Set Global Options from the Print menu).

Determine your default font's characters per inch measurement. Measure some printed output and count the number of characters.

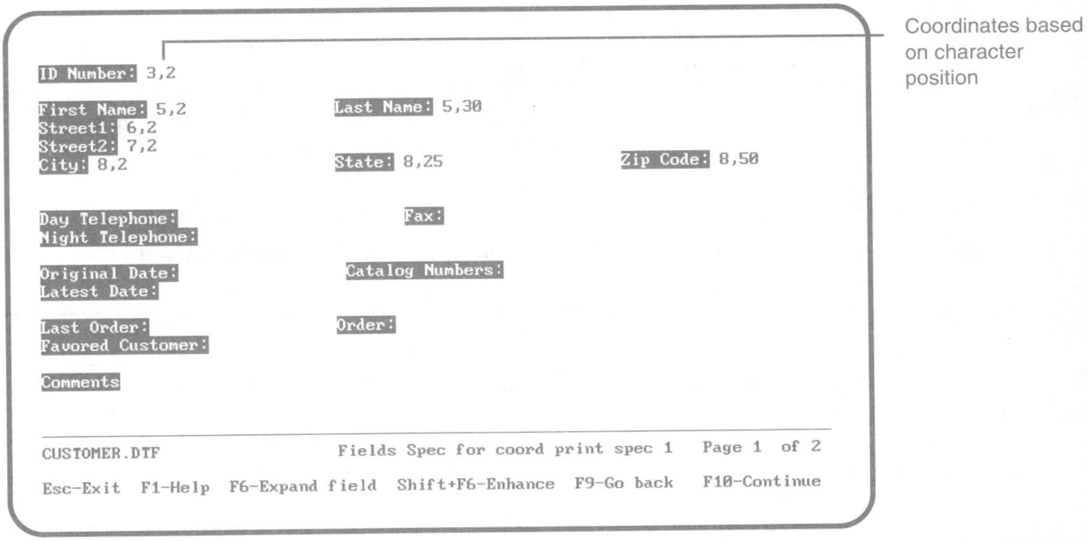

```
 ID Number: 3,2

 First Name: 5,2          Last Name: 5,30
 Street1: 6,2
 Street2: 7,2
 City: 8,2                State: 8,25         Zip Code: 8,50


 Day Telephone:              Fax:
 Night Telephone:

 Original Date:           Catalog Numbers:
 Latest Date:

 Last Order:              Order:
 Favored Customer:

 Comments


 CUSTOMER.DTF              Fields Spec for coord print spec 1    Page 1  of 2

 Esc-Exit  F1-Help  F6-Expand field  Shift+F6-Enhance  F9-Go back  F10-Continue
```

Coordinates based
on character
position

*Figure 5.8   A Field Spec for a coordinate style printout*

**127**

If you are using inches or centimeters, measure the starting coordinates for each field and write them down. The first coordinate is the position on the row or line, which is measured from the top of the page. Either count the number of lines or measure in inches or centimeters.

The second coordinate is the position in the column, which is measured from the left margin. Either count the number of characters or measure in inches or centimeters. (See Table 5.4 for examples of coordinates and their meanings.)

*Table 5.4   Coordinate Entries*

| Entry | Meaning |
| --- | --- |
| 8,1 | Print this field eight lines from the top margin and one character from the left margin. |
| 1",2" | Print this field one inch from the top margin and two inches from the left margin. |
| 1cm,2cm | Print this field one centimeter from the top margin and two centimeters from the left margin. |
| 2,3,10 | Print the first ten characters of this field two lines from the top margin and three characters from the left margin. |

*(continued)*

*Table 5.4  (continued)*

| Entry | Meaning |
|---|---|
| 1",2",L | Print the field label and then the field, one inch from the top margin and two inches from the left margin. |
| 1",2",L(Name) | Print Name (instead of the field label), followed by the field, one inch from the top margin and two inches from the left margin. |

 **Filling In the Fields Spec: Coordinate Printing**

1. For each field to be printed, type coordinates separated by a comma. If you need to expand a field to completely fill it in, press F6.

    Q&A gives you an expanded space in which to type coordinates.

2. If you prematurely leave the Fields Spec to go to the File Print Options screen, press F9.

    Q&A returns you to the Fields Spec.

3. After you have filled in this form, press F10.

    Q&A displays the File Print Options screen.

4. After making any changes to the File Print Options screen, press F10.

    Q&A saves the Print Spec and asks you whether you want to print the forms now.

5. Respond to the prompt with Yes or No.

    If you select Yes, the printing starts, accompanied by a prompt giving you the choice between quitting (press Esc) or editing the File Print Options (press F2). If you select No, Q&A returns you to the Print menu. □

## *Enhancing Form Output*

You can apply enhancements to form printing by using the Text Enhancement and Fonts menu.

### Q **Enhancing Form Output**

1. On the Form Spec, select the field that you want to enhance. For free-form printing, move the cursor over either the x or + code. For coordinate printing, move the cursor to the page coordinates of the field. If you want to enhance the label, move the cursor to the L. Then press Shift-F6.

   Q&A displays the Text Enhancement and Fonts menu.

2. Select an enhancement or font. Press Enter.

   Q&A closes the Text Enhancement and Fonts menu and prompts you to select the text to which you want to apply the enhancement.

3. Move the cursor to the appropriate area of the Fields Spec; then press F10.

   Q&A applies the enhancement that you specify.

## *Printing from an Existing Print Spec*

Instead of filling out a new Print Spec, you may have an existing Print Spec that meets your layout needs. If that is the case, select Print Forms from the Print menu.

## *Q* Printing from an Existing Print Spec

1. Select Print Records from the Print menu to print from an existing Print Spec.

   Q&A displays the List of Print Specs in Database screen.

2. Move the highlight to the name you want or type the name in the Enter Name field. Then press F10.

   Q&A asks if you want to make any temporary changes to the Print Spec.

3. Respond to the prompt with Yes or No.

   If you select No, the job prints immediately. If you select Yes, Q&A displays the Retrieve Spec related to this Print Spec.

**130**

4. Make temporary changes, such as expanding a field, sorting, or listing the Retrieve Specs related to this database. Then press F10.

   Q&A displays the File Print Options screen, which you can change if you wish.

   □

## *Setting Global Options*

Select Set Global Options from the Print menu to change File Print Options or the Define Page screens for either individual form or multiple page print jobs. Remember that you initiate single-form printing by pressing F2 as you are adding or updating data.

If you want to change either the File Print Options or Define Page Defaults for a new Print Spec, do so before you start the design. Q&A incorporates the latest defaults into new Print Specs, not existing Print Specs. The following paragraphs describe each field of the Define Page screen.

*Page width* is the width of a page, from 10 to 240 columns. The default width for the File page is 80.

*Page length* is the length of a page, from 1 to 32,750 lines. The default length for the File page is 66. If you have a laser printer, you can change the page length to as many as 90 lines in order to reset the number of lines per inch. As a result, Q&A scales text automatically.

*Left margin* is the number of characters from the left edge of the page to the starting print position for a line. The default is 0.

*Right margin* is the number of characters from the left edge of the page to the ending print position for a line. The default is 80. The right margin must be at least two characters greater than the left margin and cannot exceed the page width.

*Top margin* is the number of lines between the top edge of the page and the first printed line. The default is 3.

*Bottom margin* is the number of lines between the bottom edge of the page and the last printed line. The default is 3. The value of both margins cannot exceed the page length.

**131**

*Characters per inch* is the number of characters that your printer attempts to print on a horizontal inch. For example, if you select 10, Q&A selects a font that it thinks prints 10 characters per inch. If you have enhanced text, the characters per inch setting may be overridden. If you have a PostScript printer, it may ignore the characters per inch setting.

> ▶ **Tip:** If you have a PostScript printer, you can store PostScript program files and specify them in the Printer Control Codes field of the Print Options screen. Refer to your printer's reference guide for instructions.

*Header* allows you to enter three lines of information that appear at the top of every page of printed output.

*Footer* allows you to enter three lines of information that appear at the bottom of every page of printed output.

## *Maintaining Print Specs*

Select Rename/Delete/Copy a Spec from the Print menu to maintain your Print Specs for this database.

### Renaming a Print Spec

1. From the Rename/Delete/ Copy menu, select Rename a Print Spec.

   Q&A adds a dialog box to the bottom of the screen.

2. Type the name of the Print Spec that you want to rename and press Enter, or select one from the list and press F10.

   Q&A adds another line to the dialog box (Figure 5.9).

3. Type in a new, unique name for the Print Spec and press Enter.

   Q&A changes the name of the Print Spec and closes the dialog box. □

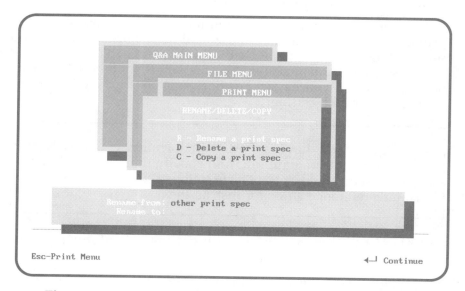

*Figure 5.9 Q&A then adds another line into which you type the new name for this Print Spec*

You also use the Rename/Delete/Copy menu if you want to delete a Print Spec.

## Deleting a Print Spec

1. From the Rename/Delete/Copy menu, select Delete a Print Spec.

   Q&A adds a dialog box to the bottom of the screen.

2. Type the name of the Print Spec that you want to delete and press Enter or select one from the list and press F10.

   Q&A displays a warning message (Figure 5.10).

3. Select Yes to delete the spec.

   Q&A returns you to the Rename/Delete/Copy menu.

4. If you decide not to delete the spec, select No.

   Q&A returns you to the List of Print Specs in Database screen. □

**133**

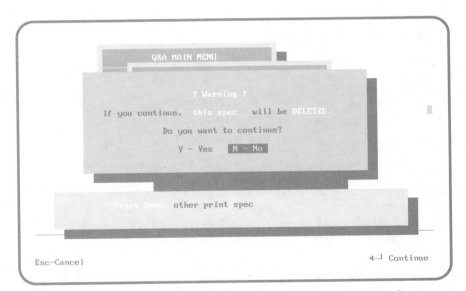

*Figure 5.10   Before Q&A deletes this Print Spec, it displays a warning message*

Copying a Print Spec is the third use of the Rename/Delete/Copy menu.

## Copying a Print Spec

1. From the Rename/Delete/Copy menu, select Copy a Print Spec.

   Q&A adds a dialog box to the bottom of the screen.

2. Type the name of the Print Spec that you want to copy and press Enter or select one from the list and press F10.

   Q&A adds another line to the dialog box (Figure 5.11).

3. Type in a new, unique name for the copy and press Enter.

   Q&A copies the Print Spec and closes the dialog box. □

**134**

Now you have two copies of the same Print Spec. You can edit one and keep the original as is.

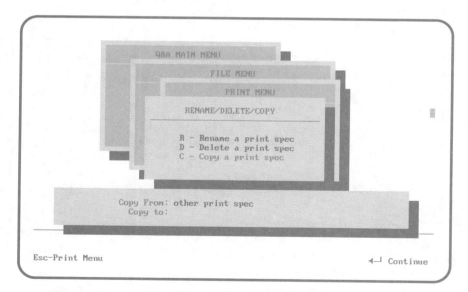

*Figure 5.11    Q&A adds another line to the dialog box into which you type a new name for the copied Print Spec*

# Updating an Entire Database

Q&A offers the mass update operation, which allows you to change the information in two or more forms at once. You can update in three ways:

1.  Change information in a field by direct action (for example, if a manufacturer changes a part number, changing it in your database).
2.  Perform calculations in one field (for example, subtracting 10% from the retail price of a group of closeout items).
3.  Calculate the value in one field to change the value in another (for example, calculating a bonus by multiplying each employee's base salary by 5% and adding the result to the amount that you have already put in the Bonus field).

Q&A does not support certain programming statements during a mass update. For example, Q&A does not execute form navigation programming statements and does not allow any GOTO or GOSUB statements on the Update Spec. For more information about Q&A programming, see Chapter 12.

**135**

> ⊘ **Caution:** Before doing a mass update for the first time, create a small test database with which to experiment.

### Ⓠ Doing a Mass Update

1.  Select Mass Update from the File menu.

    Q&A adds a dialog box to the bottom of the screen and asks you for the name of the file that you want to update.

2.  Accept the file name in the dialog box or enter another or press Enter to have Q&A display a list of files. After selecting a file, press Enter.

    Q&A displays the Retrieve Spec.

3. Fill in the Retrieve Spec to select only those records that you want to update. Optionally, press F8 so that you can fill in the Sort Spec. When you have finished with the Retrieve Spec and the Sort Spec, press F10.

Q&A displays the Update Spec (Figure 5.12).

4. Type # and a unique number in every field that you want to update or will use in a calculation. Press F8.

Q&A displays the Calculation Options screen (Figure 5.13) and asks `Are on record entry statements executed?`

5. Respond to the prompt with Yes or No.

If you select Yes, Q&A executes programming statements that occur when the record is entered, then asks `Are calculation statements executed?`

6. Respond to the prompt with Yes or No.

If you select Yes, Q&A executes programming statements that occur in each field, then asks `Are on record exit statements executed?`

7. Respond to the prompt with Yes or No.

If you select Yes, Q&A executes programming statements that occur when the record is exited.

8. Press F10.

Q&A displays a message stating how many records will be updated and offering you the chance to confirm each update as it is ready to occur (Figure 5.14). If you select No, the update takes place.

9. Press Esc.

Q&A returns to the Retrieve and Update Specs.

10. Press Ctrl-F10.                    Q&A updates the rest of the records without confirmation.

11. Press Shift-F10.                   Q&A confirms the current record.

12. Press F10.                         Q&A returns you to the File menu without updating.  □

```
ID Number:

First Name:                  Last Name:
Street1:
Street2:
City:                        State:                    Zip Code:


Day Telephone:                     Fax:
Night Telephone:

Original Date:               Catalog Numbers:
Latest Date:

Last Order:                  Order:
Favored Customer:

Comments


_____
CUSTOMER.DTF                 Update Spec               Page 1  of  2

Esc-Exit     F1-Help  F6-Expand  F8-Options  Alt+F8-List  ↑F8-Save  F10-Continue
```

*Figure 5.12   Use the Update Spec to define the changes that you want to make to the database*

**137**

⊘ **Caution:** A mass update can take a long time to run. Don't try to do anything else with Q&A during the time that it takes a mass update to execute.

To change any format on the Global Format Options using mass update, follow these steps. First, select Design File from the File menu. Then select Redesign a File and Press F10 repeatedly until you reach the Global Format Options. Change the default format to the new format. Select Mass Update and retrieve all the records by leaving the Retrieve Spec blank. On the Update Spec, move to the field that you want to change and type #1= #1. Press F10 to run the update.

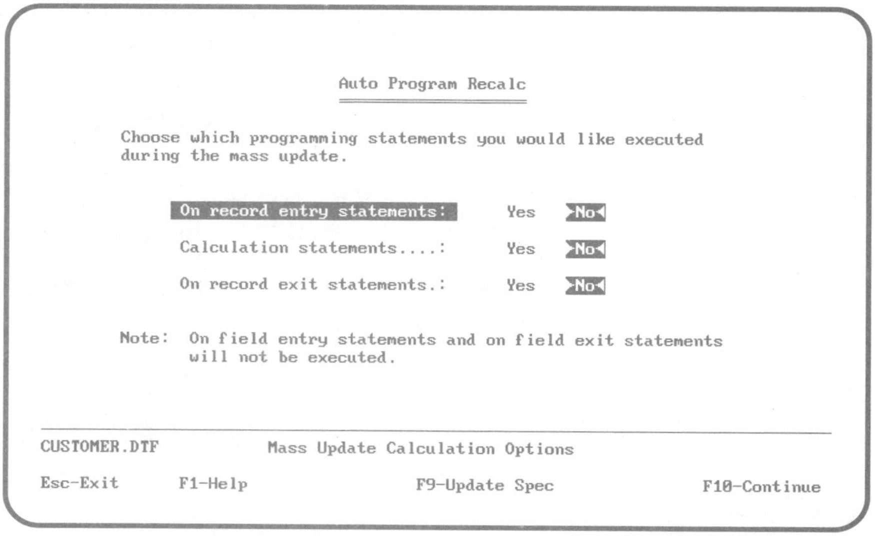

```
                              Auto Program Recalc
                              ─────────────────────

         Choose which programming statements you would like executed
         during the mass update.

                 On record entry statements:      Yes   ►No◄

                 Calculation statements....:       Yes   ►No◄

                 On record exit statements.:       Yes   ►No◄


         Note:  On field entry statements and on field exit statements
                will not be executed.
         ───────────────────────────────────────────────────────────────
         CUSTOMER.DTF          Mass Update Calculation Options

         Esc-Exit      F1-Help            F9-Update Spec        F10-Continue
```

*Figure 5.13   The Calculation Options screen gives you a chance
to decide what, if any, programming statements are executed*

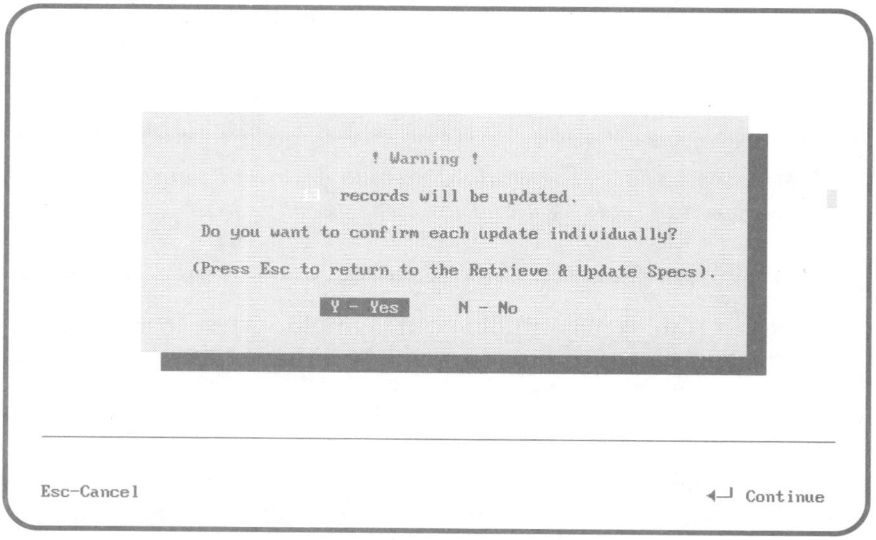

```
                              ! Warning !

                        13   records will be updated.

                 Do you want to confirm each update individually?

               (Press Esc to return to the Retrieve & Update Specs).

                        Y - Yes        N - No
```

```
         Esc-Cancel                                        ←┘ Continue
```

*Figure 5.14   Q&A asks you whether you want to confirm the
update record by record*

To add a number field to your database and add numbers to your existing records, select Design File from the File menu. Select Redesign a File and enter the file name. Add the number field to the database and define the new field as a number information type. Select Mass Update and retrieve all the records by leaving the Retrieve Spec blank. On the Update Spec, move to the new number field and type `#1= @NUMBER`. (If you need to press F6 to open more space in which to enter the value, do so.) Press F10 and then allow the update to take place without confirmation.

# Sending Data from One Database to Another

Use the Post command to send information from a source field in one database to a target field in another database. As the information travels between the two, Q&A can perform calculations on it. You can use the Post command to create a new database, piece by piece, from several databases, building the new database with the best parts of the old ones.

139

Remember these qualifications when you are posting data:

▶ The source field and target field must match and must be the same information type.
▶ The target field must be a speedy field.
▶ If either database or field has been secured, you need to get access.

> ▶ **Tip:** The target database must already exist, so if you want to start a new database, create it before you start the Post process.

## Q Using the Post Command

1. Select Post from the File menu.

   Q&A displays a dialog box with the message Post FROM Q&A file.

2. Enter the name of the source database or press Enter for a list of files. After selecting a name, press Enter.

   Q&A adds the line Post TO Q&A file.

3. Enter the name of the target database.

   Q&A displays the Retrieve Spec.

4. Fill in the Retrieve Spec to specify the records that you want to retrieve from the source database. Then press F10.

   Q&A displays the Posting Spec, which looks like the Retrieve Spec. If you leave the Retrieve Spec blank, you retrieve all records.

5. Select the fields that you wish to post to the target database. Then press F7.

   Q&A displays a box over the Posting Spec (Figure 5.15). In addition, Q&A highlights the source field.

6. Specify the label of the field to which you want to post, and specify the source and target matching fields. If you want to see a list of field names that may match, press Alt-F7. Then select the operation.

   Q&A displays a box, which contains a list of field names, over the right side of the Posting Spec.

7. Replace the target with the source field (the default). Add the source to the target field. Subtract the source from the target field. Multiply the target by the source field. Divide the source field by the target field. Optionally, press F8.

   Q&A displays the Calculation Options (Figure 5.16) and asks Are on record entry statements executed?

| | |
|---|---|
| 8. Respond to the prompt with Yes or No. | If you select Yes, Q&A executes programming statements that occur when the record is entered, then asks `Are calculation statements executed?` |
| 9. Respond to the prompt with Yes or No. | If you select Yes, Q&A executes programming statements that occur in each field, and asks `Are on record exit statements executed?` |
| 10. Respond to the prompt with Yes or No. | If you select Yes, Q&A executes programming statements that occur when the record is exited. |
| 11. Press F10. | Q&A displays the Batch Posting Spec, which shows the post fields of the source database. |
| 12. Press F10 again. | Q&A asks whether you want to post now. If you do, Q&A displays the matching and posting process on screen. □ |

**141**

> ▶ **Tip:** You can use an existing Batch Posting Spec, rather than creating one. The IA can run an existing Batch Posting Spec for you.

# File Utilities

In Chapter 3, you learned two options on the File Utilities menu— backing up a database and recovering a database. The File Utilities also enable you to link to SQL in order to import data, and to import or export other data.

You can set
up another
database
that uses
an ID
number to
connect
with the
original
database.

```
ID Number:

First Name:                    Last Name:
Street1:
Street2:
City:                          State:                    Zip Code:

Day Telephone:                       Fax:
Night Telephone:

Ori
Lat      Post the value of field   ID Number
         ... into external field:
Las      When the field:
Fav      ... matches the external field              in  TESTING.DTF

Com    Operation:      >Replace<   Add    Subtract   Multiply   Divide


CUSTOMER.DTF                     Posting Spec                  Page 1 of 2

Esc-Exit   F1-Help   F7-End Post   AltF7-List of Field Names   F10-Continue
```

**142**

*Figure 5.15    Q&A displays this box for you to enter posting
values*

```
                    Auto Program Recalc


    Choose which programming statements you would like executed
    during the batch post.


        On record entry statements:        Yes   >No<

        Calculation statements....:        Yes   >No<

        On record exit statements.:        Yes   >No<


    Note:  On field entry statements and on field exit statements
           will not be executed.



CUSTOMER.DTF            Batch Post Calculation Options

Esc-Exit    F1-Help              F9-Batch Post Spec        F10-Continue
```

*Figure 5.16    Use the Calculation Options screen to indicate
which programming statements are to be used as posting takes
place*

## Link-to-SQL

For a Link-to-SQL option to work, you must have either SQLBase or ORACLE database servers on local area networks (LANs). Structured Query Language (SQL) is a standard for databases—especially those on mainframes. If you are going to use Q&A to import SQL data, you may have to know a database ID, user name, password, server ID, and SQL table name. For other Q&A network information, see Appendix C.

 **Importing SQL Data**

1. Start your SQL software, then start Q&A and select File.

   Q&A displays the File menu.

2. Select Utilities.

   Q&A displays the File Utilities menu.

3. Select Link-to-SQL.

   Q&A displays the Link-to-SQL menu.

4. Select either SQLBase or ORACLE. Provide all requested information and press F10.

   If Q&A is successful in establishing the link, it asks for the name of a table, which is the source database.

5. Enter a table name and press Enter or press Enter without entering a name to see a list of table names.

   Q&A asks for the name of the target Q&A database.

6. Enter a database name and press Enter or press Enter without entering a name to see a list of file names.

   Q&A displays the Retrieve Spec, which represents the SQL table file but does not use your customary Retrieve Spec programming. If the destination database is new, Q&A displays a Format Spec, which enables you to define information types. Q&A then displays the Merge Spec, which tells Q&A where to put the source data.

143

7. Fill out the Merge Spec to match the fields that you are importing. Press F10.

Q&A imports the data.

☐

## Import Data

Import Data allows you to import from several formats.

 **Importing Data**

1. From the Main menu, select File.

   Q&A displays the File menu.

2. Select Utilities.

   Q&A displays the File Utilities menu.

3. Select Import Data.

   Q&A displays the Import menu.

4. Select the type of file format from which you want to import.

   Q&A adds a dialog box to the bottom of the screen and asks you for the name of the ASCII file name, which is the source.

5. Type a file name and press Enter or press Enter to see a list of files. After selecting a file, press F10.

   Q&A asks for a Q&A file name.

6. Type a file name and press Enter or press Enter to see a list of database files. After selecting a file, press F10.

   Q&A displays the Merge Spec.

7. If the fields in the external file are arranged in the same order as those in the Q&A database and you want to merge all the data, press F10. If you want to merge some of the data, type a number that corresponds with the position of the field in the source file into each target field. Then press F10.

Depending on the type of data you are importing, Q&A may display an options screen.

8. Fill out the options screen and press F10.

If Q&A can import the file, it does so; otherwise, it displays a message stating that the file does not have the proper format. □

**145**

## *Working with Non-Q&A Formats*

The following list contains general information that you should watch for when you are working with non-Q&A file formats. If you want to import data, you might want to create a small test source file before importing "real" data.

Many of these formats are fully or partially compatible with Q&A, and Q&A may create an appropriate form design, depending on the source of the data. Q&A adds the source information to the end of a Q&A database that has data.

Modify a file before you import it if there are more than ten pages in a form or if the source file has a colon (:) followed by a nonspace character.

Information from the first source field goes into the first target field, the second into the second, and so on.

Q&A imports different specs and formulas that may or may not work.

If you have attachment fields, type a field label and set the length of the field.

If you have problems importing data, try using either one of the ASCII options or DIF.

## Export Data

Export Data exports Q&A data to other programs. Q&A creates the source file in the new format but your original database remains the same.

146

### *Q*Exporting a Database File

| | |
|---|---|
| 1. From the Q&A Main menu, select File. | Q&A displays the File menu. |
| 2. Select Utilities. | Q&A displays the File Utilities menu. |
| 3. Select Export Data. | Q&A displays the Export menu. |
| 4. Select the file format to which you want to export your data. | Q&A adds a dialog box to the bottom of the screen and asks for the name of a Q&A file, which is the source file. |
| 5. Type a file name and press Enter or press Enter to see a list of databases. After selecting a file, press F10. | Q&A adds a line to the dialog box and asks for a file to export to. |
| 6. Type a file name and press Enter or press Enter to see a list of files. After selecting a file, press F10. | Q&A displays a warning message stating that the target file will be overwritten. |

7.  If you want to continue, select Yes.

Q&A displays the Retrieve Spec.

8.  Fill in the Retrieve Spec; then press F10.

Q&A displays the Merge Spec.

9.  Press F10 to export all fields in the same order that they appear on your form, or enter numbers on the fields of the Merge Spec to select fields and the order in which you want them. For every field in a Fixed ASCII file, enter a number representing the column number of the starting position of the field and the length of the field. Separate these numbers with a comma. Press F10.

Depending on the type of data you are exporting, Q&A may display an options screen.

**147**

☐

# What You Have Learned

▶ Q&A provides advanced search techniques to retrieve ranges, exact matches, and nonstandard values, using single and multiple restrictions and search logic.

▶ You can print a single form or all the forms you've added as you add data.

▶ The Print Spec allows you to retrieve certain fields, sort them, define page layout and enhancements, and save these specifications for future print jobs.

▶ The free-form style of printing enables you to print mailing labels or reports; coordinate printing, used primarily for preprinted forms, allows you to determine exactly where a field appears on a page.

▶ Mass updating is used for changing the information in two or more forms at the same time, either by direct action, by calculating in one field, or by calculating in a field and placing the results in another field.

▶ The Post command sends data from one Q&A database to another.

▶ The File Utilities allow you to import SQL data and to either import other database information to Q&A or export Q&A data to other databases.

**148**

# Q&A Report: Generating Reports

## In This Chapter

▶ *Generating columnar and cross tab reports*

▶ *Designing a report*

▶ *Filling out the Column/Sort or Cross Tab Spec*

▶ *Using calculations in a report*

▶ *Customizing a report through codes, page layout, and print options*

▶ *Changing defaults for future reports*

▶ *Maintaining your list of reports*

The Q&A Report module uses your instructions to select and format database information so that it can either be printed or displayed on your computer screen. Use an existing report specification or create one to tell Q&A what information to select, how to sort and calculate it, and what it will look like when displayed or printed.

Q&A allows you to design and save as many as 200 report formats, or specs, for a single database. Every time you work on a database, you easily can get its list of report specs in order to reuse a report design.

Q&A provides two types of reports—columnar and cross tabs.

Columnar reports are displays of fields and related calculations organized in columns. Data from each record occupies a row, and each column contains the same field information. An example of a columnar report is a standard table of contents. On one side of the page is a column of chapter and section names; on the other side is the column of related page numbers. A Q&A columnar report allows you to perform calculations and programming for rows and columns, but the emphasis is on columns. For an example of a columnar report from the EMPLOYEE database, see Figure 6.1.

Each heading represents a field.

```
     Last Name          First Name        Department             Position
    -------------       ------------       ----------          -------------
    Abrams              Judy               OPS                 Manager
    Billingsgate        Rudy               ADMIN               Manager
    Brothers            John               EXEC                President
    Carter              James              SALES               Outside
    Criswell            Ernest             ADMIN               Assistant
    Darwin              Charles            R&D                 Engineer
    Dean                Sarah              SALES               Sales Administrator
    Eisenstein          Joseph             LEGAL               Chief Counsel
    Foobah              Dorian             PROMO               Manager
    Fremont             Sam                SALES               Outside
    Gallway             James              ADMIN               Manager
    Guy                 Mary               SALES               Regional Sales Manager
    Gyorfi              Natalia            SALES               Outside
    Jacobson            Will               SALES               Regional Sales Manager
    Jeffers             David              SALES               Outside
    Johnson             Charles            EXEC                Plant Manager
    Johnson             Mildred            ADMIN               Secretary
    Johnson             Nick               SALES               National Sales Manager
    Jones               Jane               SALES               Sales Administrator

    EMPLOYEE.DTF

    Esc-Exit  F2-Reprint    { → ← ↑ ↓ }-Scroll    Shift+F9-Redesign    F10-Continue
```

*Figure 6.1    A columnar report is made up of information organized into columns*

Cross tab reports are similar to spreadsheets in format and organization, but they summarize the information from three database fields. For example, each column of a four-column report could be headed by one of your four warehouse locations, and each row could start with the name of a specific inventory item (e.g., a table saw). Where the row and column meet, you have the total value of all of these items per warehouse. Rows and columns in a cross tab report are equally important. For an example of a cross tab report from the EMPLOYEE database, see Figure 6.2.

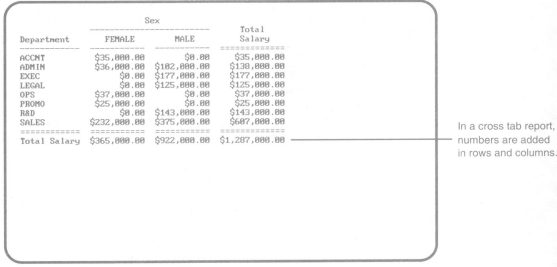

```
                          Sex
                 ---------------------------     Total
    Department      FEMALE        MALE           Salary
    ----------   ------------  -------------   =============
    ACCNT        $35,000.00         $0.00      $35,000.00
    ADMIN        $36,000.00    $102,000.00     $138,000.00
    EXEC             $0.00     $177,000.00     $177,000.00
    LEGAL            $0.00     $125,000.00     $125,000.00
    OPS          $37,000.00         $0.00      $37,000.00
    PROMO        $25,000.00         $0.00      $25,000.00
    R&D              $0.00     $143,000.00     $143,000.00
    SALES       $232,000.00    $375,000.00     $607,000.00
    ============ ============  ============    =============
    Total Salary $365,000.00   $922,000.00   $1,287,000.00
```

In a cross tab report, numbers are added in rows and columns.

*Figure 6.2   A cross tab report is formatted like a spreadsheet*

**151**

# Designing a Report

Planning the design of a report is just as important as planning the design of a database. You might want to put your initial design on paper, just as you did when you planned your first database.

Lay out a report page containing titles, column headings (and for cross tab reports, row headings), detail lines with the record information, and lines for results of calculating and programming. Ensure that your layout has enough space for both fields and totals, which may be one or two digits longer than the data item. Think of the way you want information to look on the page.

The report title should clearly identify the purpose of the report, your company name, and today's date. You might also want to include sorting information, the current time, the company or division address, and for long reports, page numbers.

Column and row headers often are abbreviated so that more information can be squeezed on a page. If you have to abbreviate headers, try to keep them meaningful. Arrange headers by category and try to allow room for totals near the right margin. Leave at least two spaces between each header, but make sure that you allow enough room for the longest data on the detail lines that follow. Consider enhancing both titles and header information so that readers can identify them easily.

Most reports require that the data be sorted, in ascending or descending order, and also placed in related groups. For example, if you want to analyze customers by ZIP code, it won't do much good to retrieve every record without sorting by ZIP code first. It also looks better for the records within groups to be sorted in some other way, such as by last name in alphabetical order.

When you decide to sort more than one field at a time, Q&A sorts automatically by the field's column location. This makes column position quite important.

*Breaks*, which are separations between groups of data (for example, the change from one state to another) can be followed by the results of calculations. Whether or not there are calculations, it is a good formatting practice to skip a line or start printing on the next page after a break.

The following Quick Steps outline the basic process of producing a report. The rest of the chapter explains each step in greater detail.

## Q Designing a Report

1. Select Report from the Main menu.

   Q&A displays the Report menu.

2. Select Design/Redesign a Report.

   Q&A adds a dialog box to the menu and asks for a file name.

3. Enter the name of the file or press Enter for a list of files. After selecting a file, press Enter or F10.

   Q&A displays the List of Reports in Database screen (Figure 6.3).

4. Type in the new report specification, which can be up to 30 characters long and contain spaces; then press Enter.

   Q&A displays the Report Type screen.

5. Select either a Columnar report or a Cross tab report.

Q&A displays the Retrieve Spec.

6. Fill out the Retrieve Spec to identify the records for this report specification or leave it blank to retrieve all records. You also can press Alt-F8 to display a list of the current Retrieve Specs for this database. Select one or press Esc to return to the blank Retrieve Spec.

Q&A displays the Column/ Sort Spec for your report design.

□

```
                             LIST OF REPORTS IN DATABASE      To select a report, move
                             _____              this highlight.
Col. - Co. Activity by Rep.
Col. - Company Listing
Xtab - Rev. by Rep. & Country
Xtab - Rev. by Rep. & US State




                         Enter name:
_____


Esc-Exit    F1-Help  F3-Delete  F5-Copy  F7-Search  F8-Rename  F10-Continue
```

*Figure 6.3    The List of Reports·in Database displays all the report designs now associated with this database, and The WRIGHT database in the Q&A tutorial contains this list of reports*

▶ **Tip:** The List of Reports in Database screen contains both columnar and cross tab report names. For this reason, consider using some of the 30 characters to identify the type of report you are creating. For example, start each cross tab report name with x, or end each columnar report name with - col.

Select the fields on which you want to retrieve records. For example, if you want to get records for people living in California with last names ranging from A through M, fill out the Last Name and State fields with appropriate values or restrictions. You also can type programming expressions or combinations of restrictions and then press Ctrl-F7 to display the Search Option Box (in order to use logical operations on the restrictions). For a list of search restrictions as well as information about the Search Option Box, see Chapter 5. For a list of programming expressions, see Chapter 12.

The next step in building your report design is to select the fields that you want in your report and determine the order in which the records appear. For example, you could sort the records first by ZIP Code and then by Last Name; then you could display the Last Name, First Name, City, and ZIP Code fields on each line. For this, use the Column/Sort Spec.

## 154

# The Column/Sort Spec

The main screen for designing a columnar report is the Column/Sort Spec. Use it to tell Report how to use the retrieved information in this report. For example, the Column/Sort Spec identifies each field in the report as well as its column position on the page. It also determines other actions, such as the types of sorts, width of columns, calculations, column and page breaks, derived and invisible columns, and specifying keyword reports. Table 6.1 lists columnar sort and format codes and their functions.

*Table 6.1   Columnar Sort and Format Codes*

| Code | Function |
| --- | --- |
| ! | Splits a field for placement on multiple lines |
| A | Prints an average value for a column |
| AB | Breaks and does subcalculations when the first letter of field changes |
| AL(name) | Substitutes the value name for the label Average |
| AS | Sorts in ascending order |
| C | Prints the count of entries in a column |

| Code | Function |
|------|----------|
| CL(name) | Substitutes the value name for the label Count |
| CS | Cancels both subcalculations and skipped lines |
| DB | Breaks and does subcalculations when the day changes |
| DS | Sorts in descending order |
| F | Indicates that format codes follow |
| H | Indicates that heading or column codes follow |
| I | Makes the column invisible |
| K | Makes Keyword report |
| MAX | Prints the maximum value found in a column |
| MAXL(name) | Substitutes the value name for the label Maximum |
| MB | Breaks and does subcalculations when the month changes |
| MIN | Prints the minimum value found in a column |
| MINL(name) | Substitutes the value name for the label Minimum |
| P | Starts a new page with a column break |
| R | Repeats usually unrepeatable values |
| SA | Prints subaverages |
| SAL(name) | Substitutes the value name for the label Average |
| SC | Prints subcounts |
| SCL(name) | Substitutes the value name for the label Count |
| SMAX | Prints submaximum values |
| SMAXL(name) | Substitutes the value name for the label Maximum |
| SMIN | Prints subminimum values |
| SMINL(name) | Substitutes value name for the label Minimum |
| SSTD | Prints the substandard deviation |
| SSTDL(name) | Substitutes the value name for the label Standard Deviation |
| ST | Prints subtotals at column breaks |
| STD | Prints the standard deviation for all the values in a column |
| STDL(name) | Substitutes the value name for the label Standard Deviation |

**155**

*(continued)*

**Table 6.1 (continued)**

| Code | Function |
|------|----------|
| STL(name) | Substitutes the value name for the label Total |
| SVAR | Prints the subvariance for the column segment |
| SVARL(name) | Substitutes the value name for the label Variance |
| T | Prints a column total |
| TL(name) | Substitutes the value name for the label Total |
| VAR | Prints the variance for all the values in a column |
| VARL(name) | Substitutes the value name for the label Variance |
| YB | Breaks and does subcalculations when the year changes |

If you know that your report will contain subtotals and totals (along with column and page breaks), you must sort the retrieved records to ensure that similar records are grouped together on the report. Table 6.2 gives examples of coded report entries and their meanings.

**Table 6.2 Examples of Column/Sort Spec Entries**

| Code | Meaning |
|------|---------|
| 2,R | Values in the second column are to be printed even if they have been printed in the previous line or start printing them if they have been suppressed in Set Global Options. |
| 6,AB,P | Values in the sixth column break on a change in the first letter of a field, resulting in a page break. |
| 1,AS,DB | Sort the data in ascending order, place the values in the first column, and break when the date changes. |
| 1,DB,MB,YB | Values in the first column break every time the date, month, or year change. This might cause a subcalculation in another field. |
| 2,AS,F(JC,U,TR) | Values in the first column have been sorted in ascending order, and the formats include center-justified, uppercase text, and when necessary, truncate to fit the column. |

| Code | Meaning |
|------|---------|
| 4,ST,T | Values in the fourth column have subtotals printed at every column break and totals printed at the bottom of every column. |
| 2,H(10:ERA) | Values in the second column are 10 characters wide with the header ERA. |
| 2,H(2cm:ERA) | Values in the second column are two centimeters wide with the header ERA. |
| 2,H(1":ERA) | Values in the second column are one inch wide with the header ERA. |
| 6,H(12:Average!Income) | Values in the sixth column are 12 characters long with the header Average on one line and Income on the next line. |
| 6,H(12:3:Avg!Income) | Values in the sixth column are 12 characters long with the header Avg on one line and Income, which is indented three characters, on the next line. |

**157**

The following Quick Steps show how to fill out the Column/ Sort Spec. Remember, to add sort codes, type a comma after the column position number, then enter AS (for ascending sort) or DS (for descending sort). Q&A allows you to sort more than one field at a time.

## Q Filling In the Column/Sort Spec

1. Type any number from 1 to 9999 in each field that will be a column in your report. Optionally, type in any of the sort or format codes that help to customize the report design, or type in any calculation, sub-calculation, or other codes.

   Q&A sorts by the column location.

2. When you have completed the Column/Sort Spec (Figure 6.4), press F10.

   Q&A displays the Report Print Options screen, from which you can print without making any changes.  □

The codes you enter determine the order in which the column is displayed and the order of the sort.

```
ID Number:

First Name: 2                Last Name: 1,AS
Street1: 3
Street2:
City: 4                      State: 5              Zip Code:


Day Telephone:               Fax:
Night Telephone:

Original Date:               Catalog Numbers:
Latest Date:

Last Order:                  Order: 6,T
Favored Customer:

Comments


CUSTOMER.DTF        Column/Sort Spec for sample col report    Page 1  of 2

Esc-Exit      F1-Help   F6-Expand   Shift+F6-Enhance   F8-Derived Cols   F10-Continue
```

**158**

*Figure 6.4   A completed Column/Sort Spec for the CUSTOMER database*

## Using Codes to Customize Your Columnar Report

You can tell Q&A to start a new report page whenever values change in a column. This is known as a *page break*. Select a field that you want to trigger a page break and make sure that it already contains a sorting code. Add a comma and then a P, which indicates that changes in this field's value causes a page break.

If you want to use a field to produce your report, but you don't want or need to show the field in the report (for example, confidential information), define it as an *invisible column*. To define an invisible column, enter column number, sorting codes, formulas, and so on, and then add the code I, which indicates invisible.

There may be times when you want to create a report based on keywords in your database. To create a *keyword report*, enter 1K in the keyword field of the Column/Sort Spec. For example, if your company is fielding a baseball team, you can produce a simple report that retrieves all employees who listed baseball as a hobby. For an example, look at the EMPLOYEE database Activities report in the \TUT subdirectory.

A multiple-line field is a field that displays more than one line on a form in your database. You can set the indentation for the second (and subsequent) line of a multiple-line field by inserting another number after the column width setting. In order to specify indentation, you must also specify column width. See Table 6.2 for an example of this setting.

Enter format codes to define the way your report looks as output. Although these codes look similar to those you enter on File's Format Spec, they only affect the output. For a list of format codes, see Table 6.3.

*Table 6.3   Codes Used with the Format (F) Code*

| Code | Function |
| --- | --- |
| C | Displays money and numbers with commas |
| Dn | Uses date format n (where n is a number from 1 through 20) |
| Hn | Uses time format n (where n is a number from 1 through 3) |
| JC | Justifies the text at the center |
| JL | Justifies the text to the left margin |
| JR | Justifies the text to the right margin |
| M | Displays in money format |
| Nn | Formats using n decimal places |
| T | Formats as text |
| TR | Truncates to fit a column width |
| U | Displays text in uppercase |
| WC | Displays numbers without commas |

**159**

> **Caution:** Do not combine Dn, Hn, Nn, M, or T codes in one field; these codes represent the different information types.

You easily can customize a column heading or change a column width for your report. After the other codes in the field, type a comma and then H:. Type the column width (in characters, inches, or centimeters) followed by a colon. Then type the heading exactly the way you want it to look on the report. If you want to split the heading into more than one line, enter ! at the location of the split. Any column heading and width changes that you enter here override the global report settings.

You also can change fonts or apply enhancements to column headings and results of either calculations or subcalculations.

## Q Applying an Enhancement

| | |
|---|---|
| 1. On the Column/Sort Spec, move the cursor to the code that represents the field or calculation that you want to enhance. Press Shift-F6. | Q&A displays the Text Enhancement and Fonts menu. |
| 2. Apply either an enhancement or a font. | Enhancements appear highlighted on the Column/Sort Spec. |
| 3. Press F10. | Q&A closes the Text Enhancement and Fonts menu. □ |

## 160  *Using Subtotals and Totals*

To calculate within a report, add codes to columns in which you want to perform calculations. Depending on the code you enter, Q&A calculates on the entire column or whenever a value in the column breaks. Later on, you'll also learn about derived columns, which result from calculations in other columns.

## *Column Calculations*

Calculate all the values in a column, showing the result at the bottom of the column. For example, if you want to see your total orders in dollars for the month, add the contents of all Order fields.

To specify column calculations or subcalculations in the Column/Sort Spec, move the cursor to the end of the current code for the field you want to calculate and type a comma. This separates the last code from the calculation code. Enter as many calculation codes as you want.

Calculate subtotals within a column that you specify. For example, if you want to produce a subtotal for every sales region, calculate an Order subtotal.

There are times when you want to sort on a column without automatic subcalculations and column breaks. You might want a sorted column to cause a break in a column closer to the right margin, or improve the look of your report by fewer control breaks. Use the CS (cancel subcalculation) code in any column for which you don't want a subcalculation. For example, if your report is sorted by City (the fourth column), Orders is the eighth column, and these are the important columns, you might want to type CS in some of the columns between.

# Using Derived Columns in a Columnar Report

Create a derived column to show the results of calculations from existing fields, between fields and other derived columns, and from derived columns only. For example, create a derived column to show the total of vacation days plus compensation days owed to each employee.

**161**

## Creating Formulas for Derived Columns

The contents in derived columns are calculated using the formulas that you enter on the Derived Column screen. A derived column formula can contain arithmetic operators, such as / (for division), * (for multiplication), + (for addition), and – (for subtraction). Q&A processes the formulas in the order of multiplication and division first, and then addition and subtraction. You can change the order of precedence by enclosing the formulas that you want processed first with parentheses.

You can create a derived column formula for the column that holds the formula. This technique is known as *self-referencing*. For example, to add a new order amount (#7) to the Order field (#8), type the formula #7 + #8 in the Order column.

To get a value from a column, insert either the column number or the field label into the formula. You can use a value from another column in a derived column formula by inserting the column number or its label in the formula. Table 6.4 gives examples of derived column formats.

**Table 6.4  Examples of Derived Column Formulas**

| Formula | Meaning |
|---|---|
| #3 + #8 | Column 3 plus column 8 |
| #1 + #2 – #3 | Column 1 plus column 2 minus column 3 |
| #3 / #2 * #7 | Column 3 divided by column 2; multiply the result by column 7 |
| #3 * (#1 – #2) | Column 1 minus column 2; multiply the result by column 3 |
| Wholesale * .25 | Multiply the amount in the Wholesale column by 25% |

A derived formula also can include programming statements or summary functions, which either refer to calculations in other columns or retrieve column break calculations. For more information about Q&A programming, see Chapter 12. Table 6.5 lists summary functions and their returns.

**Note:** You can only use summary functions for derived columns.

**Table 6.5  Summary Functions**

| Function | Returns |
|---|---|
| @AVERAGE(x) | Grand average of the values in column x |
| @AVERAGE(x,y) | Subaverage of values in column x where a break occurs in column y |
| @COUNT(x) | Grand total count of the values in column x |
| @COUNT(x,y) | Subcount of values in column x where a break occurs in column y |
| @MAXIMUM(x) | Highest value in column x |
| @MAXIMUM(x,y) | Highest value in column x where a break occurs in column y |
| @MINIMUM(x) | Lowest value in column x |
| @MINIMUM(x,y) | Lowest value in column x where a break occurs in column y |

162

| Function | Returns |
|----------|---------|
| @TOTAL(x) | Grand total of values in column x |
| @TOTAL(x,y) | Subtotal of values in column x where a break occurs in column y |

Before you enter derived column information, make a list of the existing columns in your report and the name of the field for each.

## Q Creating a Derived Column

1. From the Column/Sort Spec screen, press F8.

   Q&A displays the Derived Columns screen containing information for four derived columns.

2. Enter a number representing column width and then a colon. Then enter the column heading. If you want to split a heading, insert an exclamation point at the point of the split. Then press Enter, Tab, Down, or Up.

   Q&A processes the width you specify.

163

3. Type in the formula used to calculate the derived column; then press Enter, Tab, Down, or Up.

   Q&A processes your formula.

4. Designate a column number and type in the specification for the derived column and press Enter.

   Q&A processes your specification.

5. Repeat steps 2 through 4 for up to 15 additional derived columns. Then press F10 (or F9).

   Q&A takes you back to the Print Options screen (or Column/Sort screen).

   ☐

For an example of a Derived Columns screen for the CUS-
TOMER database, see Figure 6.5. This report shows the total of the
Last Order (the newest order) plus the Order (the grand total) (see
Figure 6.6 for the related Column/Sort Spec).

Codes for position
and calculation

```
                              DERIVED COLUMNS
                              ==============

       Heading:
       Formula:
       Column Spec:

       Heading:
       Formula:
       Column Spec:

       Heading:
       Formula:
       Column Spec:

       Heading:
       Formula:
       Column Spec:

                                                              ▮
    _____
    CUSTOMER.DTF         Derived Columns for another sample   Page 1 of 4

    Esc-Exit        F1-Help     F9-Go back to Column/Sort Spec   F10-Continue
```

**164**

*Figure 6.5    A filled-in Derived Columns screen*

```
    ID Number:

    First Name: 2              Last Name: 1,AS
    Street1:
    Street2:
    City:                      State:                  Zip Code:

    Day Telephone:                  Fax:
    Night Telephone:

    Original Date:             Catalog Numbers:
    Latest Date:

    Last Order: 3,T            Order:4,T
    Favored Customer:

    Comments
                                                              ▮
    _____
    CUSTOMER.DTF         Column/Sort Spec for another sample   Page 1  of 2

    Esc-Exit     F1-Help   F6-Expand  Shift+F6-Enhance  F8-Derived Cols  F10-Continue
```

*Figure 6.6    This Column/Sort Spec is related to the Derived
Columns screen illustrated in Figure 6.5*

## *Saving and Printing the Report*

When your report design is complete, the Report Print Options screen is displayed. If you press F10, Q&A displays a dialog box stating that your report design is saved. You can choose to print the report or not. If you select No, you are returned to the Report menu. If you select Yes, the report is printed and then you are returned to the Report menu.

After your report design has been saved, you can use it anytime you wish to print an updated version of the report. If you want to print a report that you or someone else previously created, you can select Print a Report from the Report menu.

# The Cross Tab Spec

A cross tab report is made up of three fields—row, column, and summary. A row, which contains related values arranged horizontally, ends with the row summary. A column, which contains related values arranged vertically, ends with a column summary.

> ▶ **Note:** Although a cross tab report does not use every code that a columnar report does, many of the codes are identical and you enter them in the same way.

You can design a cross tab report using many of the same tools as those used to create a columnar report. However, there are some important differences.

### Designing a Cross Tab Report

| | |
|---|---|
| 1. From the List of Reports in Database screen, type in the name of a new report, starting the name with X or XTAB. | Q&A displays the Report Type screen. |
| 2. Select a Cross tab report. | Q&A displays the Retrieve Spec. |

3. Fill out the Retrieve Spec to identify the records for this report specification (Figure 6.7). To retrieve all the records in the database, leave the Retrieve Spec blank. To retrieve some records, type restrictions into the fields that you are using to select the records. Optionally, press Alt-F8.

Q&A displays a list of the current Retrieve Specs for this database.

4. After completing the Retrieve Spec, press F10.

Q&A displays the Cross Tab Spec ready to be filled in. □

**166**

```
 ID Number:

 First Name:                  Last Name:
 Street1:
 Street2:
 City:                        State:              Zip Code: >12800..<→

 Day Telephone:                      Fax:
 Night Telephone:

 Original Date: >1/1/91        Catalog Numbers:
 Latest Date:

 Last Order:                  Order:
 Favored Customer:                                                    ▮

 Comments


 ─────────────────────────────────────────────────────────────────────
 CUSTOMER.DTF              Retrieve Spec for sample xtabs      Page 1 of 2

 Esc-Exit   F1-Help   F3-Clear  F6-Expand  Alt+F8-List  ↑F8-Save  F10-Continue
```

*Figure 6.7    This Retrieve Spec is designed to retrieve records entered after January 1, 1991 and that have ZIP codes within a range of 12800 to 20000*

The next Quick Steps show you how to proceed by filling in the Cross Tab Spec.

## **Q** Filling In the Cross Tab Spec

1.  Type COL in the field whose values are to comprise the columns of the report. Type ROW in the field whose values are to comprise the rows of the report. Type SUM in the field whose values are to be calculated and placed in the row and column summaries. Optionally, type in any summary calculation. You also can enhance all rows or columns by pressing Shift-F6.

    Q&A displays the Text Enhancements and Fonts screen. (Q&A specifies a default calculation if you do not select a summary calculation.)

2.  When you have completed the Cross Tab Spec, press F10. (See Figure 6.8 for a look at the filled-in Cross Tab Spec for our sample.)

    Q&A displays the Cross Tab Print Options screen (Figure 6.9.)

3.  Change print and page settings at this point or by selecting Print a Report from the Report menu. (For an example of our printed Cross Tab report, see Figure 6.10.)

    Q&A displays the completed Cross Tab Spec.

Q&A sorts cross tab row and column titles in ascending order automatically, but you can override the default sort order by entering either AS or DS.

You can scale numbers up or down so that the report is easier to read. Type SCALE(n), where n represents the factor by which you want to change the current value. For example, if you have many numbers with six or eight trailing zeros, scaling the numbers down to remove some of the zeros looks more professional.

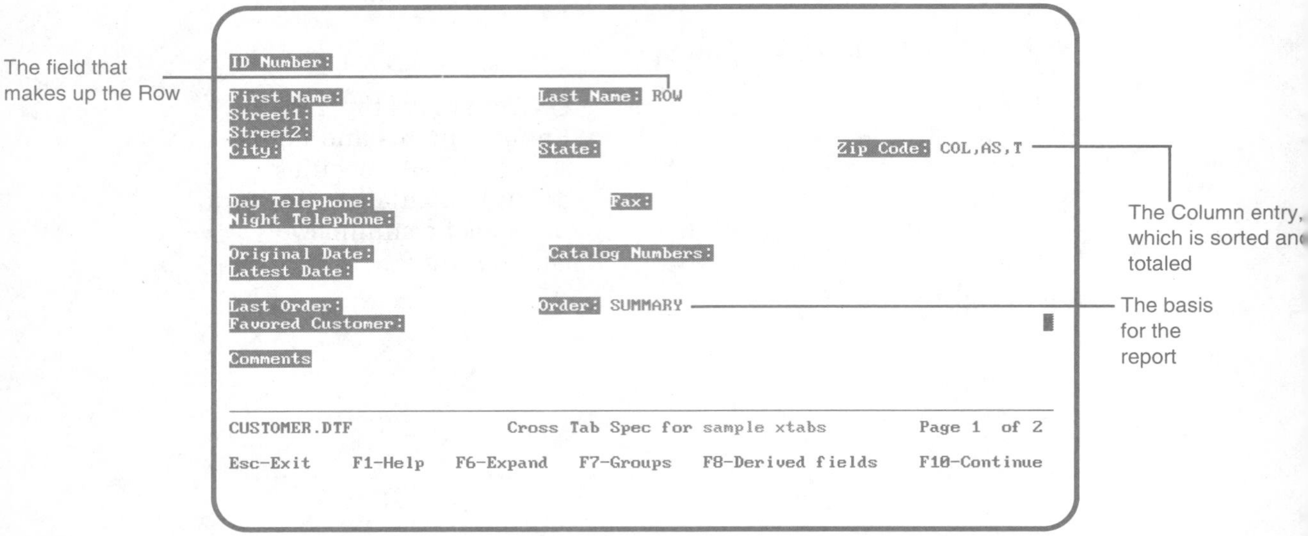

The field that
makes up the Row

```
 ID Number:

 First Name:                 Last Name: ROW
 Street1:
 Street2:
 City:                       State:              Zip Code: COL,AS,T

 Day Telephone:                    Fax:
 Night Telephone:

 Original Date:              Catalog Numbers:
 Latest Date:

 Last Order:                 Order: SUMMARY
 Favored Customer:

 Comments

 CUSTOMER.DTF           Cross Tab Spec for sample xtabs       Page 1  of 2

 Esc-Exit    F1-Help   F6-Expand   F7-Groups   F8-Derived fields   F10-Continue
```

The Column entry,
which is sorted and
totaled

The basis
for the
report

**168**

*Figure 6.8    The sample Cross Tab Spec for our first report*

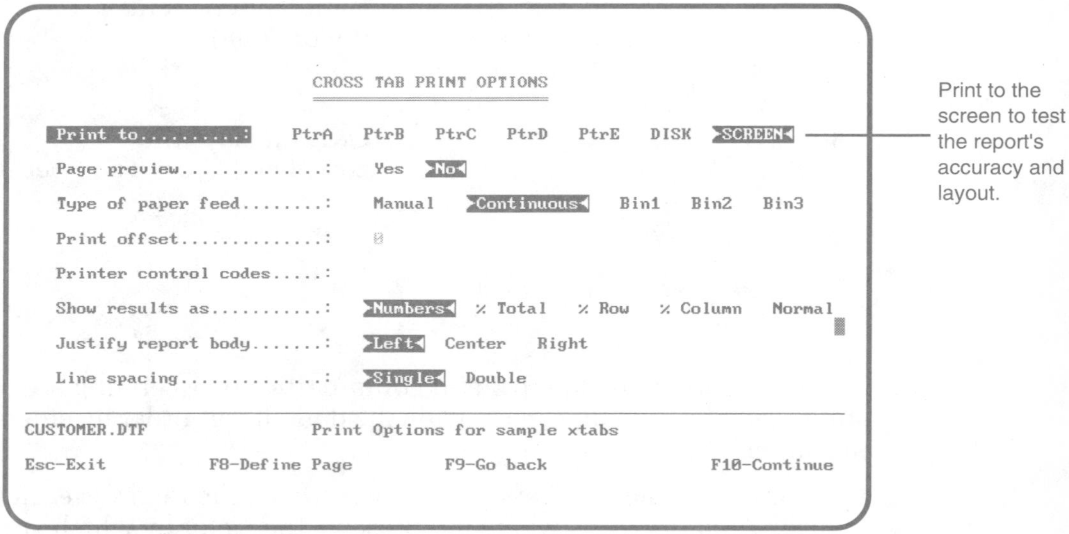

```
                        CROSS TAB PRINT OPTIONS

   Print to..........:    PtrA   PtrB   PtrC   PtrD   PtrE   DISK  ▶SCREEN◀

   Page preview...........:    Yes   ▶No◀

   Type of paper feed........:    Manual   ▶Continuous◀   Bin1   Bin2   Bin3

   Print offset.............:    0

   Printer control codes.....:

   Show results as..........:   ▶Numbers◀   % Total   % Row   % Column   Normal

   Justify report body.......:   ▶Left◀   Center   Right

   Line spacing.............:   ▶Single◀   Double

 CUSTOMER.DTF           Print Options for sample xtabs

 Esc-Exit          F8-Define Page        F9-Go back              F10-Continue
```

Print to the
screen to test
the report's
accuracy and
layout.

*Figure 6.9    The Cross Tab Print Options screen is almost
identical to the Report Print Options screen*

**Table 6.6   Cross Tab Enhancement Codes**

| Code | Enhancement |
|------|-------------|
| AL | The AVERAGE label |
| CL | The COUNT label |
| DL | A double separator line for the totals at the bottom of the report |
| H | The heading of the specified column, row, or summary field |
| HS | Separator lines for the main title |
| MAXL | The MAX label |
| MINL | The MIN label |
| SH | The subheading of the column or row field |
| SL | A single separator line between a column heading and the data |
| STDL | The STD label |
| TL | The TOTAL label |
| VARL | The VAR label |

**169**

```
                              Zip Code
              ----------------------------------------------------    Total
Last Name     12809-      12834-      12838-      12887-     Order
-----------   ----------  ----------  ----------  ----------  =======
Adams            $0.00       $0.00       $0.00      $88.00     $88.00
Atherton        $64.00       $0.00       $0.00       $0.00     $64.00
Clover           $0.00       $0.00      $32.98       $0.00     $32.98
Dragonette       $0.00     $325.54       $0.00       $0.00    $325.54
Fort             $0.00       $0.00     $125.88       $0.00    $125.88
Jennings        $14.98       $0.00       $0.00       $0.00     $14.98
Rabide           $0.00      $23.00       $0.00       $0.00     $23.00
Underwood      $145.99       $0.00       $0.00       $0.00    $145.99
Wills           $88.00       $0.00       $0.00       $0.00     $88.00
===========   ==========  ==========  ==========  ==========  =======
Total Order    $312.97     $348.54     $158.86      $88.00    $908.37
                                                                        ▮


CUSTOMER.DTF

Esc-Exit  F2-Reprint    { → ← ↑ ↓ }-Scroll    Shift+F9-Redesign    F10-Continue
```

*Figure 6.10   The printed cross tab report to which you can add titles and enhancements*

## *Using Derived Fields in a Cross Tab Report*

For cross tab reports, the counterpart of derived columns for columnar reports is the derived field, which can be used for columns, rows,
or summary fields.

### **Q Entering a Derived Field**

| | |
|---|---|
| 1. From the Cross Tab Spec, press F8. | Q&A displays the Derived Fields Spec. |
| 2. Type heading information for the first derived field; then press Enter, Tab, Down, or Up. | Q&A processes your heading information. |
| 3. Type in the formula used to calculate the derived field; then press Enter, Tab, Down, or Up. | Q&A processes your formula. |
| 4. Type ROW, COL, or SUM. You can enter a calculation code (A, C, T, or V) or a sort code (AS or DS) following SUM. | Q&A enters your derived fields. |
| 5. Repeat steps 2 through 4 for up to three additional derived fields. When you are finished, press F10 (or F9). | Q&A displays the Print Options screen (or the Cross Tab Spec). |

**170**

## *Using the Grouping Spec*

You can specify groupings of data at the Grouping Spec, for example,
to select Order in $50 increments. If our database were larger, we
would use the Grouping Spec. Table 6.7 lists predefined groupings.

*Table 6.7    Predefined Groupings for Cross Tab Reports*

| Grouping | Groups By |
|---|---|
| @ALL | Each unique value |
| @ALPHA | The first letter |

| Grouping | Groups By |
|----------|-----------|
| @DAY | Each unique date |
| @DOM | Each day of the month |
| @DOW | Each day of the week |
| @I or @INTERVAL | Interval that Q&A determines |
| @I(n) or @INTERVAL(n) | Interval that you specify |
| @MONTH | Month |
| @MOY | Months of the year |
| @R(x,y,z) or @RANGE(x,y,z) | Ranges that you specify |
| @YEAR | Year |

An example of a specific range that could be used in a grouping spec is `<= 50` or `101. . .151`.

**171**

## Filling In the Grouping Spec

1. From the Cross Tab Spec, press F7.

   Q&A displays the Cross Tabs Groupings Spec (Figure 6.11).

2. Move the cursor to the Row or Column groupings and enter a function or a specific range of values, one on each line. Optionally, enhance specific rows or columns by pressing Shift-F6.

   Q&A displays the Text Enhancements and Fonts screen.

3. When you have completed the Spec, press F10.

   Q&A displays the Cross Tab Print Options screen.    □

# Printing or Modifying a Report

If you select Print a Report from the Report menu, you can use a Report Spec to print and to customize temporarily a report before printing.

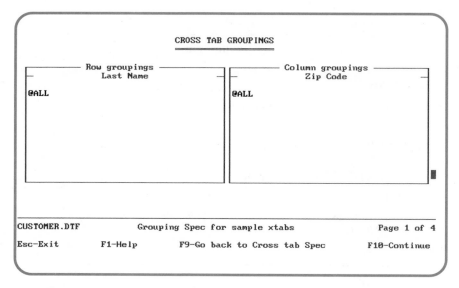

```
                        CROSS TAB GROUPINGS
                        ═══════════════════

        ┌─── Row groupings ───┐      ┌── Column groupings ──┐
        │      Last Name       │      │      Zip Code         │
  ┌─────┴──────────────────────┴──┬───┴───────────────────────┴─────┐
  │ @ALL                          │ @ALL                            │
  │                               │                                 │
  │                               │                                 │
  │                               │                                 │
  │                               │                                ▓│
  │                               │                                 │
  └───────────────────────────────┴─────────────────────────────────┘

  CUSTOMER.DTF          Grouping Spec for sample xtabs          Page 1 of 4

  Esc-Exit        F1-Help        F9-Go back to Cross tab Spec      F10-Continue
```

Figure 6.11   *A Cross Tab Groupings Spec indicating that all selected records are grouped.*

## Q Printing or Modifying a Report

1. Select Print a Report from the Report menu.

   Q&A requests the name of the database whose reports you want to print. If you have been working with a database, Q&A proposes that name.

2. Enter the name of the file or press Enter for a list of files. After selecting a file, press Enter or F10.

   Q&A displays the List of Reports in Database screen.

3. Select the name of an existing database report; then press F10.

   Q&A asks whether you want to make any temporary changes to the report.

4. Respond with Yes or No.

   If you select No, Q&A begins printing. If you select Yes, Q&A displays the Retrieve Spec for the report.  □

## *Defining Page Attributes*

Use the Define Page screen to set the page width and length, margins, characters per inch, and to define header and footer lines.

### Defining Page Attributes

1. Press F8 from the Print Options screen.

   Q&A displays the Define Page screen (Figure 6.12).

2. Press Tab, Enter, Up, or Down until the cursor highlights the option you want to change. For page and margin options, type a new value. For characters per inch, press the Spacebar to move the highlight to your desired choice. Move the cursor to the Header or Footer area and type appropriate text.

   Q&A processes the attributes you specify.

3. When you have completed the screen, press F10 to finish the report design or press F9.

   If you press F9, Q&A returns to the Print Options screen.

**173**

```
                          DEFINE PAGE


            Page width..: 85        Page length..: 66

            Left margin: 5          Right margin.: 80

            Top margin.: 3          Bottom margin: 3

            Characters per inch:   10   12   15   17
    ─────────────────────────── HEADER ───────────────────────────
         1:
         2:
         3: ─────────────────────────── FOOTER ───────────────────────────
         1:
         2:
         3:
    ────────────────────────────────────────────────────────────
    CUSTOMER.DTF              Define page for sample xtabs

    Esc-Exit      F1-Help        F9-Go Back to Print Options      F10-Continue
```

Define header and footer text here

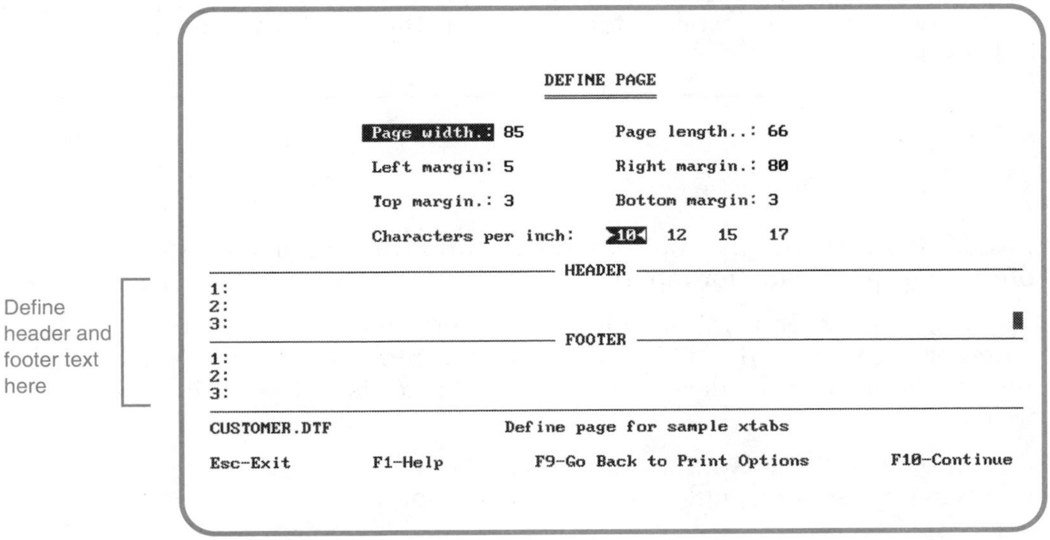

*Figure 6.12    The Define Page screen offers the same options for both types of reports*

---

> ▶ **Tip:** If you want to change settings just for this report, use the Define Page screen. If you want to change settings for all reports, select Set Global Options from the Report menu.

You can use special symbols to either format or add text to headers and footers. To justify header or footer text, insert exclamation points. For example, enter

```
@DATE(1) ! Customers Sorted by Zip Code ! @TIME(1)
```

and the result is today's date (in date format 1), left-justified, with the title centered, and the current time (in time format 1) right-justified. Remember, text before the first exclamation point is left-justified, and text after the second exclamation point is right-justified. If there is no text before the first exclamation point, the text immediately following is centered.

174

A pound sign (#) indicates that you want to print a page number on every report page. For example, enter

```
@DATE(2) ! December Hand Tool Sales ! Page #
```

and the result is today's date (in date format 2) left-justified, with the title centered and a page number right-justified.

---

> ▶ **Tip:** If you want an exclamation point or pound sign printed in the header or footer, precede the symbol with a backslash ( \ ).

---

## Print Options for a Report

Besides the standard print options, the Report Print Options screen offers two specifically for reports.

*Print totals only* is for columnar reports only and defines whether Q&A prints the totals (the summary information) in your reports rather than the data from individual records as well as the totals.

*Show results as* is for cross tab reports only and defines the following ways that calculation results are displayed:

▶ Numbers displays results as numbers. This is the default.

▶ % Total displays results as a percentage of the total value for all Summary field values.

▶ % Row displays results as a percentage of the total or count for the row.

▶ % Column displays the results as a percentage of the total or count for the column.

▶ Normal displays the results as an amount above or below average, which is a value of 100.

> ▶ **Tip:** If the value in a sorted column changes, Q&A skips a line. You can either change the Global Format Options from the Report menu or enter CS (cancel subcalculations) in the sorted field.

**175**

## Setting Print Options and Printing a Report

| | |
|---|---|
| 1. Press F10 from the Column/Sort Spec, Cross Tab Spec, or Derived Spec. | Q&A displays the Report Print Options screen. |
| 2. If you want to change an item on this screen, press a combination of cursor movement keys until the item that you want to change is highlighted. Type a value or press Enter to select an option. Optionally, change settings for your page layout by pressing F8. | Q&A displays the Define Page screen. |
| 3. After making all the desired changes, press F10. | Q&A asks if you want to start printing. |
| 4. Respond with Yes or No. | If you select Yes, Q&A starts printing the report. If you select No, Q&A returns you to the Report menu. ☐ |

## *Modifying a Report*

You can redesign a report by returning to the Report menu and selecting Design/Redesign a Report.

> ▶ **Tip:** You also can make temporary changes to a report by choosing Print from the Report menu and following the prompts.

Use the Redesign menu to move quickly to the spec that you want to change. To use the Redesign menu to change a report, follow these Quick Steps.

**Q** **Changing a Report with the Redesign Menu**

1. During the print process, press Shift-F9.

   A box opens at the bottom of the screen, giving you a choice of going to several specs (Figure 6.13).

2. Type the letter of the spec you want to alter (Retrieve, Column/Sort, Derived Columns, Print Options, or Define Page).

   Q&A displays the spec you want to alter.

3. Make changes to the specification and press F10.

   Q&A resumes printing.

   □

# Setting Global Options

Select Set Global Options and either Columnar or Cross Tab Global Options to change column heading and widths, and to define format, print, and page options for all future reports. All current report designs have default global options already.

```
                             Zip Code
              -----------------------------------------------  Total
   Last Name  12809-     12834-     12838-     12887-          Order
   ---------- ---------- ---------- ---------- ----------      =======
   Adams        $0.00      $0.00      $0.00     $88.00        $88.00
   Atherton    $64.00      $0.00      $0.00      $0.00        $64.00
   Clover       $0.00      $0.00     $32.98      $0.00        $32.98
   Dragonette   $0.00    $325.54      $0.00      $0.00       $325.54
   Fort         $0.00      $0.00    $125.88      $0.00       $125.88
   Jennings    $14.98      $0.00      $0.00      $0.00        $14.98
   Rabide       $0.00     $23.00      $0.00      $0.00        $23.00
   Underwood  $145.99      $0.00      $0.00      $0.00       $145.99
   Wills       $88.00      $0.00      $0.00      $0.00        $88.00
   ========== ========== ========== ========== ==========    =======
   Total Order $312.97   $348.54    $158.86     $88.00       $908.37



   _____

   Which spec?  R-Retrieve  C-Cross tab  D-Drvd Flds  G-Group  P-Print  A-Page
```

A shortcut to redesigning a report

*Figure 6.13    Press Shift-F9 to open this box at the bottom of the report displayed on the screen*

**177**

## Setting Global Options

| | |
|---|---|
| 1. Select Set Global Options from the Report menu. | Q&A asks for the name of the database you want to use. |
| 2. Enter the name of the database or press Enter for a list of files. After selecting a file, press Enter. | Q&A displays the Global Options menu. |
| 3. Select either Columnar Global Options or Cross Tab Global Options. | Q&A offers options to allow you to set column heading/ widths, format options, print options, or page options. □ |

## Column Headings and Widths

Q&A default column headings and widths are whichever is longer— the column heading or the longest value in a column. Define a specific column width or rename the heading, which is normally the same name as the database field label.

You can define column headings with as much as three lines of text, and you can make a column as wide as 80 characters. However, remember that once you have defined the column width, Q&A no longer adjusts the width to fit the longest value. For example, if a numeric value is longer than the new width, Q&A replaces the numbers with asterisks (*).

## **Q** Setting Column Headings and Widths

1. From the Columnar or Cross Tab Global Options screen, select Set Column Heading/Widths or Set Col/Row Headings, respectively.

   Q&A displays the Column Headings/Width or Cross Tab Headings Spec.

2. Press a combination of cursor movement keys to move to a field. For a columnar report design only, specify the new width of this column by typing a number from 1 to 80.

   Q&A processes your specification.

3. For either a columnar or cross tab report, type the new column heading. Press F10 when you have completed the Spec.

   Q&A displays the completed spec.

For columnar reports, to specify a number as a heading, type a colon and then the number, for example, :24. To change the width and column, use a format that contains two colons, for example, H(12::24). If you want to specify a number as a heading for a cross tab report, simply type it in.

For derived columns in columnar reports, type a colon before the name to specify a heading that includes a number. For example, type :1st Division. Otherwise, Q&A will misinterpret your entry as a one-character column followed by the heading "st Division."

## *Format Options*

Q&A provides the chance to change report format settings. These settings are in addition to setting print and page options:

▶ *# of spaces between columns* indicates whether a set number of spaces is placed between each column or whether Q&A sets a variable (the default) number of spaces instead.

▶ *Default to repeating values* (for columnar reports) indicates whether Q&A prints identical values for a field (e.g., the last name of Smith, Smith, and Smith) or only the first occurrence of the same value, the default.)

▶ *Action on blank value* indicates whether Q&A prints a zero or leaves a blank space when a field does not contain a number or money value.

▶ *Action on column break* (for columnar reports) indicates whether Q&A prints on the next line or skips a line when there is a changed value in a field set for a column break. Q&A normally skips a line.

▶ *Show "no entry" columns/rows* (for cross tab reports) indicates whether fields with no values are printed or not. The default is to not show a blank entry.

**179**

See Figure 6.14 for an example of the Report Global Format Options screen, and Figure 6.15 for the Cross Tab Global Format Options screen.

```
                    REPORT GLOBAL FORMAT OPTIONS
                    ═══════════════════════════════


    # of spaces between columns:   ►Variable◄  1   2   3   4   5   6   7   8   9

    Default to repeating values:   Yes  ►No◄

    Action on blank value......:   Print 0  ►Leave blank◄

    Action on column break.....:   ►Skip line◄  Don't skip line
                                                                          ▮

    ─────────────────────────────────────────────────────────────────────────

    Esc-Exit                                                  F10-Continue
```

*Figure 6.14   The Report Global Format Options screen enables format changes to a columnar report design*

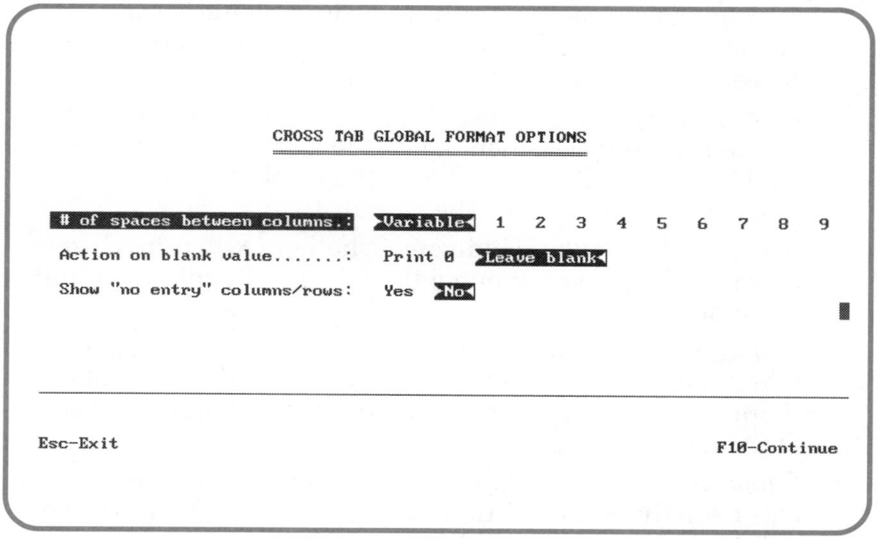

```
                    CROSS TAB GLOBAL FORMAT OPTIONS
                    ══════════════════════════════════

    # of spaces between columns.:  ►Variable◄  1   2   3   4   5   6   7   8   9

    Action on blank value.......:  Print 0  ►Leave blank◄

    Show "no entry" columns/rows:  Yes  ►No◄                                    █


    ───────────────────────────────────────────────────────────────────

    Esc-Exit                                                    F10-Continue
```

180

*Figure 6.15   The Cross Tab Global Format Options screen*
*allows you to further customize a cross tab report design*

# Rename/Delete/Copy a Report Design

The renaming, deleting, and copying options are similar to those
offered in other Q&A modules. For detailed descriptions, see Chapter 11.

**Q** **Renaming, Deleting, or Copying a Report Design**

1. From the Main menu,            Q&A displays the Report
   select Report.                 menu.

2. Select Rename/Delete/          Q&A adds a dialog box to
   Copy.                          the bottom of the screen.

3. Enter the name of the          Q&A displays the Rename/
   database or press Enter for    Delete/Copy menu.
   a list of files. After
   selecting a file, press Enter.

4. Select one of the options.

   Q&A adds an appropriate dialog box to the bottom of the screen.

5. Enter the name of the report or press Enter.

   Q&A displays the List of Reports in Database screen.

6. From the List of Reports in Database screen, delete a file (by pressing F3), copy a file (by pressing F5), search for one or more files (by pressing F7), or rename a file (by pressing F8).

   Q&A deletes, copies, searches for, or renames the file you specify and returns you to the Rename/Copy/Delete menu.

7. To rename a report from the Rename/Copy/Delete menu, fill in Rename From and Rename To in the dialog box. Then press Enter.

   Q&A renames the report you specify and returns you to the Rename/Copy/Delete menu.

**181**

8. To delete a report, enter its name and press Enter.

   Q&A displays a warning message that the file is to be deleted, and allows you to cancel the deletion. If you delete the file, Q&A returns you to the Rename/Copy/Delete menu.

9. To copy a report, fill in Copy From and Copy To in the dialog box and press Enter.

   Q&A copies the report you specify and returns you to the Rename/Delete/Copy menu. □

# What You Have Learned

▶ You can design as many as 200 reports for one database.
▶ Columnar reports are displays of data organized in columns.
▶ Cross tab reports are similar to spreadsheets in format and organization.

▶ Planning the design of a report is just as important as planning the design of a database.

▶ Q&A provides many codes that you can use to embellish your report's appearance; you can use most of these codes for columnar and cross tab reports.

▶ You can either calculate on an entire column or subcalculate whenever the value in a column changes.

▶ You can quickly redesign a report during the printing process.

▶ Q&A allows you to define the look of future report designs through global format options.

# Chapter 7

# Q&A Write: Fundamentals

## In This Chapter

▶ *Starting the Write word processing module*
▶ *Creating and editing a Write document*
▶ *Navigating a Write document*
▶ *Formatting a Write document on a page-by-page basis*
▶ *Printing a Write document*
▶ *Saving a Write document*

## Word Processing with Q&A

Write is a word processing program that fully supports Q&A's other modules. However, you can also use Write as a standalone word processor to create letters, memoranda, reports, and proposals.

Write's features include

- ▶ Simple to complex search and replace
- ▶ Page layout
- ▶ Font customization
- ▶ Print options
- ▶ Multiple columns
- ▶ Import and export of files from other programs
- ▶ Spellcheck
- ▶ A thesaurus
- ▶ Mail merge

Our catalog company can use Write to build a collection of form letters for every occasion—from "Thank you for your business" to "Sorry for the delay." We can also make our reports easier to understand and more readable.

**184**

# Starting the Write Module

All documents are created or edited on the Type/Edit screen. Perhaps the most important fact about this screen is that it has many of the same features and works in much the same way as the Form Design screen. You fill in this screen, but with text, not with fields. There are some new function keys listed at the bottom of the screen, but there are also some with which you are familiar. For example, Esc and F1 work the same way in Write as they do throughout Q&A.

### Q Creating a Document in the Type/Edit Screen

| | |
|---|---|
| 1. From the Main menu, select Write. | Q&A displays the Write menu (Figure 7.1). |
| 2. Choose Type/Edit from the Write menu. | Q&A displays the Type/Edit screen. □ |

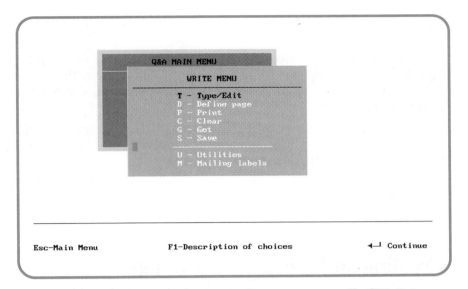

*Figure 7.1    The Write menu is the gateway to all of Write's features*

**185**

On the Type/Edit screen, look for a small line on the left side of the screen. This shows you the border between the *header* (the top six lines of this document) and the rest of the document. There is a similar line near the bottom of the page; this indicates the *footer* area (the bottom six lines of the page). As you add pages to a document, each page displayed on the screen shows the same markers. You'll learn how to use the header and footer areas in Chapter 8.

At the bottom of the Type/Edit screen are the *ruler line* and three *status lines.*

The ruler line shows margin settings, tab locations, and spacing between text lines. The left ([) and right (]) margins indicate the horizontal width of a line of text. There are two tab settings—T represents left-aligned text, and D represents numeric tab settings that are aligned to the decimal point. The character to the right of the left margin indicator is an s, d, or t, which tells you whether your text is currently single-, double-, or triplespaced.

On the status lines, Q&A displays other information about this file; sometimes Q&A displays messages and prompts. On the left side of the bottom of the screen, Q&A displays the name of the document on which you are working. If you have not saved this document,

Q&A refers to it as `Working Copy`; otherwise, Q&A displays its file name.

Q&A knows how much memory the document is using. When you start working on a document, the computer memory that it uses is 0%, or none. As you add lines of text, the percentage of memory usage increases.

Q&A always knows where the cursor is—its horizontal position on the line, the current line number, the current page number, and the total pages in this document.

At the very bottom of the screen is a display of keys and key combinations that aid you while you are using Write.

# Creating and Editing a Document

**186**

To start typing a document on the Type/Edit screen, place the cursor anywhere below the header area and begin to type. For example, you might want to prepare a form letter to a mail order customer stating that the item that a customer has ordered is temporarily out of stock (Figure 7.2).

## Using the Tab and Shift-Tab keys

You can move the cursor anywhere on the screen to start typing text, but if you want to quickly move the cursor to a specific screen location, press the Tab key. The default left margin is 10 and the first tab position on the ruler line is 15; then tabs are set for every tenth character. To move the cursor from the left margin to the tab at column 45, press Tab four times. If you want to move back toward the left margin, press the Shift-Tab key combination.

If you want to start the new line of a document, press Enter.

As you type, the cursor on the ruler line follows the cursor position on the screen. When text reaches the end of a line, the cursor does not stop at the right margin. Instead, Write starts putting text at the left margin of the next line and both cursors move to the beginning of the left margin. This is called *word wrap*.

You can move around your document by using keys and key combinations, the mouse, and the GO TO command.

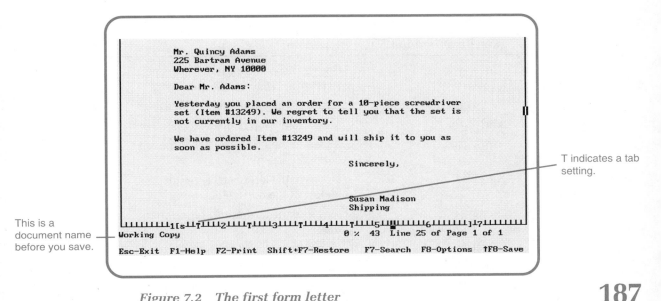

This is a document name before you save.

T indicates a tab setting.

*Figure 7.2   The first form letter*

**187**

## Using Keys and Key Combinations

Press any combination of keys and key combinations to move the cursor anywhere in your document. See Table 7.1 for a list of cursor movement keys and key combinations.

*Table 7.1   Write Cursor Movement Keys*

| Key/Key Combination | Function |
| --- | --- |
| Left | Moves left one character or space |
| Right | Moves right one character or space |
| Up | Moves up one line |
| Down | Moves down one line |
| F9 | Scrolls the screen up one line |
| Shift-F9 | Scrolls the screen down one line |
| Ctrl-Left | Moves to the beginning of the previous word |
| Ctrl-Right | Moves to the beginning of the next word |
| PgUp | Scrolls up one screen display (20 lines) |
| PgDn | Scrolls down one screen display (20 lines) |

*(continued)*

*Table 7.1* *(continued)*

| Key/Key Combination | Function |
|---|---|
| Ctrl-F7 | Goes to a specific existing page, line, or page and line combination |
| Ctrl-PgUp | Moves to the top of the previous page |
| Ctrl-PgDn | Moves to the top of the next page |
| Ctrl-Home | Moves to the first character at the top of the document |
| Ctrl-End | Moves to the last character at the bottom of the document |
| Home | Moves to the beginning of the current line |
| Home Home | Moves to the top of the screen |
| Home Home Home | Moves to the top of the page |
| Home Home Home Home | Moves to the top of the document |
| End | Moves to the end of the line |
| End End | Moves to the bottom of the screen |
| End End End | Moves to the bottom of the page |
| End End End End | Moves to the bottom of the document |

## Using the Mouse

To display text above the current cursor location, press and hold the left mouse button and push the mouse toward the top of the document. Write highlights the text as it scrolls toward the first line. When the text that you want to edit (or just look at) is on the screen, release the mouse button. You can use the highlight to perform a block operation on the text (see Chapter 8), or you can remove the highlight by moving the mouse cursor off the text and then pressing the button (see Figure 7.3).

To move toward the bottom of the document, press and hold the left mouse button and push the mouse toward the bottom of the document. Again, Write highlights the text as it scrolls.

```
        Mr. Quincy Adams
        225 Bartram Avenue
        Wherever, NY 10000

        Dear Mr. Adams:

        Yesterday you placed an order for a 10-piece screwdriver
        set (Item #13249). We regret to tell you that the set is
        not currently in our inventory.

        We have ordered Item #13249 and will ship it to you as
        soon as possible.

                          Sincerely,



                          Susan Madison
                          Shipping
```

```
TESTLTR1.DOC                      0 %  31  Line 14 of Page 1 of 1

Esc-Cancel   F3-Delete   F5-Copy   ↑F5-Move   ↑F6-Enhance   F8-Block operations
```

*Figure 7.3   You can use either keys or a mouse to highlight or mark text*

⊘ **Caution:** If you move the cursor to the ruler line and quickly click the mouse button, you may set new tab positions rather than move the text.

To move to a specific line on the screen, move the cursor up (or down) the left or right border until it is positioned at the desired line; then click once. The cursor moves to either end of the desired line.

To move to a specific character on the screen, move the cursor to that character and then click the button.

## Using the GO TO Command

Jump directly to a particular page and/or line with the GO TO command.

## Jumping to a Page, Line, or Line and Page

1. As you are editing your document, press Ctrl-F7 to move any place within the document.

   Q&A displays the GO TO dialog box (Figure 7.4). If you have previously used this command during this session, the last Page and Line setting appear.

2. Enter either a page number or line number on that page, or both. Use the Up, Down, Tab, Shift-Tab, or Enter keys to move between Page and Line. Press F10.

   Because our form letter is not a multiple-page document, you get the message Location doesn't exist if you select Page 2.

   □

190

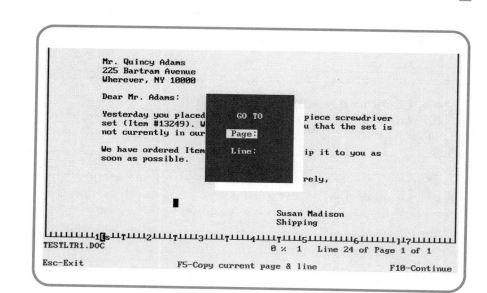

*Figure 7.4   This GO TO dialog box prompts you for page and line numbers*

> ▶ **Note:** If you enter a page and line number, the cursor is positioned at the beginning of the line on that page. If you specify only a page number, the cursor is positioned at the top of the page you specify. If you specify only a line number, the cursor is positioned at the specified line, which is calculated by counting from the top of the first page.

You can also use the GO TO command to mark the current cursor location so that you can return to this place in your document at a later time in this Q&A session.

### *Q* Returning to a Page and Line

1. Move the cursor to any place to which you will want to return later in this Write session. Press Ctrl-F7 to open the GO TO dialog box.

   Q&A displays the GO TO dialog box.

2. Press F5 to record the current page and line location in the GO TO dialog box.

   The GO TO dialog box leaves the screen but remembers the page and line location it has saved.

3. When you want to return to the page and line saved in the GO TO dialog box, press Ctrl-F7 and then F10.

   Unless you have used GO TO since saving the page and line, the cursor jumps to the page/line location. □

**191**

Write lets you use keys and key combinations to edit, get information, define page layout, print, and more. In this way, you can take shortcuts and decrease your use of menus for many Q&A operations. Table 7.2 contains a list of keys and key combinations. For each function on the table, there is a brief description, whether it also appears on the Options menu (OM), and the chapter of this book in which you'll find a detailed explanation.

**Table 7.2    Write Function Keys**

| Key/Key Combination | OM | Chapter | Function |
| --- | --- | --- | --- |
| Alt-F1 | Y | 8 | Thesaurus |
| Ctrl-F1 | Y | 8 | Spellcheck word |
| Shift-F1 | Y | 8 | Spellcheck |
| F2 | N | 7 | Prints this document |
| Ctrl-F2 | Y | 8 | Prints a block of text |
| Shift-F2 | N | 12 | Uses Q&A macros |
| F3 | Y | 8 | Deletes block of text |
| Ctrl-F3 | Y | 8 | Reports document statistics |
| F4 | N | 7 | Deletes word (also Ctrl-T) |
| Ctrl-F4 | N | 7 | Deletes from cursor to end of line |
| Shift-F4 | N | 7 | Deletes this line (also Ctrl-Y) |
| F5 | Y | 8 | Copies block of text within this file |
| Alt-F5 | Y | 8 | Moves block of text to another file |
| Ctrl-F5 | Y | 8 | Copies block of text to another file |
| Shift-F5 | Y | 8 | Moves block of text within this file |
| F6 | Y | 8 | Sets temporary margins |
| Alt-F6 | Y | 8 | Hyphenates |
| Ctrl-F6 | N | 7 | Goes to Define Page screen |
| Shift-F6 | Y | 8 | Enhances text |
| F7 | Y | 8 | Performs search and replace |

**192**

| Key/Key Combination | OM | Chapter | Function |
|---|---|---|---|
| Alt-F7 | Y | 8 | Lists fields |
| Ctrl-F7 | Y | 7 | Goes to page, line, or page and line |
| Shift-F7 | Y | 7 | Restores text (undo function) |
| F8 | N | 8 | Goes to the Options menu |
| Ctrl-F8 | Y | 7 | Saves this document as an ASCII file |
| Shift-F8 | N | 7 | Saves this document as a Write file |
| Alt-F9 | Y | 8 | Calculates |
| Ctrl-F9 | Y | 8 | Makes font assignments |

**193**

## Deleting Text

To delete a character, you can use either the Del or Backspace key. Move the cursor to the character that you want to delete and press Del, or move the cursor to the right of the character that you want to delete and press Backspace.

If you move a cursor anywhere on a word but the first letter, press F4 to delete all the characters from the cursor location to the end of the word. To delete the whole word, move the cursor to the first letter of the word you want to delete and press F4 to delete the word and the space after it.

To delete all text from the cursor location to the end of the line, press Ctrl-F4. If you want to delete the whole line, move the cursor to any location on the line that you want to delete and press Shift-F4.

If you want to restore any text that you have just deleted, copied, or moved, press Shift-F7 before performing any other Q&A function. Write allows you to restore a maximum of about a page of text; you may not be able to restore more than that.

> ▶ **Tip:** If you want to insert the same text in several places in your document, enter that text anywhere in your document. Then press F3 to delete it. Move the cursor to the first location in which you want to insert the text; then press Shift-F7. Move to the next location and press Shift-F7. Repeat this until you have inserted the text in every desired location.

## Using Overtype and Insert Modes

Write starts in overtype mode, in which you type new text over the old and the new characters replace the old. When you change to insert mode, the text that you type pushes the old text ahead of it toward the right margin. When the characters reach the right margin, they are pushed to the next line, starting at the left margin. To move between overtype mode and insert mode, press the Ins key. When you press Ins to switch to insert mode, notice that the Ins indicator appears near the bottom of the screen. The cursor also changes shape from a blinking line to a blinking square. When you switch to the overtype mode, the Ins indicator disappears and the cursor changes back to a blinking line.

If you want to delete old text in the same area as you want to add new text, use the overtype mode.

## Entering Literal Characters

Someday you may need to put special characters or symbols, which are not represented by keys on your keyboard, into a Write or File document. Because each computer and printer setup is unique, refer to your computer's, printer's, or video card's reference manual for the ASCII chart that you can use. Q&A supports the characters below 032 (or on some charts, 32) and above 127. The characters between 032 and 127 are the standard alphabetic and numeric characters, which you can type from your keyboard.

### Q Entering Literal Characters

1. Press Alt-F10.                    Q&A knows that the next
                                      character that you enter
                                      will be a literal character.

2. While holding down the Alt key, use the numeric keypad to enter the three-digit ASCII code that you have found on your chart.

If you have entered a valid code, a literal character appears at the current cursor location when you release the Alt key (Figure 7.5).  □

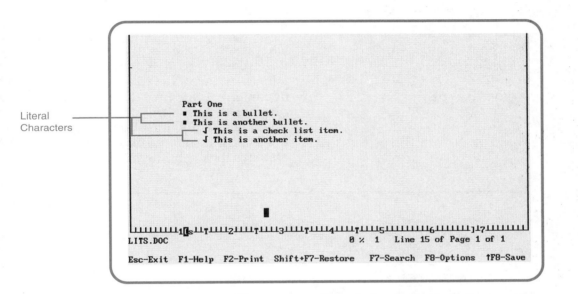

Figure 7.5   *You can use two literal characters in a document*

> **Caution:** Be careful when experimenting with literal characters. If you do not refer to an ASCII chart related to your computer system, you may see some strange results (for example, page breaks and the cursor moving from one part of the document to another).

# Formatting Documents

Write provides formatting functions for the whole document as well as for its paragraphs, words, and characters. To set the "look" for a document, use the Define Page screen to edit margins, page width and length, the number of characters per inch, headers and footers, and page numbers.

## **Q Defining the Page**

1. From the Main menu, choose Write.

   Q&A displays the Write menu.

2. Choose Define page or press Ctrl-F6.

   Q&A displays the Define Page screen (Figure 7.6). If you are not working on a document at this time, Q&A displays default attributes. If you have a document on the Type/Edit screen, Q&A displays its attributes. □

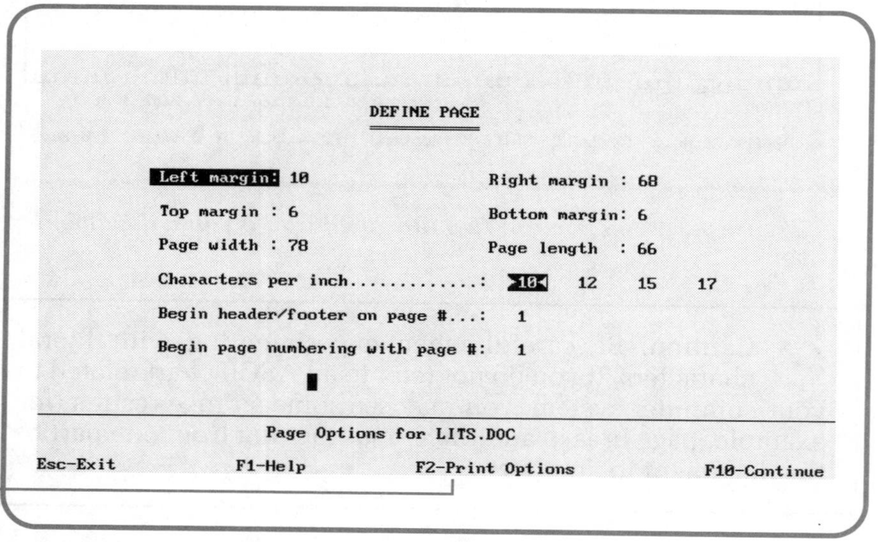

```
                          DEFINE PAGE


     Left margin: 10              Right margin : 68

     Top margin : 6               Bottom margin: 6

     Page width : 78              Page length  : 66

     Characters per inch.............:   ▶10◀   12     15     17

     Begin header/footer on page #...:    1

     Begin page numbering with page #:    1

                           ▮
     _____
                    Page Options for LITS.DOC

     Esc-Exit           F1-Help          F2-Print Options        F10-Continue
```

You can go directly to the Print Options screen

*Figure 7.6   The Define Page screen*

When you define page attributes for a document, the values stay with a document until you change them. For example, if you decide to print a letter using a type size of 12 characters per inch, that is the permanent setting. If you then change to 10 characters per inch, that new setting is permanent—even after you end that Q&A session. You can either return to your document or go to the Print Options screen after you have filled in the Define Page screen.

Margin settings represent the borders extending from the outside of the paper on which a document is printed to the location of the printed matter. For example, if all margins are set to 0 inches, the margins are quite small. If you set both left and right margins to 2 inches, the amount of white space on either side of the text is approximately 2 inches wide.

Enter left and right margin settings in any combination of column location, inches, and centimeters. Left margins start at 0 and right margins cannot be higher than the maximum page width, which is 240 columns (or approximately 24 inches). Q&A does not accept a negative margin setting. The default left margin is 10 columns and the default right margin is 68.

> ▶ **Note:** If you use column settings, the right margin is measured from the left side of the document. For example, a 0 left margin and 5 right margin results in an odd-looking printout that is about five columns wide and aligned on the left margin. A right margin of 68 columns is a lot better!

The total of the top and bottom margins cannot be greater than 18 lines or approximately 3 inches. The default top (and bottom) margins are 6 lines from the top (or bottom) of the page. For information about setting temporary margins, see Chapter 8.

*Page width* is the width of a page, up to a maximum of 240 columns. The default page width is 78 columns.

*Page length* is the length of a page, up to a maximum of 192 lines. The default page length is 66 lines.

*Characters per inch* is the number of characters that can fit in a horizontal inch of printed line. Q&A gives you a choice of 10, 12, 15, or 17. The higher the number, the smaller the text looks when printed.

*Begin header/footer on page #* is the page number on which headers and footers start printing. The maximum value is a number over 32,700, and the default is to start printing headers and footers on the first page. For more information about using headers and footers in Write documents, see Chapter 8.

*Begin page numbering with page #* is the page number on which page numbering begins. The maximum value is approximately 9,000, and the default is to start printing page numbers on the first page. For more information about using page numbering in Write documents, see Chapter 8.

# Printing Documents

There are many ways to print a Write document. You can select a document for printing from the Type/Edit, Define Page, and Print Options as well as their associated screens. Here is one way to get to the Print Options screen.

**198**

**Q Printing a Document**

1. From the Main menu, choose Write.

    Q&A displays the Write menu.

2. Choose Print or press F2.

    Q&A displays the Print Options screen (Figure 7.7). If you are not working on a document at this time, Q&A reminds you that you need to get a document before you can print it. If you are working on a document, Q&A displays the print options associated with it. □

*From page* is the first page that you want to print. Q&A knows how many pages are in your document so it does not print a document for which you define an invalid number. The default starting page number is 1.

*To page* is the last page that you want to print. You can enter an ending page number that is out of the actual page range of your document. To print one page of a document, the From and To values should be identical (for example, if you want to print the ninth page, both values should be 9). The default ending page number is END.

*Number of copies* is the number of copies of your document that you want to print. The default number of copies is 1.

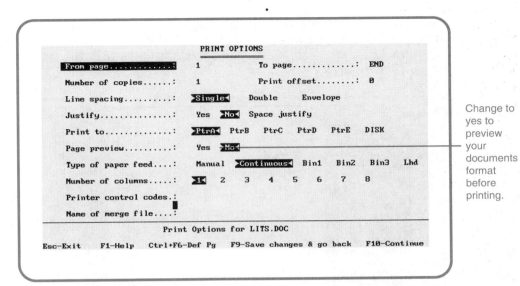

```
                         PRINT OPTIONS

    From page............:    1            To page............:    END

    Number of copies......:   1            Print offset........:    0

    Line spacing..........:  ▶Single◀   Double      Envelope

    Justify...............:   Yes  ▶No◀  Space justify

    Print to..............:  ▶PtrA◀  PtrB   PtrC   PtrD   PtrE   DISK

    Page preview..........:   Yes  ▶No◀

    Type of paper feed....:  Manual  ▶Continuous◀  Bin1   Bin2   Bin3   Lhd

    Number of columns.....:  ▶1◀  2    3    4    5    6    7    8

    Printer control codes.:

    Name of merge file....:
    ─────────────────────────────────────────────────────────────────
                     Print Options for LITS.DOC

    Esc-Exit    F1-Help   Ctrl+F6-Def Pg   F9-Save changes & go back   F10-Continue
```

Change to yes to preview your documents format before printing.

*Figure 7.7    The Print Options screen*

199

*Print offset* leaves a larger margin on the left margin. If you have a pin-fed printer, use this option to move the print head for better alignment along the left side of the paper. The default is 0.

*Line spacing* offers you the choice of Single, Double, or Envelope. If your document line spacing is single or double, and for some reason, you want to leave this setting alone, you can use this option to single- or doublespace your printed output. The default is Single. For detailed information about printing envelopes, see Chapter 9.

*Justify* offers you the choice of Yes, No, and Space Justify. Both Yes and Space Justify offer right justification. The Yes option microjustifies your document—if your printer supports it. This process measures the line to be printed and places equal spaces between the words from the left to the right margin. The Space Justify option places uneven spaces between the words from the left to the right margin. The No option, the default, prints a line with an unjustified or ragged right margin.

*Print to* indicates the printer to which you want to print this file. If you have more than one printer (or multiple modes for one printer), select a printer to which you want to print. If you select DISK, your file, along with its print codes, prints to a disk file; then you can print this file on a printer later. The default printer is your primary printer, PtrA.

Page Preview offers you the opportunity to see what your document will look like when it prints. For a list of Page Preview function keys, see Table 7.3. For an example of a Page Preview screen, see Figures 7-8, 7-9, and 7-10.

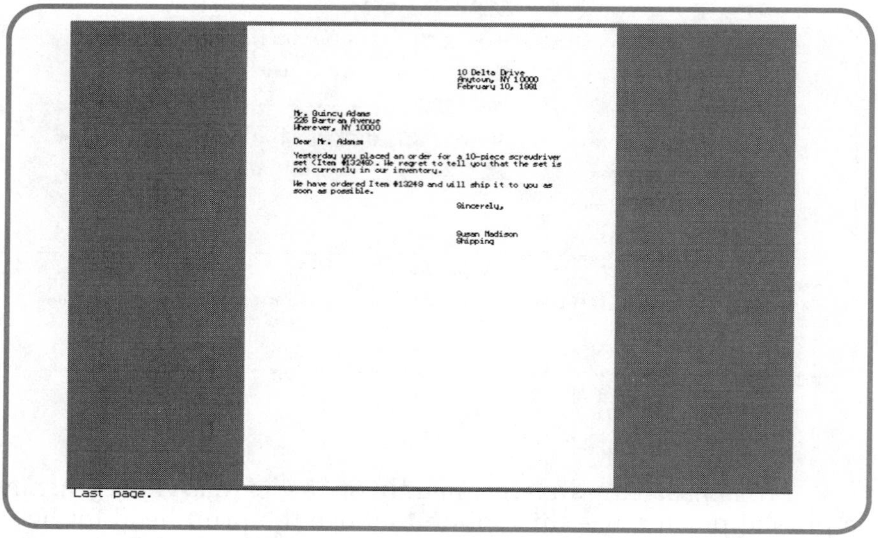

*Figure 7.8    The Full Page preview screen*

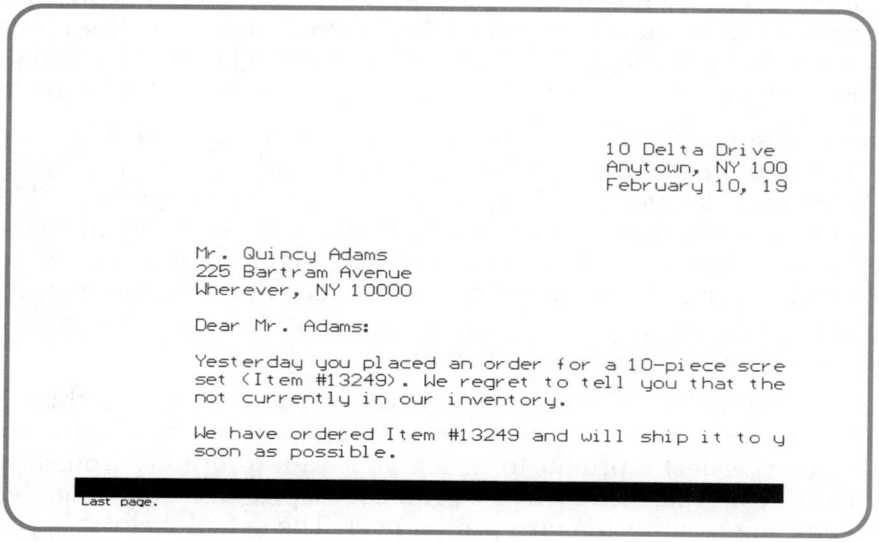

10 Delta Drive
Anytown, NY 100
February 10, 19

Mr. Quincy Adams
225 Bartram Avenue
Wherever, NY 10000

Dear Mr. Adams:

Yesterday you placed an order for a 10-piece scre
set (Item #13249). We regret to tell you that the
not currently in our inventory.

We have ordered Item #13249 and will ship it to y
soon as possible.

Last page.

*Figure 7.9    The file in Figure 7.10 shown in Normal mode*

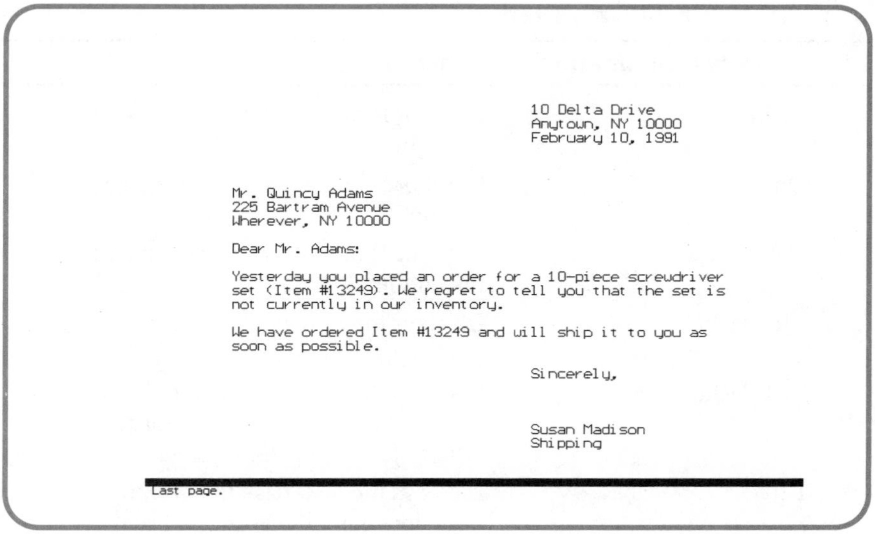

*Figure 7.10   Half Page mode is halfway between Full and Normal modes*

*Table 7.3   Page Preview Function Keys*

| Key/Key Combination | Function |
| --- | --- |
| F | Full mode, displays a printed page |
| H | Half mode, displays a half page |
| N | Normal mode, displays 25 lines per screen |
| PgDn | Scrolls the page down by one screen unless you are in F mode |
| PgUp | Scrolls the page up by one screen unless you are in F mode |
| 2 | Displays facing pages (the even-numbered page on the left side, the odd-numbered page on the right side) |
| + (plus) | Zooms in on part of the document, from F to H to N mode, then stops |
| – (minus) | Zooms out from part of the document, from N to H to F mode, then stops |
| Left | For N or H mode, moves the cursor to the left |

*(continued)*

Table 7.3   (continued)

| Key/Key Combination | Function |
|---|---|
| Right | For N or H mode, moves the cursor to the right |
| Up | For N or H mode, moves the cursor to the top |
| Down | For N or H mode, moves the cursor to the bottom |
| Ctrl-PgUp | Displays the previous page in a multiple-page document |
| Ctrl-PgDn | Displays the next page in a multiple-page document; if on the last page, returns to the Type/Edit screen |
| F10 | Displays the next page in a multiple-page document;if on the last page, returns to the Type/Edit screen |
| F2 | Returns to the Print Options screen |

After previewing your document, either press F10 or Esc to return to the Write menu or press F2 to return to the Print Options screen (from which you can print the document). If your computer does not have a graphics card, you cannot use Page Preview. Occasionally, Q&A won't be able to show you how a special character or font looks before printing. In this case, Q&A does not replace that part of the document with something that does preview; it doesn't show anything. The default setting for Page Preview is No.

*Type of paper feed* indicates what sort of paper you are using—Continuous, Manual, Bin, or Lhd. If you are printing continuous-form paper (this can also include a single tray of papers in a laser printer), select Continuous, the default. If you need to hand-feed paper or envelopes, choose the Manual option. If your printer has several bins, select the appropriate one for this print job. Lhd (Letterhead) allows you to print the first sheet (on letterhead) from Bin1 and subsequent sheets (on plain paper) from Bin2.

*Number of columns* prints from one to eight columns. For example, if you are printing a form letter or a plain instruction sheet, you are printing one column. If you are printing a newsletter, you might select 2 or 3. The default is 1.

*Printer control codes* indicates that your printer supports special options that are sent to your printer before any document is printed. Refer to your printer's manual to see if it uses printer control codes.

*Name of merge file* names the database file for which there is a merge document. You'll learn more about merging documents in Chapter 9.

# Saving Documents

Saving a document is as important as backing up a document. Don't wait until you are completely finished editing to save; save every few minutes. Everyone who has more than a couple of months of computer experience has a story about how he or she worked on a file or document for a long time without saving it—then suddenly the lights went out and all the work was lost!

**203**

**Saving a Document**

1. Press Shift-F8.

   Q&A displays the Save dialog box (Figure 7.11).

2. Type in a name up to eight characters long, type a period, and then any extension from one to three characters and press Enter.

   Q&A saves your text and returns you to the Type/Edit screen.

3. When you have finished working on your text and want to exit from your document, press Esc after you save the last time.

   Q&A returns you to the Write menu.

   □

---

⊘ **Caution:** If you try to exit from the Write menu and you have not saved your document, Write warns you that the document has not been saved. Write then gives you an opportunity to save it. If you do not save the text, it is lost forever.

> ► **Tip:** Use a standard extension, such as .DOC, for all your Write documents.

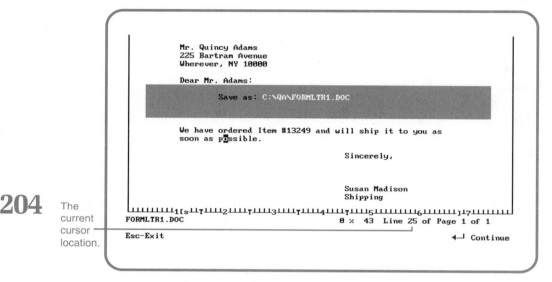

Mr. Quincy Adams
225 Bartram Avenue
Wherever, NY 10000

Dear Mr. Adams:

         Save as: C:\QA\FORMLTR1.DOC

We have ordered Item #13249 and will ship it to you as soon as possible.

                              Sincerely,


                              Susan Madison
                              Shipping

FORMLTR1.DOC                        0 %  43  Line 25 of Page 1 of 1
Esc-Exit                                           ◄┘ Continue

The current cursor location.

*Figure 7.11   The Save screen*

# What You Have Learned

- ► You use the Type/Edit screen and the Form Design screen in about the same way—you fill them in.
- ► Although Write supports Q&A's other modules, it is also a word processor that can be used for non-Q&A purposes.
- ► The Type/Edit screen has a ruler line and three status lines.
- ► You can use keys, a mouse, or the GO TO command to navigate a Write document.
- ► Write provides you with many keys and key combinations so that you can edit a document without going through menus.

204

► You can define the formatting style of a document as a whole; Write also gives you the ability to format smaller segments of a document.

► You can preview what a Write document will look like when printed, you can print a Write document now, or you can save it to file for later printing.

► Save a document while you are editing it as well as when you finish working on it.

# Q&A Write: Advanced Operations

## In This Chapter

▶ *Getting a document*
▶ *Using the Options menu to perform many functions*
▶ *Searching and replacing*
▶ *Using the Write Utilities*
▶ *Importing and exporting documents*

## Getting an Existing Document

When you want to work on a document that already exists, you access it with the Get command. Choose one of the following:

▶ The Get option on the Write menu
▶ The Get a Document option from the Documents submenu on the Options menu

You also can use the name of the document itself if it is listed on the Documents submenu on the Options menu.

Regardless of the way you get a document, it is displayed on the Type/Edit screen. The following steps tell you how to use the Get option on the Write menu.

## **Q** Getting a Document with the Get Command

1. Choose Write from the Main menu.

   Q&A displays the Write menu.

2. Choose Get.

   Q&A adds a dialog box below the Write menu that shows the current Q&A default drive and directory.

3. Enter the name of a document file or press Enter to get a list of files. After you have selected a document, press Enter.

   Q&A displays the document, which is on the Type/Edit screen.

4. Edit the document you retrieved.

   Q&A processes your editing instructions.    □

You also can get a document from the Type/Edit screen by pressing F8 to display the Options menu. You learn about using that menu later in this chapter.

Regardless of whether there is a document displayed on the Type/Edit screen, you can get another document.

## **Q** Getting a Document at the Type/Edit Screen

1. From the Type/Edit screen, press F8.

   Q&A displays the Options menu.

2. Highlight Documents (the second entry on the menu).

   Whenever you move the highlight on the Options menu, the options change on the submenu on the right (Figure 8.1).

3. Press Enter, Tab, or Right to move to (or activate) the submenu. If you need to move back to the Options menu, either press Left or Shift-Tab.

   The Documents submenu displays up to 12 of the last files on which you worked, even in past Q&A sessions.

208

4. If the name of the document you want is on the submenu, highlight the document name and press Enter. If the name of the document is not on the submenu, choose Get a Document and press Enter. Either enter a document name or press Enter to get a list of files.

If you have used Get a Document, and if there is a document on the Type/Edit screen and you have changed it in any way, Write warns you to save the document before retrieving the new document. Otherwise, you get a document without the warning.

5. If you want to save before getting the new document, select N.

Write returns you to the Type/Edit screen, from which you can save the current document.

6. If you want to continue getting a new document, select Y.

Write displays the file on the Type/Edit screen.

□

**209**

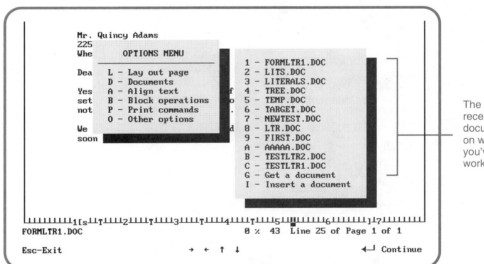

*Figure 8.1    The Options menu offers you six options, including Documents*

The Documents submenu also has two commands—Get a Document and Insert a Document—with which you can retrieve a document for editing or inserting into another document, respectively.

# The Options Menu

In Chapter 2, you learned about using the Options menu (in particular, block operations) for File's Form Design screen. The Options menu offers even more options for Write. See Table 8.1 for a list of each Option menu option and suboption, along with the key or key combination that you press to implement it, and whether it is supported in File, Write, or both.

*Table 8.1  Options Menu*

| Option/Suboption | Key | Module(s) |
|---|---|---|
| *Lay Out Page* | | |
| Edit Header | | Write/File |
| Edit Footer | | Write/File |
| Set Tabs | | Write/File |
| Newpage | | Write |
| Draw | | Write/File |
| *Documents* | | |
| Get a Document | | Write |
| Insert a Document | | Write |
| *Align Text* | | |
| Left | | Write/File |
| Center | | Write/File |
| Right | | Write |
| Temp Margins | F6 | Write |
| Single Space | | Write |
| Double Space | | Write |
| Triple Space | | Write |
| *Block Operations* | | |
| Copy | F5 | Write/File |
| Move | Shift-F5 | Write/File |
| Delete | F3 | Write/File |
| Copy to File | Ctrl-F5 | Write/File |

| Option/Suboption | Key | Module(s) |
|---|---|---|
| Move to File | Alt-F5 | Write/File |
| Enhance | Shift-F6 | Write |
| Print | Ctrl-F2 | Write/File |
| Capitalize | | Write/File |
| Lowercase | | Write/File |
| Title | | Write/File |

### Print Commands

| Option/Suboption | Key | Module(s) |
|---|---|---|
| Date | | Write |
| Filename | | Write |
| Graph | | Write |
| Join | | Write |
| Justify | | Write |
| Linespacing | | Write |
| Postfile | | Write |
| Postscript | | Write |
| Printer | | Write |
| Program | | Write |
| Queue | | Write |
| QueueP | | Write |
| Spreadsheet | | Write |
| Stop | | Write |
| Time | | Write |

### Other Options

| Option/Suboption | Key | Module(s) |
|---|---|---|
| Spellcheck | Shift-F1 | Write/File |
| Spellcheck Word | Ctrl-F1 | Write/File |
| Thesaurus | Alt-F1 | Write/File |
| Statistics | Ctrl-F3 | Write/File |
| Hyphenate | Alt-F6 | Write |
| Search & Replace | F7 | Write/File |
| Restore | Shift-F7 | Write/File |
| GO TO Page/Line | Ctrl-F7 | Write/File |
| List Fields | Alt-F7 | Write |

211

*(continued)*

**Table 8.1** *(continued)*

| Option/Suboption | Key | Module(s) |
|---|---|---|
| Save | Shift-F8 | Write |
| Save as ASCII | Ctrl-F8 | Write |
| Assign Fonts | Ctrl-F9 | Write |
| Calculate | Alt-F9 | Write/File |

> ▶ **Tip:** A quick way to select options is to press F8, Enter, the first letter of the option on the Option menu, Enter, the first letter that Q&A gives to the option (e.g., F-Edit Footer) on the submenu, and Enter.

**212**

## Lay Out Page Options

The Lay Out Page options enable you to define documentwide characteristics (see Figure 8.2).

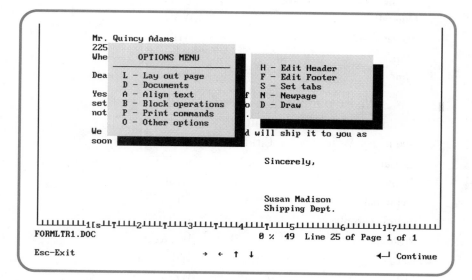

**Figure 8.2** *The Lay Out Page options include editing headers and footers, setting tabs, defining page breaks, and drawing*

*Edit Header/Edit Footer.* A header or footer is an area that encompasses as much as the top or bottom six lines of each page of your document. These areas can contain page numbers, chapter numbers and titles, a company name and address, and so on. To edit a header or footer, press F8 to display the Options menu. Choose Lay Out Page and select either Edit Header or Edit Footer. Enter appropriate header or footer information and then press F10.

*Set Tabs.* To set tabs for the current document on the Type/Edit screen, press F8 to display the Options menu. Choose Lay Out Page and select Set Tabs on the submenu. The cursor is positioned on the ruler line. Move the cursor along the ruler line until you reach a position in which you want a tab stop. Either enter T (for a regular, left-aligned tab) or D (for a decimal tab). After you have completed setting tab stops, press F10 to resume editing.

*Newpage.* To define a page break (to start a new page) at the cursor location, move the cursor to any position on the line on which you want to break. Then press F8 to display the Options menu. Choose Lay Out Page and select Newpage on the submenu.

**213**

> ▶ **Tip:** If the current document does not have its page length defined, choose the Define Page menu and type an appropriate number (such as 66) in the Page Length field. This tells Q&A how many lines to print on a page before starting to print the next page.

*Draw.* To draw lines or boxes in a document, move the cursor to any position from which you want to start drawing; then press F8 to display the Options menu. Choose Lay Out Page and select Draw on the submenu, and press the appropriate key to start drawing. For detailed information about drawing lines and boxes, refer to Chapter 2. For an example of a form created with Write, see Figure 8.3.

## Documents Options

The Documents options allow you to retrieve a document, either from a list of up to 12 documents on which you last worked, or by choosing one of the two options on the submenu.

```
┌─────────────────────────────────────────────────────────┐
│  ┌─────────────────────────────────────────────────┐    │
│  │Name ──────────────────────────────────────────  │    │
│  │Address ───────────────────────────────────────  │    │
│  │City/State/Zip ────────────────────────────────  │    │
│  │Page┬Stock┬Color┬Description═══════════┬Qty┬Price │    │
│  │    │     │     │                      │   │     │    │
│  │    │     │     │                      │   │     │    │
│  │    │     │     │                      │   │     │    │
│  │    │     │     │                      │   │     │    │
│  │    │     │     │                      │   │     │    │
│  │    │     │     │                      │   │     │    │
│  │    │     │     │                      │   │     │    │
│  │ ═══ Payment Method ═══  ┌───────────────────────┐│    │
│  │ ┌─────────────┬───────┐ │         Total │       ││    │
│  │ │             │       │ │           Tax │       ││    │
│  │ └─────────────┴───────┘ │      Shipping │       ││    │
│  │                         │   Grand Total │     ■ ││    │
│  └─────────────────────────┴───────────────────────┘    │
│ ⊔⊔⊔⊔⊔⊔⊔⊔1[s⊔⊔T⊔⊔⊔2⊔⊔⊔T⊔⊔⊔3⊔⊔⊔⊔T⊔⊔⊔4⊔▮▮T⊔⊔⊔5⊔⊔⊔⊔⊔⊔6⊔⊔⊔⊔⊔17⊔⊔⊔⊔ │
│  FORMLTR3.DOC                    0 %  33  Line 19 of Page 1 of 1 │
│                                                           │
│  Esc-Exit  F1-Help  F2-Print  Shift+F7-Restore  F7-Search  F8-Options  ↑F8-Save │
└─────────────────────────────────────────────────────────┘
```

*Figure 8.3   This order form is an example of the line-drawing capabilities of Write*

*Get a Document.* Get a Document retrieves a document and displays it on the Type/Edit screen. You can get a document in any format; if it is in a non-Write format, Write displays the Import Document menu automatically.

*Insert a Document.* Insert a Document retrieves a document that is to be inserted into another document. Before you display the Options menu, be sure to move the cursor to the location in the current document after which you want the document inserted, then press F8 and select Document, Insert a Document, and the document you want to insert.

## Align Text Options

The Align Text options enable you to align text along the left or right margin or to center text (see Figure 8.4).

*Left/Center/Right.* To align text, move the cursor to any position on the line that you want to align; then press F8 to display the Options menu. Choose Align Text and select Left, Center, or Right on the submenu. Once you select the alignment, the text moves to the appropriate place on the screen.

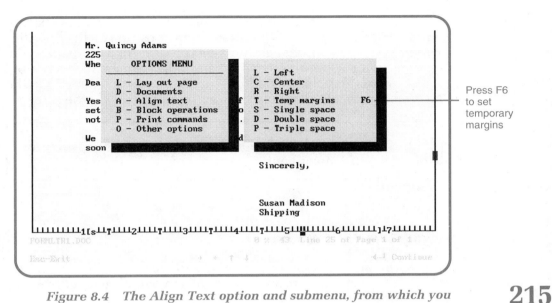

*Figure 8.4   The Align Text option and submenu, from which you can align text, set temporary margins, and set line spacing for part of a document*

**215**

*Temp Margins*. Temp Margins sets temporary margins for a paragraph. Because the first line of a paragraph is not changed by setting temporary margins, this option is ideal if you use hanging indentations for bulleted or numbered lists.

### Setting Temporary Margins

1. Move the cursor to the column in which you want a temporary margin. Press F6. If you want to use the Options menu to set a temporary margin, press F8. Choose Align Text and then select Temp Margins on the submenu.

   Q&A adds the Set Temporary Margin box to the bottom of the screen.

2. To create a temporary left margin, enter L. To create a temporary right margin, enter R. To clear a temporary margin and return to the default margin, enter C.

   Q&A sets the margin you designate.

*Single Space/Double Space/Triple Space.* To set line spacing within a document, move the cursor to any position on the line after which you want to change the spacing. Press F8 to display the Options menu. Choose Align Text and select Single Space, Double Space, or Triple Space on the submenu. Once you select the alignment, the text moves to the appropriate place on the screen.

> ▶ **Tip:** Use the Print Options menu to change line spacing for an entire document.

## Block Operations Options

Block Operations options enable you to work with blocks of text ranging in size from lines to paragraphs to pages (see Figure 8.5).

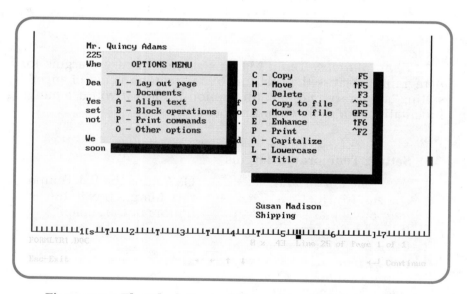

*Figure 8.5   The Block Operations options enable you to process blocks of text*

To select a block of text, use any cursor movement key to mark the beginning and end of the range of text. If you want to select larger blocks of text at a time, Q&A provides shortcut keys (see Table 8.2).

> ▶ **Note:** In most cases, if you press repeatedly the key with which you started a block operation, Q&A selects the next larger block, starting with a word, sentence, paragraph, or page, and ending with the entire document.

*Table 8.2*   ***Block Selection Keys***

| Key | Function |
| --- | --- |
| A-Z a-z | Selects the text from the current cursor position through the next occurrence of an alphabetic character |
| . , ? | Selects the text from the current cursor position to the next occurrence of a punctuation symbol |
| Enter | Selects the text from the current cursor position to the next occurrence of the carriage return character |
| Spacebar | Adds the next word to the text that you have already marked |
| End | Selects the text from the current cursor position to the end of the line (press End again to select text through the last character on the screen, press End again to select text through the end of the document) |
| Home | Selects the text from the current cursor position to the beginning of the line (press Home again to select text through the first character on the screen, press Home again to select the text through the top of the document) |
| Ctrl-End | Selects text through the end of the document |
| Ctrl-Home | Selects text through the beginning of the document |

*Copy*. The Copy option copies a block of text from one place in a document to another place in the same document. The end result is two copies—one in both the original and new location.

Move the cursor to the beginning of the area that you want to copy; then press F8 to display the Options menu. Choose Block Operations and select Copy on the submenu. Press Enter or F10. Q&A prompts you to mark the rest of the text that you want to copy. Press F10. Q&A then prompts you to move the cursor to the location in which you want to put the copy and press F10 again. The copied block of text is now in both locations.

You also can copy a block of text while you edit a document on the Type/Edit screen. First, move the cursor to the beginning of the area that you want to copy and press F5. Then follow the instructions in the prior paragraph.

*Move.* The move option moves a block of text from one place in a document to another place in the same document.

> ⊘ **Caution:** Move is a destructive action—the original block of text is destroyed.

Move the cursor to the beginning of the area that you want to move; then press F8 to display the Options menu. Choose Block Operations and select Move on the submenu. Press Enter or F10. Q&A prompts you to mark the start of the text that you want to move. Press F10. Q&A prompts you to mark the rest of the text that you want to move. Press F10. Q&A then prompts you to move the cursor to the location in which you want to put the moved text and press F10 again. The moved block of text is now located in its new place in the document.

You also can move a block of text while you edit a document on the Type/Edit screen. First, move the cursor to the beginning of the area that you want to move and press Shift-F5. Then follow the instructions in the prior paragraph.

*Delete.* The Delete option erases a block of text. Move the cursor to the beginning of the area that you want to delete; then press F8 to display the Options menu. Choose Block Operations and select Delete on the submenu. Press Enter or F10. Q&A prompts you to mark the rest of the text that you want to erase; then press F10. The block of text is now deleted.

You also can delete a block of text while you edit a document on the Type/Edit screen. First, move the cursor to the beginning of the area that you want to delete. Press F3. Then follow the instructions in the last paragraph.

*Copy to File.* Copy to File copies a block of text to another document. If the document already exists, the copied text overwrites (replaces) the contents of that file. You can create a new document with this operation if you give the document a new, unique name.

Move the cursor to the beginning of the area that you want to copy; then press F8 to display the Options menu. Choose Block Operations and select Copy to File on the submenu. Press Enter or

F10. Q&A prompts you to mark the rest of the text that you want to copy; then press F10. Q&A displays a dialog box so that you can enter the name of the document where you want the text copied. Press Enter or F10. If you use a file name that already exists, Q&A warns you that the target document will be overwritten and asks if you want to continue. If you answer Yes, Q&A overwrites the target document with the block of text. The end result is two identical blocks of text—one is located in the original document and one is in the target document.

You also can copy a block of text to another file while you edit a document on the Type/Edit screen. First, move the cursor to the beginning of the area that you want to copy and press Ctrl-F5. Then follow the instructions in the prior paragraph.

*Move to File*. Move to File moves a block of text to a new document. If the document already exists, the moved text overwrites the contents of that file. You can create a new document with this operation if you give the document a new, unique name.

**219**

Move the cursor to the beginning of the area that you want to move; then press F8 to display the Options menu. Choose Block Operations and select Move to File on the submenu. Press Enter or F10. Q&A prompts you to mark the rest of the text that you want to move; then press F10. If you use a file name that already exists, Q&A displays a dialog box so that you can enter the name of the document where you want the text moved. Press Enter or F10. Q&A warns you that the target document will be overwritten and asks if you want to continue. If you answer Yes, Q&A overwrites the target document with the block of text. The end result is one copy of the block of text in the target document.

You also can move a block of text to another file while you edit a document on the Type/Edit screen. First, move the cursor to the beginning of the area that you want to move; then press Alt-F5. Then follow the instructions in the last paragraph.

---

⊘ **Caution:** When using either Copy to File or Move to File, be sure that the file name you give to the target document is not a name that you have given to any other file in the current directory. Remember that either option overwrites the contents of an existing file.

---

*Enhance*. This option allows you to format a block of text with text enhancements.

Move the cursor to the beginning of the area that you want to enhance; then press F8 to display the Options menu. Choose Block Operations and select Enhance on the submenu. Q&A displays the Text Enhancements and Fonts menu. Select one of the following—Bold, Underline, Superscript, Subscript, Italics, Strikeout, Regular, Font 1 through Font 8, or Assign Fonts. After making a selection from the screen, press Enter or F10. Q&A prompts you to mark the rest of the text that you want to enhance; then press F10. The block of text is now enhanced. You can see the change to the text on the Type/Edit screen.

You also can enhance a block of text while you edit a document on the Type/Edit screen. First, move the cursor to the beginning of the area that you want to enhance and press Shift-F6. Then follow the instructions in the last paragraph. Later in this chapter you'll get detailed information about assigning fonts.

> ▶ **Tip:** To remove an enhancement from a block of text, select Regular on the Text Enhancements and Fonts menu.

*Print.* You can print any block of text from a document, including the entire document. Do not confuse this option with the Print command (F2), which displays the Print Options screen. This is more like your computer's Print Screen command, which gives you a printed version of the screen image. This printout does not include any enhancements that you might have added.

Move the cursor to the beginning of the area that you want to enhance; then press F8 to display the Options menu. Choose Block Operations and select Print on the submenu. Q&A prompts you to mark the rest of the text that you want to print; then press F10.

You also can print a block of text while you edit a document on the Type/Edit screen. First, move the cursor to the beginning of the area that you want to print and press Ctrl-F2. Then follow the instructions in the prior paragraph.

*Capitalize.* To change a block of text to all uppercase letters, move the cursor to the beginning of the area that you want to capitalize; then press F8 to display the Options menu. Choose Block operations and select Capitalize on the submenu. Q&A prompts you to mark the rest of the text that you want to capitalize; then press F10.

*Lowercase.* To change a block of text to all lowercase letters. move the cursor to the beginning of the area that you want to change. Press F8 to display the Options menu. Choose Block Operations and select Lowercase on the submenu. Q&A prompts you to mark the rest of the text that you want to change to lowercase; then press F10.

*Title.* Use this option to produce headings, college degrees, and other titles (such as Mr. or Mrs.). Move the cursor to the beginning of the area to which you want to add initial uppercase letters. Then press F8 to display the Options menu. Choose Block Operations and select Title on the submenu. Q&A prompts you to mark the rest of the text to which you want to apply initial uppercase letters; then press F10.

## Print Commands Options

**221**

You can embed print commands in a Write document to perform operations as the document prints. For an illustration of the Print options and submenu, see Figure 8.6. Table 8.3 lists Q&A print commands.

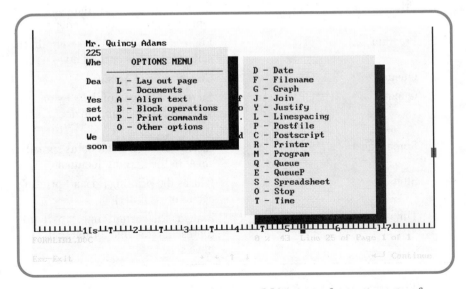

*Figure 8.6    The Print options enable you to format parts of your document or embed information in it*

**222**

### Table 8.3   Print Commands

| Option | Command | Function |
|--------|---------|----------|
| Date | *@DATE(n) | Embeds the current date, where (n) represents the date format that you have selected |
| File name | *FILENAME* | Inserts the name of the current document into itself |
| Graph | *G* | Inserts pictures from Lotus or Symphony (.PIC extension) or PFS Graph in a document, if your printer supports printing graphics |
| Join | *J* | Joins two or more Write documents in this document |
| Justify | *JY* | Turns microjustification on or off |
| Linespacing | *LS* | Changes line spacing in a segment of the current document |
| Postfile | *PF* | Inserts a Postscript program file in the current document |
| Postscript | *PS* | Inserts a Postscript code in a document |
| Printer | *P* | Embeds the ASCII decimal equivalent for a printer control code |
| Program | *PG* | Embeds a valid Q&A programming statement in the current document |
| Queue | *Q* | Creates a print queue |
| QueueP | *QP* | Increments page numbers by one as you print more than one document in row |
| Spreadsheet | *SS* | Inserts all or part of a Lotus spreadsheet in the current document |
| Stop | *S* | Pauses the printing (to start printing again, press Enter) |
| Time | *@TIME(n) | Embeds the current time, where (n) represents the time format that you have selected |

The format of the Graph command is

```
*GRAPH fn density*
```

where fn is the file path and name, and density is S, D, or Q, which represents single, double, or quadruple density, respectively. (Quadruple has the best resolution, the "finest" looking characters.) When you use Lotus or Symphony .PIC files, you also can specify fonts as well as graph size and rotation.

To turn microjustification on, use

```
*JY Y*
```

or

```
*JUSTIFY Yes*
```

To turn microjustification off, use

```
*JY N*
```

or

```
*JUSTIFY No*
```

The format for the Linespacing command is

```
*LINESPACING n*
```

where n is an integer ranging from 1 through 9. This is the only line spacing that is not displayed on the screen; it just displays when it is printed.

The format for the Postfile command is

```
*POSTFILE filename*
```

where filename is a Postscript ASCII file.

The format for the Postscript command is

```
*POSTSCRIPT code*
```

where code represents a Postscript code.

To print several documents, one after another, enter

```
*QUEUE docname*
```

to specify each of the documents in the print queue. When you print the first document, the rest follow. You don't have to issue the commands to print them.

## Other Options

Q&A also provides miscellaneous options with Other Options (see Figure 8.7).

All the options have keys and key copmbinations for easy use.

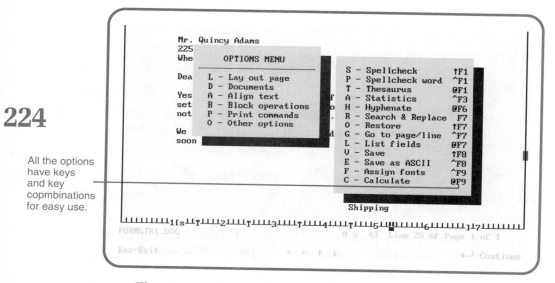

*Figure 8.7    The Other Options and submenu*

*Spellcheck* and *Spellcheck Word*. These options check the spelling of either all words in the current document or a single word in the document.

When you check the words in the current document, Spellcheck uses two dictionaries—the main one (QAMAIN.DCT) and your personal dictionary (QAPERS.DCT). To prepare for checking an entire document, move the cursor to the first character on the first line. To prepare for checking a single word, move the cursor either on the word or in the space to the right of the word.

To use either Spellcheck operation, press F8 to display the Options menu. Choose Other Options and select either Spellcheck or Spellcheck Word on the submenu. From the Type/Edit screen, you can press Shift-F1 for the Spellcheck or Ctrl-F1 for Spellcheck Word.

For a spellcheck of the entire document, Q&A checks each word following the cursor position, comparing it against the main dictionary and your personal dictionary. When it finds a word not listed in either dictionary, it highlights the word on the screen and super-imposes a box on top of your document (see Figure 8.8). For a spellcheck of a single word, Q&A checks that word. It either tells you that the word is spelled correctly or superimposes the box.

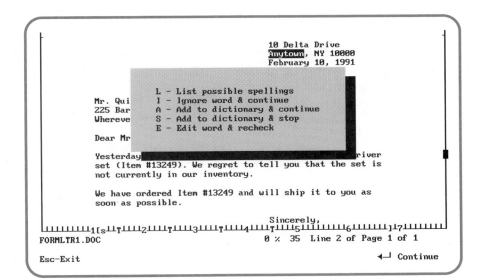

*Figure 8.8   When Spellcheck questions a word, it highlights it and superimposes a box on your document*

If the box is superimposed, you can select one of these five operations:

1. List the possible spellings that the spellcheck associates with your word; you can either accept or ignore the suggestions.
2. Ignore the word and continue the spellcheck.
3. Add the word to your personal dictionary and continue the spellcheck.
4. Add the word to your personal dictionary and stop the spellcheck.

5. Change the word to a new spelling and then recheck it. When you select this option, Q&A displays a dialog box in which you can enter your correction.

You can create or edit your personal dictionary without going through the spellcheck process.

## Q Creating Your Personal Dictionary

| | |
|---|---|
| 1. From the Main menu, choose Write. | Q&A displays the Write menu. |
| 2. Choose Type/Edit. | Q&A displays the Type/Edit screen. |
| 3. If QAPERS.DCT already exists, get it by pressing F8, Select Documents, and Get a Document, and typing QAPERS.DCT. Press Enter. Select ASCII, then press Enter. | Q&A displays your personal dictionary. |
| 4. QAPERS.DCT does not exist if you have not done a spellcheck. Do so by pressing F8, Select Documents, and Get a Document. Get any document and perform a spellcheck by pressing F8, Other Options, and Spellcheck. | Q&A runs a spellcheck until it comes across a word it does not recognize and displays a menu over your document. |
| 5. Choose either Add to Dictionary and Continue or Add to Dictionary and Stop. | Q&A begins setting up QAPERS.DCT. |
| 6. Type words on the screen in alphabetical order, in the appropriate combination of uppercase and lowercase letters. When you have completed entering the last word, press Ctrl-F8. (Do not use Save to save this file!) | Q&A recognizes that you want to save this as an ASCII file. |
| 7. Type QAPERS.DCT; then press Enter. | Your personal dictionary file is created. ☐ |

*Thesaurus.* To check a selected word in your document for synonyms, move the cursor to the word and press F8. Choose Other Options and select Thesaurus on the submenu. From the Type/Edit screen, you can press Alt-F1 to access the Thesaurus.

If the thesaurus has a list of synonyms associated with the word, the Thesaurus screen is superimposed over your document. If you want to replace the word in your document with one listed on the screen, move the cursor to the word that you want to select; then press F10. If you have had a previous (or next) list of synonyms, press F9 (or Shift-F9) to display that list. You also can look up a word on the synonym list by pressing Alt-F1.

*Statistics.* This option counts words, lines, and paragraphs, and gives you totals for text before the cursor, after the cursor, and for the entire document.

Press F8 to display the Options menu. Choose Other Options and select Statistics on the submenu. Q&A superimposes the Document Statistics box (see Figure 8.9) over the current document. Press Esc to return to your document. You also can press Ctrl-F3 from the Type/Edit screen to display the statistics box.

**227**

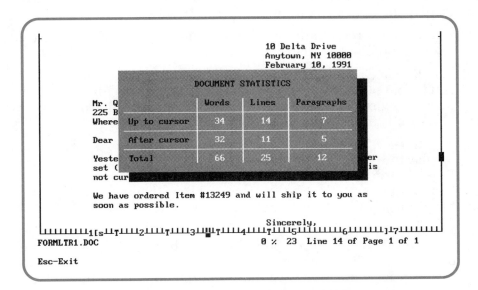

**Figure 8.9** *The Document Statistics box displays word, line, and paragraph counts for your document*

*Hyphenate.* A hyphen that improves the format of the printed line is a soft hyphen. A hard hyphen is a permanently placed one. For example, a soft hyphen is useful to break a long word and not leave a big gap at the end of a line.

> ▶ **Tip:** Please refer to a dictionary to find the proper place-ment of a soft hyphen in a given word if you are not sure where the word breaks.

To use the Hyphenate option, move the cursor to the location on the line before which you want to insert a soft hyphen. Write allows you to enter a soft hyphen anywhere in a word except in the first character. Press F8 to display the Options menu. Choose Other Options and select Hyphenate on the submenu. Q&A applies the soft hyphen. You also can press Alt-F6 from the Type/Edit screen to add a soft hyphen.

**228**

*Search & Replace.* Press F8 to display the Options menu. Choose Other Options and select Search & Replace on the submenu. Press Enter or F10. Q&A adds a dialog box to the screen. You also can display the dialog box from the Type/Edit screen by pressing F7.

For more information about this option, see the section entitled "Search and Replace" later in this chapter.

*Restore.* To restore the last deleted, copied, or moved block of text before performing another Q&A function, press Shift-F7. Each press produces an additional copy. You can continue copying the block until you start another block operation.

*GO TO Page/Line.* To use the GO TO operation, press F8 to display the Options menu. Choose Other Options and select GO TO Page/Line on the submenu. Q&A adds a dialog box to the screen for you to fill in with the desired page and line; then press F10. If you have typed valid values, that page/line combination is now dis-played.

You also can go to a page and/or line while you edit a document on the Type/Edit screen. Press Ctrl-F7. Then follow the instructions in the prior paragraph. For more information about the GO TO operation, see Chapter 7.

*List Fields.* This option enables you to insert data from a database into a form letter. As you type your letter, when you reach an area into which you want to insert data, press F8 to display the

Options menu. Choose Other Options and select List Fields on the submenu. Q&A asks you to select the database from which you want to get information; then press F10. Q&A lists all the fields in the database. Choose the appropriate field by moving the highlight over it and pressing Enter. Notice that the field name, which is surrounded by asterisks, is embedded in your document. From the Type/Edit screen, you can press Alt-F7 to use the List Fields operation. For information about form letters and mail merge, see Chapter 9.

*Save*. Press F8 to display the Options menu. Choose Other Options and select Save on the submenu. Q&A adds a dialog box to the screen for you to fill in with an appropriate file name—either a new, unique file name or the name of a current file. Press F10. If you have entered the name of a current file, Q&A warns you that the file will be overwritten. If you want to proceed anyway, select Yes. If you don't want to proceed with that file name, you can type another name in the dialog box.

You also can save a document from the Type/Edit screen. Press Shift-F8, then follow the instructions in the prior paragraph. For more information about the Save operation, see Chapter 7.

*Save as ASCII*. This option saves a file without Write formatting so you can export it to another program. To use the Save as ASCII operation, press F8 to display the Options menu. Choose Other Options and select Save as ASCII on the submenu. Q&A adds a dialog box to the screen for you to fill in with an appropriate file name—either a new, unique file name or the name of a current file. Press F10. If you have entered the name of a current file, Q&A warns you that the file will be overwritten. If you want to proceed anyway, select Yes. If you don't want to proceed with that file name, you can type another name in the dialog box.

You also can save a document from the Type/Edit screen. Press Ctrl-F8. Then follow the instructions in the prior paragraph.

*Assign Fonts*. During the last stages of Q&A installation, the Install program asked if you wanted to install font description files. If your printer has fonts and you want to use fonts with Q&A, it is a good idea to install fonts description files.

**229**

> ▶ **Note:** You must have installed font description files to assign fonts.

Before you get started with assigning fonts, review the font terms mentioned in this section:

*Abbr.* The abbreviation for this font name. Q&A displays this name on the status line when the cursor is located on enhanced text.

*Fixed font.* A font whose characters are the same width. For example, an *i* takes the same horizontal space as a *w*.

*Font name.* The name of a font as it is known to Q&A. These names are commonly used by printers, artists, and desktop publishers.

*Font file.* A font description file that is supplied with Q&A.

*Pitch.* The horizontal measurement of the characters that fit in an inch. Ten characters per inch is 10 pitch. P indicates proportional fonts, E indicates an enhancement, and a number indicates fixed fonts.

*Point.* The vertical height of a character measured from the top of letters such as *b* or *t* to the bottom of letters such as *q* or *p*. The point size is either a number (such as 10 or 12) or E, which indicates a special font enhancement supported by your printer.

*Proportional font.* A font whose characters vary in width. For example, an *i* does not take up as much horizontal space as a *w*.

**230**

 **Assigning Fonts**

| | |
|---|---|
| 1. Move the cursor to the beginning of the area that you want to enhance. Then press F8. | Write displays the Options menu. |
| 2. Choose Block Operations and select Enhance on the submenu. | Write displays the Text Enhancements and Fonts menu. |
| 3. Choose Assign Fonts. | Write displays the Font Assignments screen (Figure 8.10). |
| 4. Enter a Font file name. Or press F6 to list the available font files. Select one and press F10. To select the | Write displays the List of Available Font Descriptions screen (Figure 8.11). |

Regular font name, move the highlight to that field on the screen. Then either enter a font name or press F6.

| | |
|---|---|
| 5. Move the highlight to the desired font description. | As you move the highlight, the name in the Font name field changes. |
| 6. Press F10 to select the font name. | Write returns you to the Font Assignments screen where you are prompted to enter the point size for the font if it is scalable font, or if you can set it to almost any size. |
| 7. Either accept the displayed point size or enter one; then press F10. | The column for the Regular font name is filled in with the name, abbreviation, point, pitch, and comments. |
| 8. Assign up to eight more fonts by moving the highlight to the Font field and repeating steps 5 through 7. If you want to remove a font, highlight it and press the Spacebar. | Write returns you to the Text Enhancements and Fonts Screen. |
| 9. When you have completed the screen, press F10, then Enter. | Write returns you to the Type/Edit screen. |
| 10. Use the arrow keys to select the text the you want to enhance. | From now on, Q&A prints text in the new default font. □ |

The next time you enhance text, notice that the new fonts are displayed on the Text Enhancements and Fonts screen.

*Calculate.* You can perform five types of calculations on numbers, which are arranged either by row or column, in your document:

1. Total calculates the sum of the numbers.
2. Average computes the average of the numbers.
3. Count counts the numbers.

4. Multiply multiplies each number by the product of the previous numbers.

5. Divide divides the last number into the next-to-last number.

These settings match those on the text Enhancements and Fonts screen

```
                        FONT ASSIGNMENTS                   Pg. U-???

 Font file name:

              Font name            Abbr.  Point Pitch      Comments

 Regular:

 Font 1:
 Font 2:
 Font 3:
 Font 4:
 Font 5:
 Font 6:
 Font 7:
 Font 8:


 FORMLTR1.DOC

 Esc-Exit       F1-Help        F6-List fonts     F8-Make default    F10-Continue
```

**232**

*Figure 8.10   Use the Font Assignments screen to select a font file and assign appropriate fonts*

```
                 LIST OF AVAILABLE FONT DESCRIPTIONS

 LJet-Courier 10 Med              Univers ItaBld          Font
 LJet-Line Printer                Univers Med             descriptions
 LJet IID/P/III Cour 12 Ita       Univers ItaMed          vary
 LJet IID/P/III Cour 12 Bld       LaserJet-Courier 12 Med depending
 LJet IID/P/III Cour 12 Med       LaserJet-Courier 10 Ita on your
 LJet II/D/P/III Cour 10 Bld      LaserJet-Courier 10 Bld printer
 LJet II/D/P/III Cour 10 Ita      C01-CG Times 12 Bld     and
 LJet II/D/P/III Cour 10 Med      C01-CG Times 12 Ita     whether
 LJet II/D/P/III Line Ptr 16      C01-CG Times 12 Med     you
 CG Times Bld                     C01-CG Times 13 Bld     installed
 CG Times ItaBld                  C01-CG Times 13 Ita     these
 CG Times Med                     C01-CG Times 13 Med     files
 CG Times ItaMed                  C01-CG Times 18 Bld
 Univers Bld                      C01-CG Times 24 Bld

                                        Press PgDn for more

               Font name: LJet-Courier 10 Med

 FORMLTR1.DOC

 Esc-Exit                       F7-Search                  F10-Continue
```

*Figure 8.11   The List of Available Font Descriptions screen shows you the font descriptions in your font file*

## Q Calculating Numbers in a Document

1. Enter numbers either in a row or column format in the document. If you are using a column format, either right-align the numbers or align them by the position of the decimal point. For column math, move the cursor over the last number in the column. For row math, move the cursor to the right of the last number in the row. To use this feature from the Options menu, press F8.

   Q&A adds a dialog box at the bottom of the screen.

2. Select Other Options from the Options menu and Calculate from the submenu. To use this feature directly from the Type/Edit screen, press Alt-F9. Select T (for Total), A (for Average), C (for Count), M (for Multiply), or D (for Divide).

   Q&A prompts you to move the cursor to the screen location where the result of the calculation is to be placed.

3. Move the cursor and press F10.

   Q&A displays the result of the calculation.  □

When you are calculating numbers in a document, remember the following:

▶ Any number either preceded by a minus (–) sign or enclosed in parentheses is considered to be a negative number.

▶ The number of decimal places in a result is the same as the the largest number of decimal places in a number being calculated.

▶ For average or divide, two additional decimal places are added.

▶ Columns and rows being calculated should only contain numbers—not text.

# Search and Replace

Write gives you the ability to search for text and even some functions within a document and then, optionally, replace the search characters with other characters.

Search and replace is a valuable operation. For example, you can search for a particular font in order to change it. If you intend to export this document, in the process of saving it as an ASCII document, you lose certain formatting symbols, such as tabs. If you search for and replace tabs with a rare combination of letters (such as *qw*), you can reapply tabs by searching and replacing after the document reaches the target program, assuming that it has the capability to search and replace. For a list of special functions for which you can search, see Table 8.4.

**234**

*Table 8.4    Q&A Search and Replace Combinations*

| Key Combination | Function |
| --- | --- |
| @CR | Searches for a carriage return character |
| @TB | Searches for a tab character |
| @NP | Searches for a new page character |
| @CT | Searches for a centered line |
| @RG | Searches for any regular text |
| @BD | Searches for boldface text |
| @UL | Searches for underlined text |
| @IT | Searches for italicized text |
| @SP | Searches for superscript text |
| @SB | Searches for subscript text |
| @F1 | Searches for font 1 |
| @F2 | Searches for font 2 |
| @F3 | Searches for font 3 |
| @F4 | Searches for font 4 |
| @F5 | Searches for font 5 |
| @F6 | Searches for font 6 |
| @F7 | Searches for font 7 |
| @F8 | Searches for font 8 |

# Searching For Text or Special Functions in a Document

1. From the Type/Edit screen, press F7.

    Q&A displays a dialog box (Figure 8.12).

2. In the Search For field, enter the text or special function. Begin the search by pressing F7 or F10.

    If Write finds the text or function, it highlights it and displays a message, saying that it found the text. It also gives you the chance to search again or cancel the search.

3. Modify the characters in some way (which ends the search), press F7 to look for the next occurrence of the text, or press Esc to end the search.

    If Write does not find the text or function, it displays the text or function and the message NOT FOUND. After completing at least one match, Write tells you how many matches it has made and the type of search operation used. □

**235**

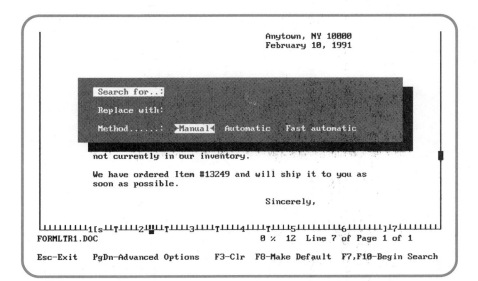

*Figure 8.12    The Search dialog box makes it easy for you to search for, and optionally replace, text or special characters*

Write starts searching at the current cursor location, goes to the bottom of the document, and then starts at the top until it reaches the cursor again. The Search dialog box has room for entering replacement text or functions. In the box, you also can select the method that you want to use for the search:

*Manual* finds a match and then waits for you to tell it to continue the search.

*Automatic* finds and acknowleges each match without waiting for a prompt.

*Fast Automatic* finds each match without waiting for a prompt or displaying that there was a match. If you are sure that the search text (including spaces) is accurate, this is a rapid way to search and replace.

You can use wildcards if you want to search for text that contains particular characters or symbols. Table 8.5 lists Q&A wildcard symbols and an explanation of each.

*Table 8.5    Q&A Wildcard Symbols*

| Wildcard | Function |
| --- | --- |
| \ | Searches for the literal character immediately following the backslash |
| ? | Searches for a single alphanumeric character at the location of the question mark |
| ..t | Searches for any word that ends with a specific character (where t represents any alphanumeric ) |
| t.. | Searches for any word that begins with a specific character (where t represents any alphanumeric character) |
| ..t.. | Searches for any word that contains a specific character (where t represents any alphanumeric character) |
| @ | Q&A special functions |

## Searching For and Replacing Text or Special Functions

1. From the Type/Edit screen, press F7.    Q&A displays the Search dialog box.

2. In the Search For field, enter the text or special function.

Q&A searches in the document for the text you type.

3. Move to the Replace With field and type the replacement text or function.

Q&A replaces the searched for text with the replacement text.

4. Move to the Method field and select either Manual, Automatic, or Fast Automatic. Press either F7 or F10 to begin the search.

After it finds the search text, Write prompts you to press F7 to search again without replacing, F10 to replace and continue, or Esc to cancel the operation.

5. Press either F7, F10, or Esc.

If you press Esc, any replacements that Write made up to this point remain. When Write completes all search and replace operations, it displays `Search and replace completed.` □

**237**

Q&A also has advanced search options, which allow you to search for exact matches of partial words, words with both uppercase and lowercase characters, and words in documents that are connected to the current document via the *JOIN*, *QUEUE*, or *QUEUEP* commands. In the following Quick Steps, you use Type, Case, and Range settings.

*Type* specifies whether you are searching for whole words, parts of words, or patterns (such as three numbers followed by four alphabetic characters or a specific format). If you specify whole word, Write looks for that word only and not part of it found in another word.

If you specify text, Write looks for that text, regardless of the fact that it is a whole word or part of a larger word. (For example, you can find the word *ran* in orange, ranging, and transfer.)

If you specify pattern, you are actually searching for a specific format. You can use this option to search for all Social Security numbers or all ID numbers—if they are formatted identically. For example, 999-999-9999 represents a telephone number (with area code), and AAAAA999 represents an ID number that starts with five alphabetic characters and ends with three numeric characters. Table 8.6 lists the pattern wildcards and their meanings.

**Table 8.6    Q&A Pattern Wildcards**

| Wildcard | Represents |
|----------|-----------|
| 9 | Any numeric character |
| a,A | Any alphabetic character |
| ? | Any alphanumeric character |
| ~ (tilde) | Any nonalphanumeric character |

*Case* tells Write whether to search for the exact combination of uppercase and lowercase letters that you have entered. *Insensitive* searches for the word, regardless of the case; *sensitive* searches for an exact match by case.

*Range* specifies whether Write searches all or part of the document and in which direction. *All* searches the entire document from the cursor position to the end and then from the beginning to the cursor position. *To End* searches from the cursor position to the bottom of the document. *To Beginning* searches from the cursor to the top of the document.

*Search Joins* tells Write to search the current document as well as documents that are connected to this one via the *JOIN*, *QUEUE*, or *QUEUEP* commands.

## Using Advanced Search Options

| | |
|---|---|
| 1. From the Type/Edit screen, press F7. | Write displays the Search dialog box. |
| 2. Press PgDn. | Write adds four more options to the dialog box. |
| 3. Select Type, Case, and Range settings. Press F7. | Q&A searches the document. ☐ |

> **Tip:** If you search again in the session, the Advanced Options screen is automatically displayed. To close this screen, press PgUp.

You can search for and replace the Spacebar character so that extra spaces can be removed from documents, especially those formatted by another word processing program. With the document on the Type/Edit screen, start the search. At the `Search for` prompt, type two backslashes separated by two spaces (\ \). At the `Replace with` prompt, type two backslashes separated by one space (\ \). Choose the Automatic option and press F10. You also can use this method to reformat sentences that are separated by two spaces rather than one.

# Using the Write Utilities

The Write Utilities are functions that help you customize the Write module:

> *Set Global Options* enables you to change the default editing options that are on the Type/Edit screen.
>
> *Change Print Defaults* allows you to access the Print Options screen (see Chapter 7).
>
> *Change Page Defaults* allows you to access the Define Page screen (see Chapter 7).
>
> *Change Import Defaults* enables you to determine the page definition for imported documents that come in ASCII, WordStar, and Lotus formats.

**239**

When you use Set Global Options, you can change the tab settings, customize the import type for the documents that you bring into Q&A Write, and show normally hidden characters for all documents on which you work. For an example of the Editing Options screen, see Figure 8.13.

# Importing and Exporting Document Files

Write gives you the capability to get documents from outside Q&A. For example, you can retrieve documents in several versions of ASCII, and in such formats as WordPerfect, Microsoft Word, and MultiMate, among others.

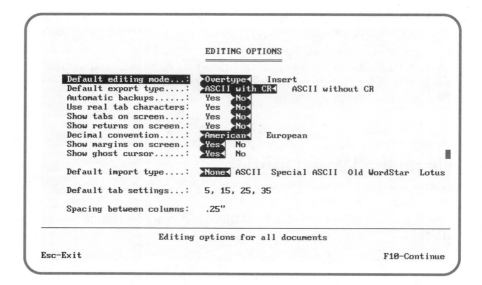

```
                        EDITING OPTIONS

        Default editing mode...:  ▶Overtype◀   Insert
        Default export type....:  ▶ASCII with CR◀   ASCII without CR
        Automatic backups......:  Yes  ▶No◀
        Use real tab characters:  Yes  ▶No◀
        Show tabs on screen....:  Yes  ▶No◀
        Show returns on screen.:  Yes  ▶No◀
        Decimal convention.....:  ▶American◀   European
        Show margins on screen.:  ▶Yes◀  No
        Show ghost cursor......:  ▶Yes◀  No

        Default import type....:  ▶None◀ ASCII  Special ASCII  Old WordStar  Lotus

        Default tab settings...:  5, 15, 25, 35

        Spacing between columns:  .25"

                Editing options for all documents

   Esc-Exit                                       F10-Continue
```

240

*Figure 8.13   Use the Editing Options screen to change Write
default editing settings*

Earlier in this chapter, you learned how to get a document via
the Options menu, Documents, and Get a document. When Write
detects a document that is not in Write format, it displays the Import
Document menu from which you select a format that is the closest
to your non-Write document.

You also can select Import a Document from the Write Utilities
menu to determine a word processing format in which to import
documents.

## Q Importing a Document

1. From the Write menu, select       Write displays the Write
   Utilities.                        Utilities menu.

2. Choose Import a Document.         Write displays the Write
                                     Import menu.

3. Select the format that most       Write adds a dialog box to
   nearly matches your non-          the screen.
   Write document. If Write
   asks you to identify the release of the program from
   which you are importing,
   do so.

4. Choose a file to be imported.     Write prompts you to give a new file name to the document.

5. Give the file a new, unique name.     Write displays a message that the document has been imported.    □

You can use the same Quick Steps to export a Write document to one of the same nine format types. In step 2, choose Export a Document.

If a document is damaged in some way (for example, if the computer is accidentally unplugged), you may have to ask Write to Recover the Document. See Chapter 3 for instructions.

The Q&A Write Utilities module offers you the chance to perform several DOS commands without leaving Q&A. You can list files and rename, delete, or copy a file. For complete instructions, see Chapter 11.

**241**

# What You Have Learned

▶   Write provides a variety of ways to perform many functions.

▶   The Options menu offers you six main options along with many suboptions.

▶   Many of the Options menu functions are available both in Write and in File.

▶   You can embed date and time information in a document to timestamp it.

▶   Write allows you to use two dictionaries—the Q&A dictionary and one that you create—to check spelling.

▶   If you have a printer with font capabilities, you can print Write documents with a polished appearance.

▶   Write provides an advanced search and replace function; you can search for parts of words, special functions, and even patterns of numbers and text.

▶   Use the Write Utilities to customize your version of Write.

▶   You can import and export documents in many formats.

*Chapter 9*

# Q&A Write: Merging and Mailing

## In This Chapter

▶ *Creating a mail merge document*
▶ *Printing from mail merge*
▶ *Merge-printing envelopes from letters*
▶ *Mailing labels*

One of the many advantages of Q&A is that the modules can work together. This chapter describes the way Write works with File to produce form letters, to print envelopes automatically, and to create mailing labels.

The operation by which a word processor uses current database information to customize each letter is called *mail merge*.

In Chapter 4, you learned how to use File to retrieve and sort selected records from your database. You can use these features to customize your mailing. For example, you can inform specific customers that you are opening a warehouse outlet in their area, or you can send a special sales flier to your favored customers.

# Creating a Mail Merge Document

Create a mail merge document as you would a normal letter, with certain exceptions.

**Q** **Creating a Merge Document**

1. From the Main menu, select Write.

   Q&A displays the Write menu.

2. Select Type/Edit.

   Q&A displays a blank Type/Edit screen.

3. Create a document but omit specific names and mailing addresses that you will get from the database (Figure 9.1).

   Q&A displays your "skeleton" letter form as you create it.

4. Move the cursor to the first place in the letter where you want to insert information from the database, and press Alt-F7.

   Q&A adds a dialog box to the screen and asks for a database name (Figure 9.2).

5. Enter the name of the database or press Enter for a list of files. After selecting a database, press Enter.

   Q&A displays an alphabetized list of all the field names from the database. If the list of names is too long to fit on the screen, Q&A displays an arrow showing you that more names follow.

6. Move the cursor to the name that you want to insert into the letter. Highlight it and then press Enter.

   Q&A inserts the name, enclosed in asterisks, into the letter at the cursor location (Figure 9.3).

7. Keep adding field names to the letter until it is complete. Press Shift-F8 to save your document.

   Q&A saves the completed document (Figure 9.4).

   □

You can use the same field more than once in the letter. You also can type fields into the document, but make sure that you enclose the name with asterisks.

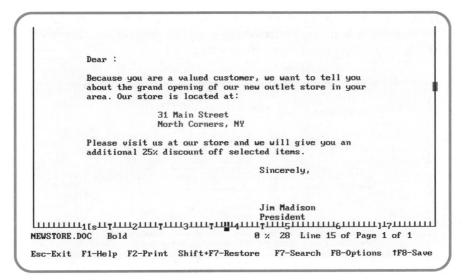

*Figure 9.1    This is the "skeleton" letter with nonspecific text*

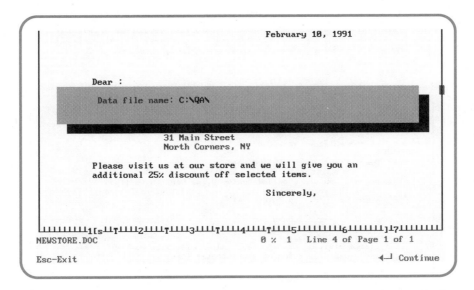

*Figure 9.2    Q&A asks for the name of the database from which you will get specific information*

When the letter is printed, the merged information starts at the left asterisk and takes only the space that it needs. Write recognizes the ending character (the right asterisk) and starts printing the next character, whether it is a letter, number, symbol, or space. Although Q&A encloses each name in asterisks in the document, the asterisks do not appear on the letter when you print.

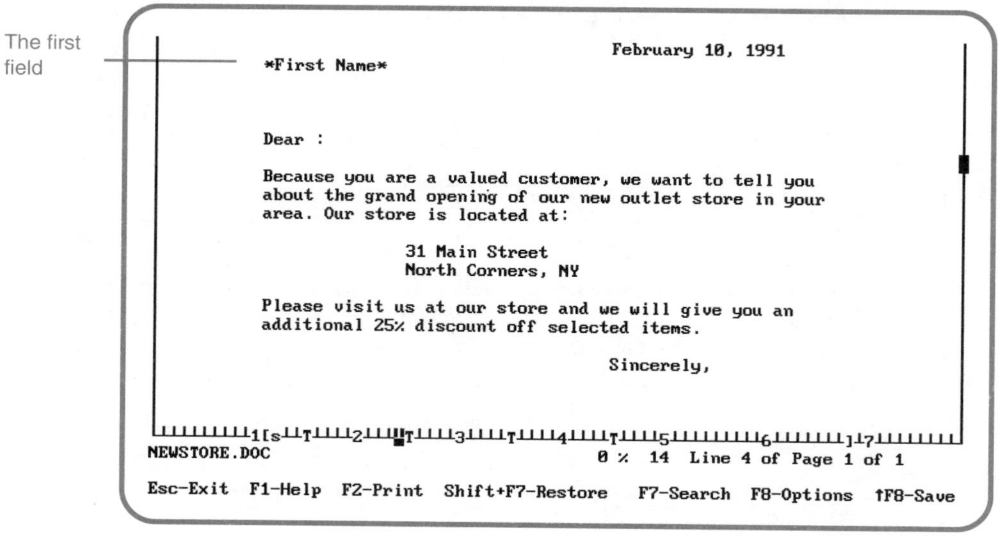

The first field

*Figure 9.3    Q&A adds the first field to the letter*

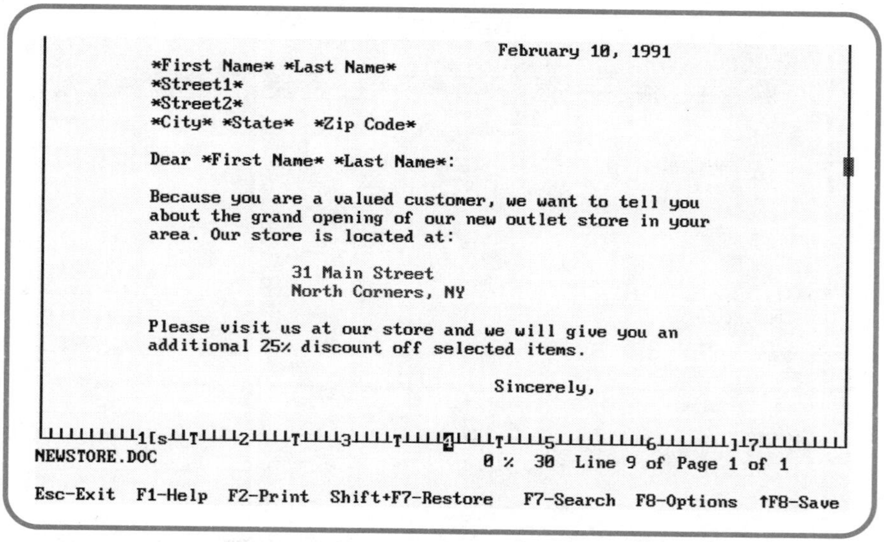

246

*Figure 9.4    The form letter with all the fields from the database*

Write allows you to add codes to refine the format of the letter: (T), (L), and (R).

(T) removes extra spaces between the field name and the end of the field (represented by the second asterisk, for example, `*Last Name(T)*`.

(L) left-justifies a column of information. For example, to align a list within a document on the left margin, enter `*First Name (L)*`.

(R) right-justifies a column of information. To align a list within a document on the right margin, enter `*Last Name        (R)*`. The extra spaces between Name and the left parenthesis allow for the maximum characters in the Last Name field.

# Mail Merge Printing

Before you print many letters, create a small test database or retrieve a few records from the database and use Q&A's Page Preview to look at your document before printing.

After the test or page preview, ensure that you have adequate space—at least two or three times the file size—on your hard drive to allow for both sorting and merging. Both of these operations can take a great deal of storage space temporarily.

**Printing a Merge Document**

1. With the merge document on the Type/Edit screen, press F2.

   Q&A displays the Print Options screen with the document name at the bottom.

2. If the Name of the merge file (that is, the database you are using as the source file) is not displayed on the Print Options screen, press any combination of cursor movement keys to move the highlight and type the database name. Make any

   Q&A makes the changes you specify.

changes to the Print Options screen to customize printing for this merge document. Optionally, you can press Ctrl-F6 to go to the Define Page screen to make appropriate changes there.

3. After completing all page and print changes, press F10.

Q&A displays a Retrieve Spec for the database.

4. Fill in the Retrieve Spec screen with whatever search restrictions you want to use to clearly identify only those records you want to merge into the document. You also can choose to sort records by pressing F8. After sorting, either press F9 to return to the Retrieve Spec or F10 to continue. When you have completed the Retrieve Spec (and optionally the Sort Spec), press F10.

Q&A displays a message telling you the number of records from your database that will be merged with the document (Figure 9.5).

**248**

5. Either press Enter to start printing or Esc to cancel.

First, Q&A rapidly displays the retrieved database records and then starts printing.  □

> **Tip:** You also can use programming expressions in the Retrieve Spec to retrieve data from more than one database or to calculate in certain fields. For more information about programming, see Chapter 12.

If you are printing many documents, sort by zip code. If the printing is interrupted, it is easier to determine the last record printed if your records are sorted.

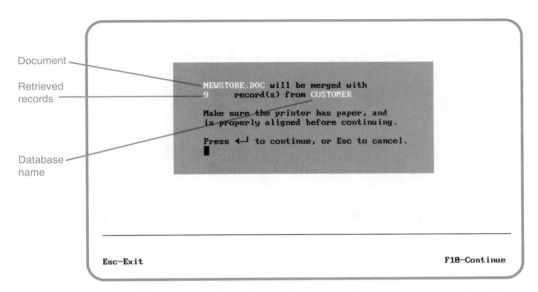

Document ⸺

Retrieved records ⸺

Database name ⸺

*Figure 9.5    Q&A tells you how many documents you will print*

**249**

Because you used the Field Names screen to fill in your document, the field names on the document and the database match. If Q&A finds a mismatch between the document and the database (see Figure 9.6), you can edit the merge field labels in the document or use the Identifier Spec, which lets you type in the field label as you typed it in the document. For example, if you typed *Last Nme* in the document and the real name in the database is Last Name, type Last Nme into the Last Name field on the Identifier Spec.

# Merge Printing Envelopes from Letters

Q&A can print automatically an envelope using the name and address you have typed into a Write letter.

---

Ø **Caution:** Printing envelopes can cause severe damage to your printer. For example, the Hewlett-Packard LaserJet III User's Manual has several pages of information and warnings about printing envelopes. Be careful about the types of envelopes you use and be sure to check your printer's manual.

---

This field
does not
agree
with your
database.

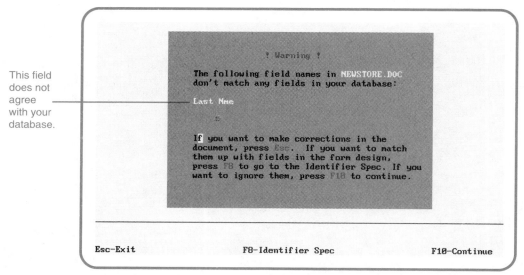

Figure 9.6   *Q&A displays a warning message when it finds field*
*names that do not match*

Write is programmed to look for more than one line of left-aligned text in a document and identify it as the text to print on an envelope. After it finds a block of text, it then looks for the first blank line and uses that to define the end of the block of text. For an example of a letter that is formatted so that Q&A finds the name and address, see Figure 9.7.

## Printing an Envelope

1. Type or Get a letter; then edit it, if needed, to ensure that the first block of text is the name and address. Be sure to leave a blank line before typing the salutation.

   Q&A displays your letter with the editing changes you made.

2. Move the cursor to the top of the letter. Insert an envelope in the printer. If appropriate, align the top of the envelope with the print head. Press F2.

   Q&A displays the Print Options screen.

3. Using any combination of cursor movement keys, highlight the Line Spacing option and select Envelope; then press F10.

Q&A displays a status message and then prints the address, starting about eight lines from the top edge and indented about 3 ¹/₂ inches from the left edge.    □

```
                                    10 Delta Drive
                                    Anytown, NY 10000
                                    February 10, 1991

        Mr. Quincy Adams
        225 Bartram Avenue
        Wherever, NY 10000

        Dear Mr. Adams:

        Yesterday you placed an order for a 10-piece screwdriver
        set (Item #13249). We regret to tell you that the set is
        not currently in our inventory.

        We have ordered Item #13249 and will ship it to you as
        soon as possible.

                        Sincerely,

FORMLTR1.DOC                              0 %  1    Line 19 of Page 1 of 1

Esc-Exit  F1-Help  F2-Print  Shift+F7-Restore  F7-Search  F8-Options  ↑F8-Save
```

The first block of text.

**251**

*Figure 9.7    Q&A uses this letter format to find a name and address to print on an envelope*

When you installed your printer, you had the opportunity to change the envelope height. If you need to change it now, select Utilities from the Main menu; then go through the Install Printer screens until you can press F8 to select Special Printer Options. You can change envelope height on the More Special Printer Options screen.

The envelope is printed in portrait mode; that is, the lines of the address are formatted in exactly the same way as your letter.

▶ **Tip:** If you have a laser printer, an alternate way to print an envelope is to use landscape mode (rotated 90 degrees from the portrait mode). For information about this, refer to your printer's manual.

# Mailing Labels

For mass mailings, putting address information on mailing labels and then sticking them on envelopes is the most practical approach. Q&A's mailing label option enables you to print names and addresses from a database on labels whether or not they come from well-known manufacturers.

**Creating Mailing Labels**

1. Select Mailing Labels from the Write Menu.

   Q&A displays the List of Mailing Labels screen.

2. Select the appropriate label by moving the highlight to your choice. If you need to change the label specifications or use the label for a unique job, ask Q&A to make a copy of the original label; press F5.

   Q&A adds a line to the screen.

3. Enter a name, which can be up to 32 characters long and can contain spaces. Press F10.

   Q&A adds your label name to its list of labels.                □

You also can edit labels with the List of Mailing Labels screen.

**Editing Mailing Labels**

1. Select Mailing Labels from the Write Menu.

   Q&A displays the List of Mailing Labels screen.

2. Select a unique name (not one predefined by Q&A) by moving the highlight to your choice. Then press F10.

   Q&A displays a label template on the upper left part of the screen (Figure 9.8).

3. Edit the label information by pressing Alt-F7.

   Q&A opens a dialog box.

4. Type the name of the database and press Enter. To have Q&A display a list of databases from which you can choose, press Enter without typing a name.

   Q&A displays the field names from your database (Figure 9.9).

5. To place field names from your database into the template, press Esc.

Q&A closes the Field Names box.

6. Delete whatever field names and the appropriate asterisks you want from the label template. Leave the cursor in the "empty" area. Press Alt-F7.

Q&A opens the Field Names box.

7. Highlight the field that you want to add to the erased area of the label template. PressEnter.

Q&A moves the field name to the label template and closes the Field Names box.

8. Repeat steps 6 through 8 until you have finished changing the field names on the label template.

Q&A repeatedly opens and closes the Field Names box in response to your actions.

**253**

9. If you want to change the label dimensions, press Ctrl-F6 with the Field Names box closed.

Q&A displays the Define Label screen (Figure 9.10).

10. Type new dimensions where needed; then press F10.

Q&A processes your label edits. □

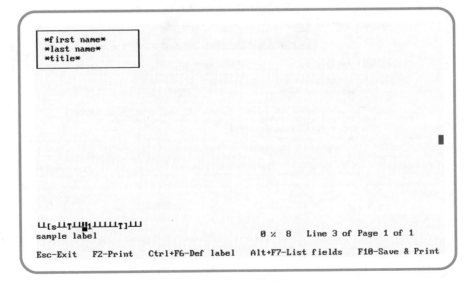

Figure 9.8    This screen shows you the fields that are defined for this label

If the names on the label do not agree with the Field Names list, edit the label.

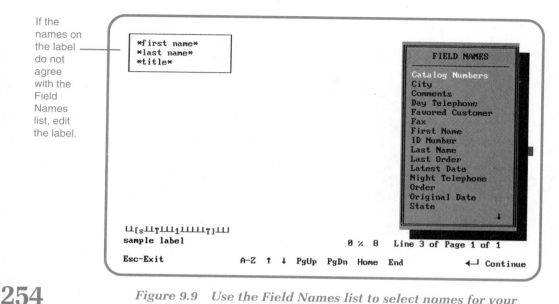

*Figure 9.9     Use the Field Names list to select names for your label*

254

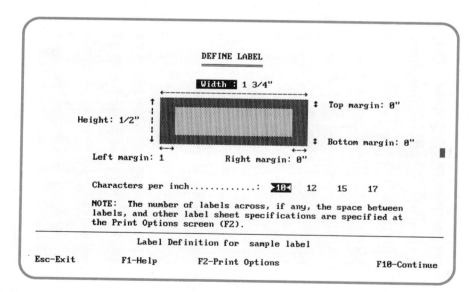

*Figure 9.10     You can change label dimensions on the Define Label screen*

Use the Define Label screen to change the dimensions of the selected label in different ways. See Table 9.1 for a list of label dimensions.

*Table 9.1    Label Dimensions*

| Dimension | Measurement |
|---|---|
| Width | From the left edge to the right edge |
| Height | From the top edge to the bottom edge |
| Left margin | From the left edge to the first character on the row |
| Right margin | From the right edge to the last character on the row |
| Top margin | From the top to the first printed line |
| Bottom margin | From the bottom to the last printed line |

Every module that allows you to print has its own Print Options screen. Q&A also provides print options unique to mailing labels. You have seen some of these options before, but some are new.

**255**

*Print offset* offers a way for you to adjust the print head.

*Lines per label sheet* indicates the number of lines either per label or inch, depending on your printer. If you have a single sheet printer, use the number of lines per page. For a pin-fed printer, use the number of lines per label.

*Blank lines at top* and *Blank lines at bottom* adjust where the printer starts (or stops) printing on the first (or last) label on the sheet. Increase the number of blank lines at the top to print higher on the first label; decrease the number of blank lines on the bottom to print lower on the last label.

## Printing Mailing Labels

If you plan on printing labels immediately, you have already "connected" your database to the label-printing process. However, to print mailing labels after doing other Q&A work in the meantime, you need to get a database file from which to get the needed data.

**Printing Mailing Labels**

| | |
|---|---|
| 1. Select Mailing Labels from the Write menu. | Q&A displays the List of Mailing Labels screen. |
| 2. Select the appropriate label by moving the highlight to your choice; then press Enter. | Q&A displays label information. |
| 3. Press F2. | Q&A displays the Mailing Label Print Options screen (Figure 9.11). |
| 4. Move the highlight to the Name of Q&A Merge File option, enter the name of the database that contains the information to be printed on the labels. Press F10. | If the fields match, Q&A displays the Retrieve Spec. If Q&A finds fields that do not match the fields on the label, it displays those names on the screen, and prompts you to identify them. |
| 5. If the fields match and you see the Retrieve Spec, go to Step 7. If they do not match, press F8. | Q&A displays the Identifier Spec. |
| 6. Fill in the Spec and press F10. | Q&A displays the Retrieve Spec. |
| 7. Use the Retrieve Spec to limit the number of records selected. Optionally, press F8 to sort the records. After completion, press F10. | Q&A displays a status message. |
| 8. Press Enter to print (or Esc to cancel). | Q&A prints your labels. □ |

**256**

## *Printing Multiple Copies*

Q&A lets you print multiple copies of a single label containing the same information. For example, you can create a label with your company name and address, save it, and then print any number of copies.

## *Q* Printing Multiple Copies

1. Select Mailing Labels from the Write menu.

   Q&A displays the List of Mailing Labels screen.

2. Select the appropriate label by moving the highlight to your choice; then press Enter.

   Q&A displays label information on the screen.

3. Move the cursor to the first character to be copied and press F5. Follow the prompts to make a copy of the label.

   Q&A copies your label.

4. Select the name of the new label from the List of Mailing Labels and press F10.

   Q&A displays the label and its current field names.

5. Type the information you want on the label, making sure to remove all the current information. Press F2.

   Q&A displays the Mailing Label Print Options screen.

6. In the Number of Copies field, type the number of labels youwant printed. Then press F10.

   Q&A prints the labels.

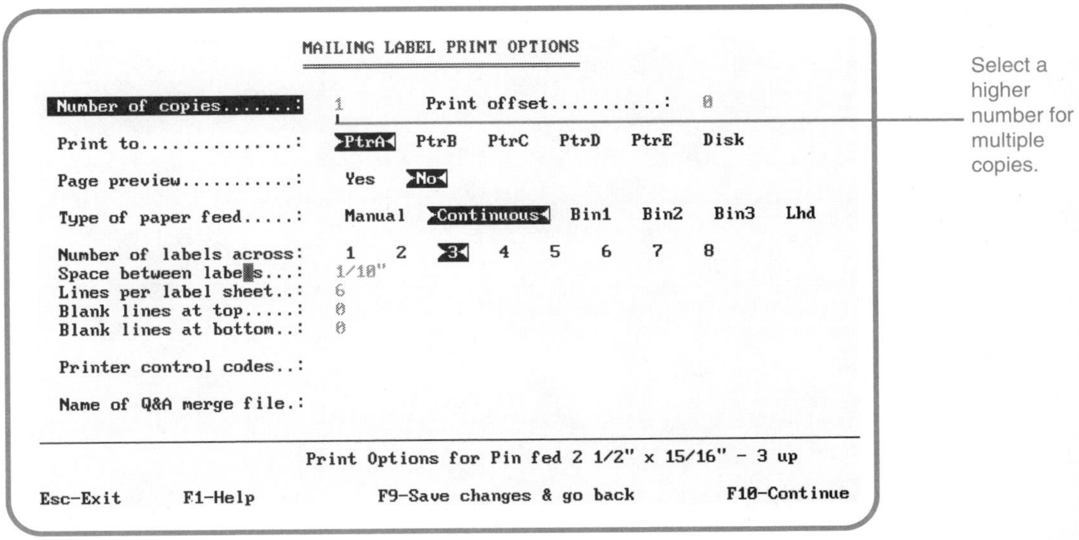

257

□

```
                    MAILING LABEL PRINT OPTIONS

  Number of copies.......:   1          Print offset..........:   0

  Print to..............:  >PtrA<  PtrB   PtrC   PtrD   PtrE   Disk

  Page preview..........:   Yes   >No<

  Type of paper feed.....:  Manual  >Continuous<  Bin1   Bin2   Bin3   Lhd

  Number of labels across:  1    2   >3<   4    5    6    7    8
  Space between labels...:  1/10"
  Lines per label sheet..:  6
  Blank lines at top.....:  0
  Blank lines at bottom..:  0

  Printer control codes..:

  Name of Q&A merge file.:

  ─────────────────────────────────────────────────────────────────────
              Print Options for Pin fed 2 1/2" x 15/16" - 3 up

  Esc-Exit      F1-Help         F9-Save changes & go back        F10-Continue
```

Select a higher number for multiple copies.

*Figure 9.11   The Mailing Label Print Options screen*

# What You Have Learned

▶ Write works with File to produce form letters, to print envelopes, and to create mailing labels.

▶ You can create a mail merge document as you would a normal letter, but omit specific information.

▶ Before printing many letters, test on a smaller database or use the Page Preview option.

▶ Q&A can print automatically an envelope from name and address information in a letter.

▶ Q&A provides you with a list of standard labels from which you can select.

258

*Chapter 10*

# Q&A Assistant

## In This Chapter

259

▶ *Using the Query Guide*
▶ *Teaching the Query Guide*
▶ *Using the Intelligent Assistant (IA)*
▶ *Teaching IA about a Database*
▶ *Asking IA Questions*

The Q&A Assistant module is another way for you to access a database in order to fill in or change a form, to calculate, to ask questions, or to produce reports.

Q&A provides two assistants—the Query Guide and the Intelligent Assistant. The Query Guide contains words and phrases that you can use to create questions; it is ideal for the new user. Use the Intelligent Assistant, which knows about 600 words and phrases, to ask questions of the Q&A File and Report modules. You can use both assistants immediately, but they work much better if you spend the time to set them up—teach them.

The first time that you use the Query Guide with a database, Q&A gives you the choice of starting it without teaching it about the database.

## Using the Query Guide before Teaching It

| | |
|---|---|
| 1. From the Main menu, select Assistant. | Q&A displays the Assistant menu (Figure 10.1). |
| 2. Select Query Guide. | Q&A displays a dialog box. |
| 3. Enter the name of the database or have Q&A display a list of files from which you can select. Press Enter. | The first time you access the database, Q&A displays a message that prompts you to allow the Query Guide to learn about your database or to just start working (Figure 10.2). |
| 4. Select No in order to start using the Query Guide now. | Q&A displays a box containing phrases which you can use to construct a request (Figure 10.3). |
| 5. Select a phrase. | Q&A displays a Select a Field screen, which shows the database fields arranged alphabetically. The phrase that you selected appears at the top of the screen. |
| 6. Press any combination of cursor movement keys to highlight a field or phrase from the list, depending on the starting phrase. Press Enter. | Q&A displays another list of options or fields that you use to add to the question. Q&A may also ask you to type a value. |
| 7. Add to the request until it is completed. | The screen contains the phrase to execute the command (Figure 10.4). |
| 8. Highlight to execute the command and press Enter. | Q&A displays the results of the query. |
| 9. If you ever want to rephrase the question during the query, press F3. | Q&A displays the first screen. ☐ |

When you start the Query Guide that is not set up, the first screen displays some phrases from which you select the first part of the sentence:

*Find ... (records)* fills out a Retrieve Spec.

*Produce a report showing the ... (fields)* creates a columnar report.

*Count ... (records)* counts the number of retrieved records.

*Summarize the data by ... (fields, with statistics)* creates a report that contains only summary information.

*Run ... (a stored procedure)* prints a report that you previously created.

*Cross-tabulate ... (statistics, by row/column categories)* creates a cross tab report arranged by ROW, COL, and SUM fields.

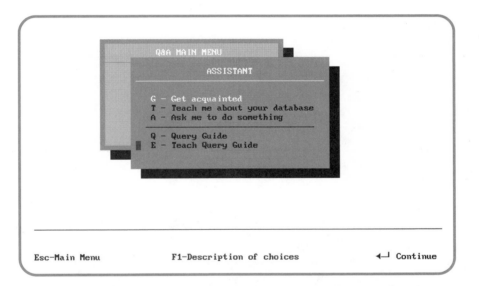

*Figure 10.1   Use the Assistant menu options to start the Query Guide or the Intelligent Assistant*

# Teaching the Query Guide

You can either choose to teach the Query Guide the first time it asks or you can teach it later by using Teach Query Guide from the Assistant menu.

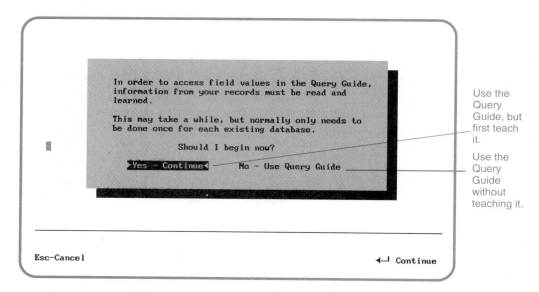

Use the Query Guide, but first teach it.

Use the Query Guide without teaching it.

*Figure 10.2   This screen is used to prompt you either to start the Query Guide or teach it first*

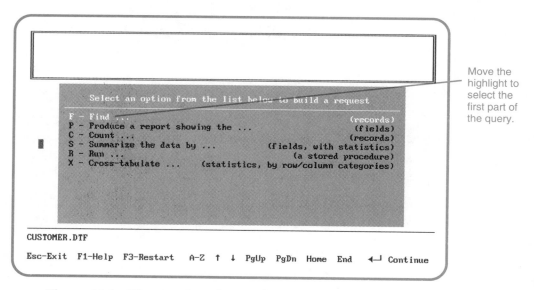

Move the highlight to select the first part of the query.

*Figure 10.3   The starting phrases for a Query Guide request can branch to several types of queries*

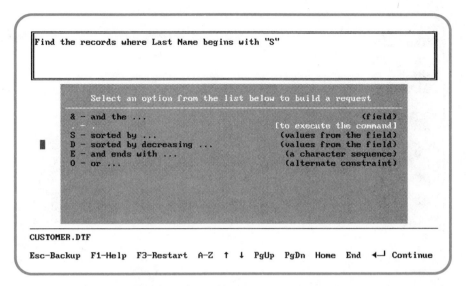

*Figure 10.4* **To execute a query, highlight** to execute the command **and then press Enter**

 **Teaching the Query Guide**

1. From the Main menu, select Assistant.

   Q&A displays the Assistant menu.

2. Select Teach Query Guide.

   Q&A displays a dialog box.

3. You can either enter the name of the database or have Q&A display a list of files from which to select. After selecting a file, press Enter.

   Q&A displays the Query Guide Teach screen (Figure 10.5).

4. Either press F5 to mark all text and keyword fields or enter a Q in any text and keyword fields to be used by the Query Guide, and press F10.

   Q&A displays a status screen and then returns to the Assistant menu.

   □

When the Query Guide knows about your database, you can use most of the same phrases to word the query but you also can restrict a query by using actual values from your database. After you have taught the Query Guide about your database, it can ask you questions that are related to the values in it.

ID Number:

First Name:                    Last Name:
Street1:
Street2:
City:                          State:                    Zip Code:

Day Telephone:                 Fax:
Night Telephone:

> Type "Q" in each text or keyword field that you wish to index
> for use by the Query Guide.  For example, if you wish to have
> access to a scrollable list of cities in your database while in
> the Query Guide, type a "Q" in the "City" field.
>
> SUGGESTION: Start by pressing F5 to mark all fields indexable by the
> query guide with "Q"s.  Then, remove the "Q"s from those fields that
> you do not wish to index.  To unteach the database, remove all Q's.

Select all
fields for
the
query.

```
CUSTOMER.DTF               Query Guide Teach              Page 1  of 2

Esc-Exit         F3-Clear spec         F5-Select all         F10-Continue
```

**264**

**Figure 10.5** *Use the Query Guide Teach screen to identify each
field that you want the Query Guide to use*

## Q Using the Query Guide after Teaching It

1. From the Main menu, select Assistant.

   Q&A displays the Assistant menu.

2. Select Query Guide.

   Q&A displays a dialog box.

3. Either enter the name of the database or have Q&A display a list of files from which you can select. After selecting a file, press Enter.

   Q&A displays a box containing phrases which you can use to construct a request.

4. Select a phrase.

   Q&A displays a Select a Field screen, which shows the database fields arranged alphabetically. The phrase that you selected appears at the top of the screen.

5. Press any combination of cursor movement keys to highlight a field or phrase from the list, depending on the starting phrase. Press Enter.

   Q&A displays another list of options or fields that you use to add to the question. Q&A may also ask you to type a value.

| | |
|---|---|
| 6. Add to the request until it is completed. | The screen contains the phrase `to execute the command`. |
| 7. Highlight `to execute the command` and press Enter. | Q&A displays the results of the query. |
| 8. If you ever want to rephrase the question during the query, press F3. | Q&A displays the first screen. □ |

Once you are comfortable with the Query Guide, take the next step and use the Intelligent Assistant (IA), which offers more types of queries. If you have already used the Query Guide for a database, you have to teach IA about it. The information from Query Guide is not passed to IA.

You can use IA to ask more sophisticated questions than you can by using File and Report. For example, you can ask questions that compare two values and follow up with related questions.

**265**

# Using the Intelligent Assistant

As with the Query Guide, you can use IA without teaching it. When you access the database, IA automatically learns certain information about it.

However, the best way to use IA is to spend a few moments teaching it more about your database—the layout, what the database is really about, the types and names of fields, synonyms for fields of the database, and more. A series of menu screens make it easy for you to provide IA with this type of information.

# Teaching IA about a Database

When you first identify your database to IA, it quickly learns about the fields on the form and learns from the data itself. You then add to IA's understanding of your database by teaching it about certain aspects of your database.

**Q** **Teaching IA about a Database**

1. From the Q&A Main menu, select Assistant.

   Q&A displays the Assistant menu.

2. Select Get Acquainted.

   Q&A displays a series of screens to scroll through (Figure 10.6).

3. Press Enter three times.

   Q&A returns you to the Assistant menu.

4. Select Teach Me about Your Database.

   Q&A displays a dialog box.

5. Either enter the name of the database or have Q&A display a list of files from which you can select. After selecting a file, press Enter.

   Q&A displays the working message at the bottom left of the screen. Then it displays the Basic Lessons menu.

6. Select Learn Values for Assistant.

   Q&A displays a message that asks you whether you want to continue the lesson or not (Figure 10.7).

7. Select Yes.

   Q&A displays status as it learns about your database, then returns you to the Basic Lessons menu.

8. Select What This Database Is About and press Enter.

   Q&A displays a screen that asks you for any words or phrases used to complete the sentence at the top of the screen (Figure 10.8).

9. Fill in the screen and press F10.

   Q&A returns you to the Basic Lessons menu. Which fields identify a form is highlighted.

10. Press Enter.

    Q&A asks you for columns (fields) that IA should always include in a report (Figure 10.9).

11. Enter the order of as many as eight columns (e.g., 1, 2, 3, and so on). Then press F10.

    Q&A returns you to the Basic Lessons menu. Which fields contain locations is now highlighted.

| | | |
|---|---|---|
| 12. | Press Enter. | Q&A asks you to indicate the database fields that indicate a location. For example, select address, city, or state fields. If your database does not include locations, don't fill in this screen. |
| 13. | Press F10. | Q&A returns you to the Basic Lessons menu. Alternate field names is now highlighted. |
| 14. | Press Enter. | Q&A asks you to enter synonyms or nicknames for any fields (Figure 10.10). |
| 15. | Press F6 to move to the previous field; press F8 to move to the next field. When you have finished, press F10. | Q&A returns you to the Basic Lessons menu. Advanced lessons is highlighted.   □ |

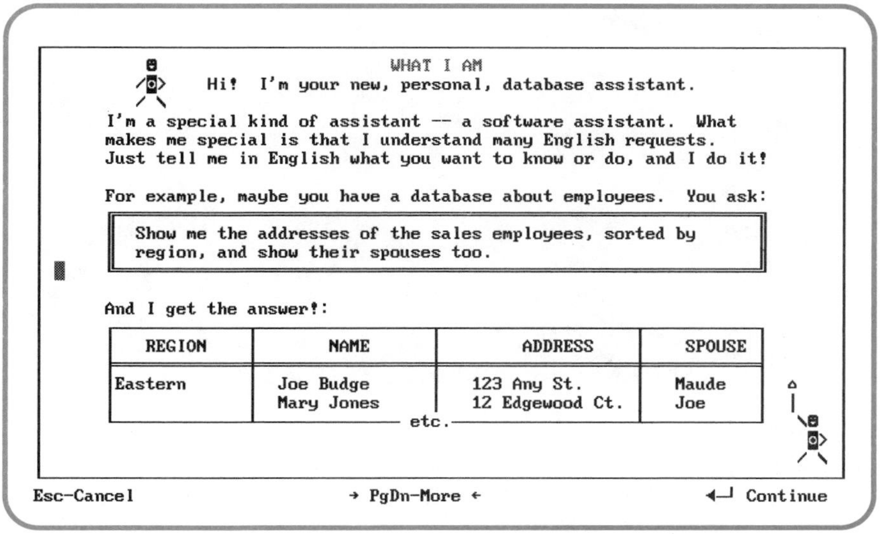

**267**

*Figure 10.6   This is the first screen in the Get Acquainted screens*

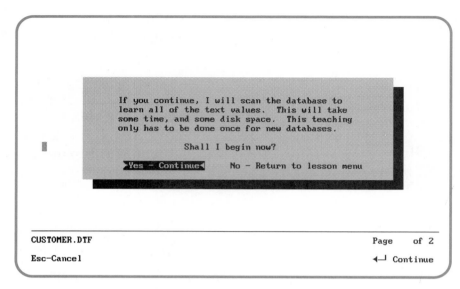

Figure 10.7    At this point, you can decide whether to have IA
learn automatically about your database's text values

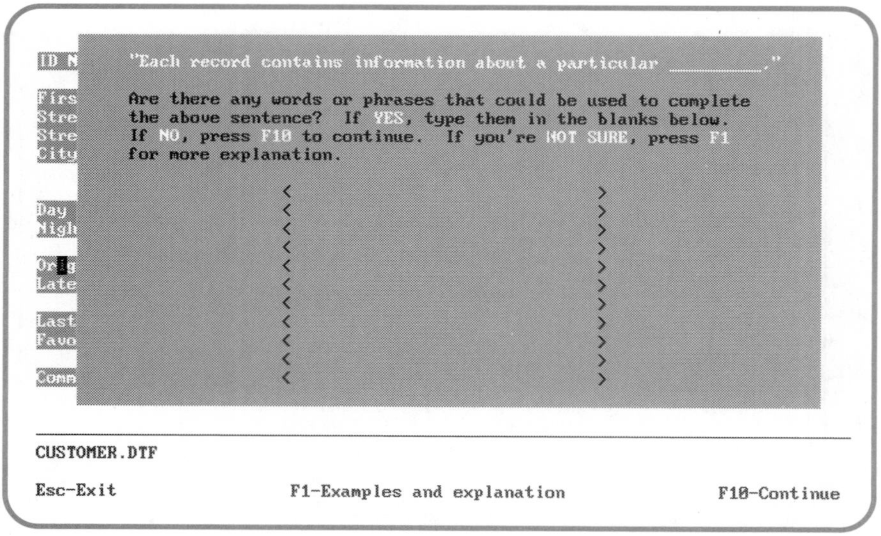

Figure 10.8    IA asks you about words or phrases for each
record

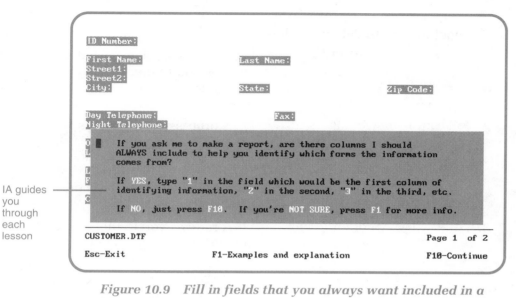

IA guides you through each lesson

*Figure 10.9    Fill in fields that you always want included in a report*

**269**

The highlighted field is reflected in the dialog box.

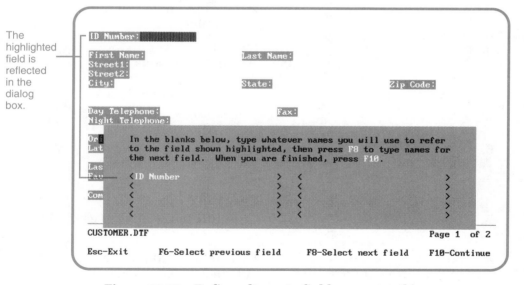

*Figure 10.10    Define alternate field names on this screen*

Once you have finished the preliminary screens, you can move on to teach IA advanced lessons.

# Q Teaching the IA Advanced Lessons

1. From the Advanced Lessons menu, with What Fields Contain People's Names highlighted, press Enter.

   Q&A displays a screen that enables you to identify any person's name (Figure 10.11).

2. Fill in the appropriate fields and press F10.

   Q&A processes the records for a short time and then asks if you will refer to the person whose name you identified by other words or phrases.

3. After you have filled in any fields, press F10.

   Q&A returns you to the Advanced Lessons menu. Units of measure is high-lighted.

4. Press Enter.

   If you do not have any number fields in your database, Q&A states that fact and prompts you to press Enter.

5. If you have number fields, you can enter information to further define these fields. Press either F6 or F8 to move between fields. After filling in number fields, press F10.

   Q&A returns you to the Advanced Lessons menu. Advanced vocabulary: adjectives is highlighted.

6. Press Enter.

   Q&A asks you if you will use adjectives in some of the database fields (Figure 10.12).

7. Fill in high- and low-value numeric or money adjectives.

   Q&A fills in the adjectives.

8. Press F6 or F8 to select the previous or next field, respectively. Press F10 after completing this screen.

   Q&A returns you to the Advanced Lessons menu. Advanced vocabulary: verbs is highlighted

9. Press Enter.

   Q&A asks you to enter verbs that you identify with specific fields (Figure 10.13).

10. Press F6 to select the previous field or press F8 to select the next field. When you have completed the screen, press F10.

Q&A returns you to the Advanced Lessons menu. `Exit lessons` is highlighted.

11. If you want to edit any of the screens that you have filled in, highlight that entry or enter the number associated with the entry. Then press Enter. If you want to exit the lessons, press Enter.

Q&A processes your edits.

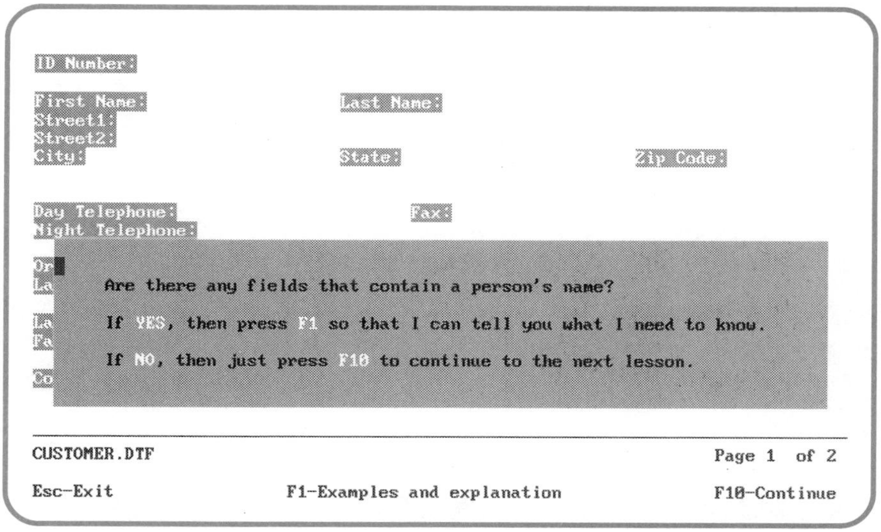

□

```
ID Number:

First Name:                    Last Name:
Street1:
Street2:
City:                          State:                    Zip Code:

Day Telephone:                      Fax:
Night Telephone:

Or
La      Are there any fields that contain a person's name?

La      If YES, then press F1 so that I can tell you what I need to know.
Fa
        If NO, then just press F10 to continue to the next lesson.
Co
───────────────────────────────────────────────────────────────────
CUSTOMER.DTF                                          Page 1  of 2

Esc-Exit              F1-Examples and explanation       F10-Continue
```

*Figure 10.11    Fill in name information on this screen*

Q&A recognizes S, ES, EN, ED and ING when you enter a verb. However, if the spelling of a verb changes beyond these, you may have to type in the word.

Table 10.1 lists abbreviations that you can use to tell IA what part of a person's name you are selecting.

▶ **Tip:** If the first, middle, and last names in a database represent one person, the codes are `1F`, `1M`, and `1L`, respectively.

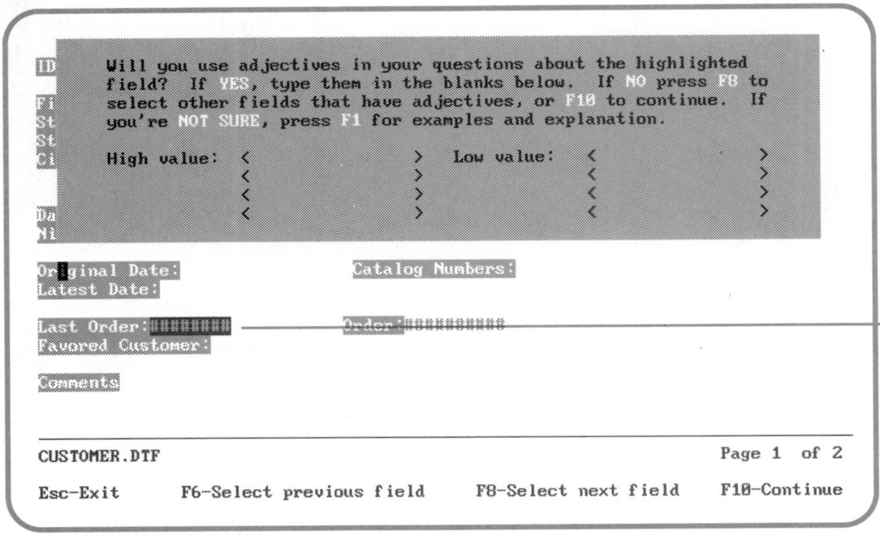

```
ID        Will you use adjectives in your questions about the highlighted
          field? If YES, type them in the blanks below.  If NO press F8 to
Fi        select other fields that have adjectives, or F10 to continue.  If
St        you're NOT SURE, press F1 for examples and explanation.
St
Ci        High value: <              >  Low value: <              >
                       <              >             <              >
                       <              >             <              >
Da                     <              >             <              >
Ni
Original Date:              Catalog Numbers:
Latest Date:

Last Order:████████ ───────── Order:█#########
Favored Customer:

Comments
_____
CUSTOMER.DTF                                        Page 1  of 2

Esc-Exit      F6-Select previous field    F8-Select next field    F10-Continue
```

IA shows you the fields for which you can define numeric adjectives.

Figure 10.12   Enter numeric adjectives on this screen, but remember that IA has a built-in vocabulary that contains common adjectives

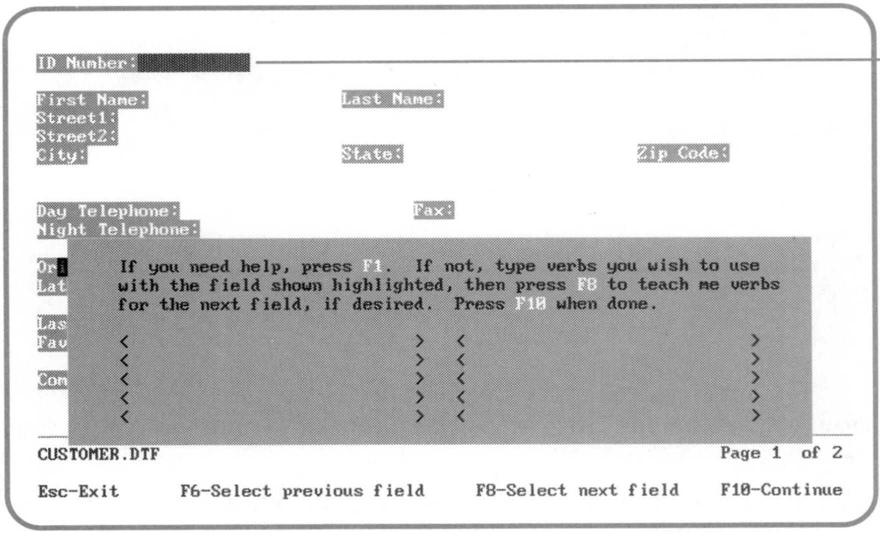

```
ID Number:██████████ ──────────────
First Name:                Last Name:
Street1:
Street2:
City:              State:                Zip Code:

Day Telephone:           Fax:
Night Telephone:
Or█     If you need help, press F1.  If not, type verbs you wish to use
Lat     with the field shown highlighted, then press F8 to teach me verbs
        for the next field, if desired.  Press F10 when done.
Las
Fav     <              >  <              >
        <              >  <              >
Con     <              >  <              >
        <              >  <              >
        <              >  <              >
_____
CUSTOMER.DTF                                        Page 1  of 2

Esc-Exit      F6-Select previous field    F8-Select next field    F10-Continue
```

You can type verbs for one highlighted field at a time.

Figure 10.13   Type verbs in the current highlighted field and then move to another field by pressing either F8 or F6

*Table 10.1    Name Codes*

| Code | Part of Name | Usage | Meaning |
|------|-------------|-------|---------|
| W | Whole | 1W | The first name is a whole name. |
| F | First | 2F | The second name is a first name. |
| M | Middle | 2M | The second name is a middle name. |
| L | Last | 1L | The first name is a last name. |
| T | Title (Ms., Mr., Miss) | 1T | The first name is a title. |
| S | Suffix (III, Jr.) | 4S | The fourth name is a suffix. |

Table 10.2 lists the adjectives that IA already knows.

*Table 10.2    Adjectives that IA Knows*

| | | |
|------|------|------|
| above | higher | many |
| below | highest | maximum (max) |
| big | large | minimum (min) |
| bigger | larger | more |
| biggest | largest | most |
| bottom (min) | least | much |
| few | less | small |
| fewer | little | smaller |
| fewest | littler | smallest |
| great | littlest | top (max) |
| greater | low | under |
| greatest | lower | |
| high | lowest | |

**273**

---

▶ **Tip:** If you redesign a database, teach IA the new or changed database components. IA remembers the information associated with old fields but needs to be taught the new fields.

# Asking IA Questions

Select the Ask Me To Do Something option to ask IA to find some records, update them, make a report, or do something else related to File and Report activities.

## Q Asking IA To Do Something

1. From the Q&A Main menu, select Assistant.

   Q&A displays the Assistant menu.

2. Select Ask Me To Do Something.

   Q&A adds a dialog box for the screen.

3. Either enter the name of the database or have Q&A display a list of files from which you can select. After selecting a file, press Enter.

   Q&A displays a dialog box into which you enter a query. Below the dialog box is useful information about how to ask a question (Figure 10.14).

4. Type a question and press Enter.

   If IA does not think that you have worded the question clearly enough, it asks you questions, one at a time. Or, if it wants to show you its interpretation of your request, it asks you to confirm its interpretation (Figure 10.15).

5. Answer each question and press Enter.

   When the question is clear to IA, it processes the records and produces an answer.

6. Press F10 after you have reviewed the results and ask your next question. (If you want to display the last question you asked, press Shift-F7.

   Q&A displays a blank screen for a new question.

7. If you want to print the report, press F2. Optionally, press F8 to teach IA more words.

Q&A displays the Report Print Options screen.     □

IA can process many questions. If it thinks that your question is unclear, it continues to ask. To help you prepare questions or statements for IA, this section contains examples and descriptions related to the CUSTOMER database.

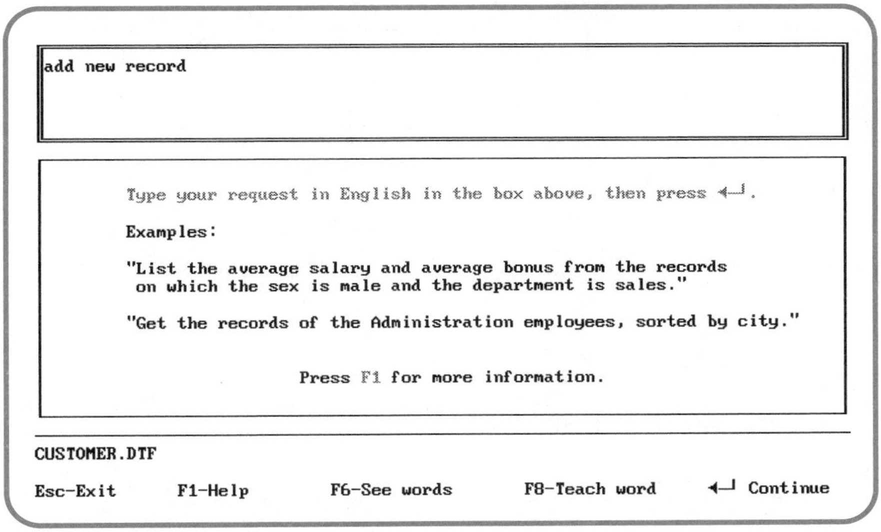

```
┌─────────────────────────────────────────────────────────────────┐
│ ┌───────────────────────────────────────────────────────────────┐ │
│ │add new record                                                 │ │
│ │                                                               │ │
│ │                                                               │ │
│ └───────────────────────────────────────────────────────────────┘ │
│ ┌───────────────────────────────────────────────────────────────┐ │
│ │                                                               │ │
│ │      Type your request in English in the box above, then press ◄┘. │ │
│ │                                                               │ │
│ │      Examples:                                                │ │
│ │                                                               │ │
│ │      "List the average salary and average bonus from the records │ │
│ │       on which the sex is male and the department is sales."  │ │
│ │                                                               │ │
│ │      "Get the records of the Administration employees, sorted by city." │ │
│ │                                                               │ │
│ │              Press F1 for more information.                   │ │
│ │                                                               │ │
│ └───────────────────────────────────────────────────────────────┘ │
│  CUSTOMER.DTF                                                      │
│                                                                   │
│  Esc-Exit      F1-Help       F6-See words      F8-Teach word    ◄┘ Continue │
└─────────────────────────────────────────────────────────────────┘
```

275

*Figure 10.14   Enter your query at the top of the screen*

## Retrieving Records

Use IA to retrieve records based on restrictions that are part of the question. IA decides whether to produce a report based on the type of question you ask.

You don't have to enter a query in any formal way—IA recognizes your queries whether or not they have initial capitalization or end with question marks or periods.

> ▶ **Tip:** If you need to rephrase a question, press Shift-F7 to display the original question and then edit it.

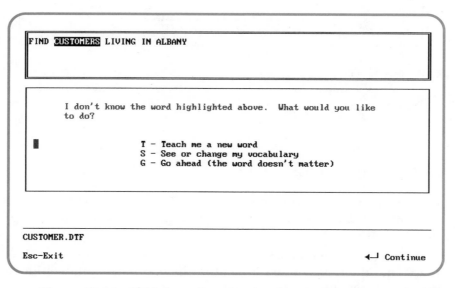

```
┌─────────────────────────────────────────────────────────────┐
│ ┌───────────────────────────────────────────────────────┐   │
│ │ ADD NEW RECORD                                          │   │
│ │                                                         │   │
│ │                                                         │   │
│ └───────────────────────────────────────────────────────┘   │
│ ┌───────────────────────────────────────────────────────┐   │
│ │                 Shall I do the following?               │   │
│ │                                                         │   │
│ │        CHANGE THE DATABASE                              │   │
│ │        by adding a new empty record for you to fill in. │   │
│ │ ▓                                                       │   │
│ │                                                         │   │
│ │          Yes - Continue        No - Cancel request      │   │
│ └───────────────────────────────────────────────────────┘   │
│                                                               │
│ ────────────────────────────────────────────────────────    │
│ CUSTOMER.DTF                                                  │
│                                                               │
│ Esc-Cancel                                    ◄┘ Continue     │
└─────────────────────────────────────────────────────────────┘
```

**276**

*Figure 10.15    IA interprets your query and asks you if it is correct*

```
┌─────────────────────────────────────────────────────────────┐
│ ┌───────────────────────────────────────────────────────┐   │
│ │ FIND CUSTOMERS LIVING IN ALBANY                         │   │
│ │                                                         │   │
│ │                                                         │   │
│ └───────────────────────────────────────────────────────┘   │
│ ┌───────────────────────────────────────────────────────┐   │
│ │     I don't know the word highlighted above.  What would you like │
│ │  to do?                                                 │   │
│ │ ▓                                                       │   │
│ │              T - Teach me a new word                    │   │
│ │              S - See or change my vocabulary            │   │
│ │              G - Go ahead (the word doesn't matter)     │   │
│ │                                                         │   │
│ └───────────────────────────────────────────────────────┘   │
│                                                               │
│ ────────────────────────────────────────────────────────    │
│ CUSTOMER.DTF                                                  │
│                                                               │
│ Esc-Exit                                      ◄┘ Continue     │
└─────────────────────────────────────────────────────────────┘
```

*Figure 10.16    If IA doesn't understand a word in a query, it asks you to clarify*

## Ad Hoc Queries

If you have taken the time to teach IA about your database, you can ask it questions as they pop into your head. For example:

```
Who has the largest order?
```

Ask this question to find out what customer has the highest value in the Order field. Because "order" is a word in IA's vocabulary, it asks you to clarify what it means to you. You can identify order as a field on your form, a word in IA's vocabulary, or something completely different.

If you ask

```
Where does Smith live?
```

IA identifies every customer named Smith and creates a report, if more than one customer is Smith.

If you ask

```
Whose order is between Adams and Carter?
```

IA prints a table if it finds more than one value.

If you have just asked a question such as

```
What person named Carter lives in Rochester?
```

you can ask a follow-up question:

```
What is his address?
```

## Creating and Running Reports

You also can ask IA specifically to produce either a columnar or cross tab report, or you can word a question in such a way that the result is a report:

```
How many customers exist in Albany?
```

277

"Exist" is defined in IA's vocabulary. If you want to teach IA the word "live," type the question

```
How many customers live in Albany?
```

IA does not know the word "live" so it gives you the following choices:

```
Edit the highlighted word.
Teach me a new word.
See or change my vocabulary.
Go ahead (the word doesn't matter).
```

If you enter

```
Cross-tab order by last name by city.
```

IA shows a cross tab report with Last Name as the column and city as the row.

You also can ask IA to run a report that you have already designed, for instance, one that is named "sample col report":

```
Run sample col report
```

## Giving IA a New Name

If the place at which you work has decided on a unique name for Assistant, simply ask IA to change its name:

```
Change your name to Helper
```

## New Words and Synonyms

You can teach IA a word that you use regularly and that it does not already have in its vocabulary.

You can press F8 as you are typing a query or even when the dialog box is empty. Or as IA asks you questions, you can add a word. After you press F8, IA asks you whether the word is for the subject of the database, a field name, a synonym, a verb, or other (which you select if you don't know the category). If the new word is a synonym, IA displays a screen into which you enter the new word and the word or phrase already in the IA vocabulary.

## Updating Records

You also can use IA to update some or even all of your records:

```
Add $50 to all last orders.
```

IA recognizes the field Last Order (even though it is all lower-case and plural) and asks you whether you want to change the data in the database, create a report with a calculated column, or look for another interpretation. If you choose to change the data in the database, this is the equivalent of a Mass Update.

> ⊘ **Caution:** Using IA to update records has the potential to be very destructive, so ask carefully.

**279**

## Adding Records

If you request it, IA gives you a blank form to fill in. After you have completed the form, you can press F10 to add another form or press Shift-F10 to save the last form and end the session. After ending the session, Q&A displays the IA query screen. Type

```
Add form
```

You also can add information to a database without IA displaying a blank form for you to fill in:

```
Fill in a new record with "Jones" in last name and "Mary"
in first name
```

After adding the information, however, IA displays the filled-in form. You can either fill in more forms or press Shift-F10 to return to the IA query screen.

> ▶ **Tip:** If you give IA information for a new record, enclose the text within quotes.

## What You Have Learned

▶ Q&A provides two assistants—the Query Guide and the Intelligent Assistant.

▶ You can use Query Guide or the Intelligent Assistant to ask questions about your database, to change or add records, or to create columnar and cross tab reports.

▶ You can use both the assistants without teaching them about your database, but it's better to teach them.

▶ Use the Query Guide, especially when you are a beginner, to build your query piece by piece.

▶ You can use the Intelligent Assistant, which has a large built-in vocabulary of words, to structure many types of queries and to perform many other functions

**280**

*Chapter 11*

# Q&A Utilities

## In This Chapter

281

- ► *Customizing printer installation*
- ► *Using font description files*
- ► *Using DOS-type commands within Q&A*
- ► *Setting global options*
- ► *Setting alternate programs*

Use the Q&A Utilities to do the odd jobs that make it easier to use Q&A, your computer, and your printer. For example, if you buy a new laser printer, you can install it and change the Q&A fonts to take advantage of the printer's capabilities. Utilities even enables you to use certain DOS functions without leaving Q&A and gives you the ability to start other programs from the Main menu. You also can change some defaults so that Q&A better meets your needs.

## Customizing Printer Installation

When you installed Q&A, you learned how to install from one to five printers. Refer to Appendix A for information on basic printer installation.

This section describes how to select a printer option so that you can print a file at a later time and how to install an Intel Connection CoProcessor fax board. You also learn how to change certain printer settings by selecting special printer options.

Select the File option to define a disk file to which you can print a file on your hard drive; then you can actually use your printer to print this file at a later time. Because you also define your printer when you select the File option, printed output is identical to any other output from your printer.

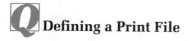

## Defining a Print File

1. If you are not currently in the Q&A directory, change to it by typing CD\QA (where QA represents the name of the directory in which you installed the program). Start Q&A by typing QA.

   Q&A displays the Title screen and then the Main menu.

2. Select Utilities and press Enter.

   Q&A displays the Utilities menu.

3. Select Install Printer.

   Q&A displays the Printer Selection screen (Figure 11.1).

4. Highlight Printer C. Look for the File option, which is under the Port heading. Press Enter.

   Q&A displays the Port Selection screen (Figure 11.2). FILE is highlighted. The Q&A printer is PtrC, and the printer model and mode is Basic (Vanilla) Non-Laser Printer, which is the default.

5. With FILE highlighted, press Enter again.

   Q&A displays the List of Printer Manufacturers screen (Figure 11.3).

6. Move the selection bar until the name of your printer's manufacturer is highlighted. If you don't see the appropriate name on the first screen, press PgDn. Press Enter.

Names of models for that manufacturer are displayed (Figure 11.4).

7. Move the selection bar until your printer's model name is highlighted. If you don't see the appropriate name on the first screen, press PgDn. Press Enter.

Q&A displays specific information about your printer (Figure 11.5) and offers several options.

8. Press Enter again to confirm that you have read the information about your printer.

Q&A displays a message stating that your printer has been installed.

9. Select Yes or No to indicate whether you want to install another printer or fax.

If you don't install another printer, Q&A returns to the Utilities menu. □

**283**

```
                        PRINTER SELECTION
                        ================

    A "Q&A PRINTER" is a combination of a PORT and a specific PRINTER MODEL
    and MODE (e.g. draft or letter).   Press F1 if you want more explanation.

    Highlight the Q&A PRINTER you want to install by pressing ↑  or ↓, then
    press ←┘.

    ┌──────────────────┬──────────┬─────────────────────────────────────┐
    │ Q&A PRINTER      │ PORT     │ PRINTER MODEL AND MODE              │
    ├──────────────────┼──────────┼─────────────────────────────────────┤
    │ Printer A (PtrA) │ LPT1     │ Basic (Vanilla) Non-laser printer   │
    │ Printer B (PtrB) │ LPT2     │ Basic (Vanilla) Non-laser printer   │
    │ Printer C (PtrC) │ LPT3     │ Basic (Vanilla) Non-laser printer   │
    │ Printer D (PtrD) │ COM1     │ Basic (Vanilla) Non-laser printer   │
    │ Printer E (PtrE) │ COM2     │ Basic (Vanilla) Non-laser printer   │
    └──────────────────┴──────────┴─────────────────────────────────────┘



    Esc-Exit                    F1-Help                    ←┘ Continue
```

Select Printer A for the printer that you use most often.

*Figure 11.1   The Printer Selection screen*

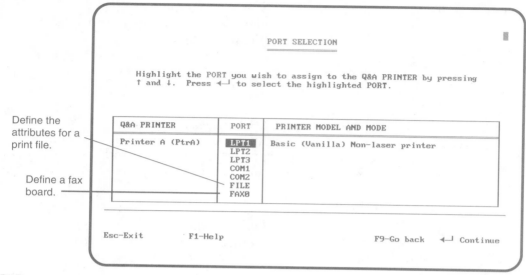

Define the attributes for a print file.

Define a fax board.

Figure 11.2   *The Port Selection screen shows you the name of the printer that you highlighted on the Printer Selection screen, along with its port, FILE*

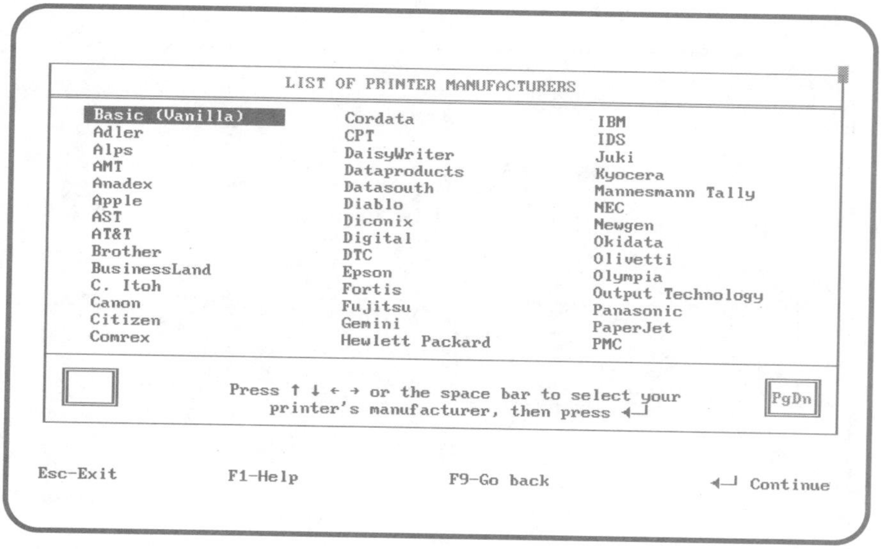

284

Figure 11.3   *The List of Printer Manufacturers displays the names of manufacturers that Q&A supports*

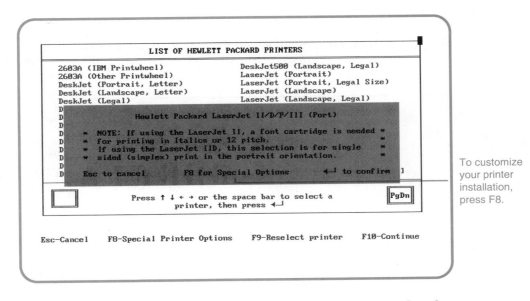

```
              LIST OF HEWLETT PACKARD PRINTERS

2603A (IBM Printwheel)              DeskJet500 (Landscape, Legal)
2603A (Other Printwheel)           LaserJet (Portrait)
DeskJet (Portrait, Letter)         LaserJet (Portrait, Legal Size)
DeskJet (Landscape, Letter)        LaserJet (Landscape)
DeskJet (Legal)                    LaserJet (Landscape, Legal)
DeskJet (Envelope)                 LaserJet (Envelope)
DeskJet + (Portrait, Letter)       LaserJet IID (Portrait,Duplex)
DeskJet + (Portrait, Legal)        LaserJet IID (Port,Leg,Duplex)
DeskJet + (Landscape, Letter)      LaserJet IID (Landscape,Duplex)
DeskJet + (Landscape, Legal)       LaserJet IID (Land,Leg,Duplex)
DeskJet + (Envelope)               LaserJet IID (Port, A4, Duplex)
DeskJet500 (Portrait, Letter)      LaserJet IID (Land, A4, Duplex)
DeskJet500 (Portrait, Legal)       LaserJet II/D/P/III (Port)
DeskJet500 (Landscape, Letter)     LaserJet II/D/P/III (Port) [NO GR]

        Press ↑ ↓ ← → or the space bar to select a      PgDn
              printer, then press ↵

Esc-Exit        F1-Help        F9-Reselect Manufacturer    ↵ Continue
```

Select from
these options
to install one
printer in up
to five modes.

*Figure 11.4   The list of models for your printer's manufacturer
gives you a choice of selecting one*

**285**

```
              LIST OF HEWLETT PACKARD PRINTERS

2603A (IBM Printwheel)              DeskJet500 (Landscape, Legal)
2603A (Other Printwheel)           LaserJet (Portrait)
DeskJet (Portrait, Letter)         LaserJet (Portrait, Legal Size)
DeskJet (Landscape, Letter)        LaserJet (Landscape)
DeskJet (Legal)                    LaserJet (Landscape, Legal)
D
D        Hewlett Packard LaserJet II/D/P/III (Port)
D
D    * NOTE: If using the LaserJet II, a font cartridge is needed *
D    * for printing in Italics or 12 pitch.                       *
D    * If using the LaserJet IID, this selection is for single    *
D    * sided (simplex) print in the portrait orientation.         *
D
D    Esc to cancel      F8 for Special Options     ↵ to confirm   ]
D

        Press ↑ ↓ ← → or the space bar to select a      PgDn
              printer, then press ↵

Esc-Cancel   F8-Special Printer Options   F9-Reselect printer   F10-Continue
```

To customize
your printer
installation,
press F8.

*Figure 11.5   This screen displays specific information related to
the printer model that you have selected*

The Utilities menu allows you to

▶ Install as many as five printers
▶ Modify font files
▶ Use DOS file facilities
▶ Set global options
▶ Set alternate programs

The Printer Selection screen shows you the names of the printers that you have installed along with their port assignments. This screen also enables you to install more printers or define a print file or Intel Connection CoProcessor fax board.

Select the Fax option to define an Intel Connection CoProcessor fax board so that you can send Q&A files to other fax machines. Fine output has 200 by 200 dots per inch. Standard output has 200 by 100 dots per inch. The 80-column option has 10 characters per inch and 66 lines per page. This option is ideal for letters or reports. The 132-column option has compressed characters and 88 lines per page. This option produces spreadsheet-type output. You must have fax software installed to define a fax to Q&A.

---

▶ **Note:** You can send almost any type of Q&A file via fax. The only exceptions are fonts, print enhancements, and the *GRAPH* command.

---

**Defining a Fax**

1. If you are not currently in the Q&A directory, change to it by typing CD \QA. Start Q&A by typing QA.

   Q&A displays the Title screen and then the Main menu.

2. Select Utilities and press Enter.

   Q&A displays the Utilities menu.

3. Select Install Printer.

   Q&A displays the Printer Selection screen.

4. With the highlight anywhere on the screen, press Enter.

   Q&A displays the Port Selection screen.

286

5. Highlight FAX0 and press Enter.

Q&A displays the Special Port Options screen.

6. Select one of the fax options and press Enter.

Q&A displays a message stating your printer is installed and asking if you want to install another. □

You can customize your printer installation by using special printer options.

## Defining Special Printer Options

1. If you are not currently in the Q&A directory, change to it by typing CD \QA. Start Q&A by typing QA.

Q&A displays the Title screen and then the Main menu.

2. Select Utilities and press Enter.

Q&A displays the Utilities menu.

3. Select Install printer.

Q&A displays the Printer Selection screen. Assuming that you have already installed a printer, you can see the port, printer model, and specific attributes about your printer definition (mode) on this screen.

4. Highlight the name of the printer (PtrA–PtrE) for which you want to define special options; then press Enter.

Q&A displays the Port Selection screen.

5. With the highlight remaining on the name of the printer for which you want to define special options, press Enter.

Q&A displays the List of Printer Manufacturers screen with the selected printer highlighted.

6. Keep the highlight on the name of your printer and press Enter.

Q&A displays a list of printer models with your printer model highlighted.

**287**

7. With the highlight on the name of your printer model, press Enter.

Q&A displays specific information about your printer and gives you the choice of pressing F8 for Special Printer Options.

8. Press F8.

Q&A displays the Special Printer Options screen (Figure 11.6).

9. Press any combination of cursor movement keys to move the highlight from option to option. Then either move the highlight from Yes to No or type a new value in Length of Timeout or Font File Name fields. Then press F9 to reselect a printer, F10 to select more options, or Esc to return to the Utilities menu.

If you press F9, Q&A returns you to the list of printer models for your printer's manufacturer. If you press F10, the More Special Printer Options screen appears (Figure 11.7).

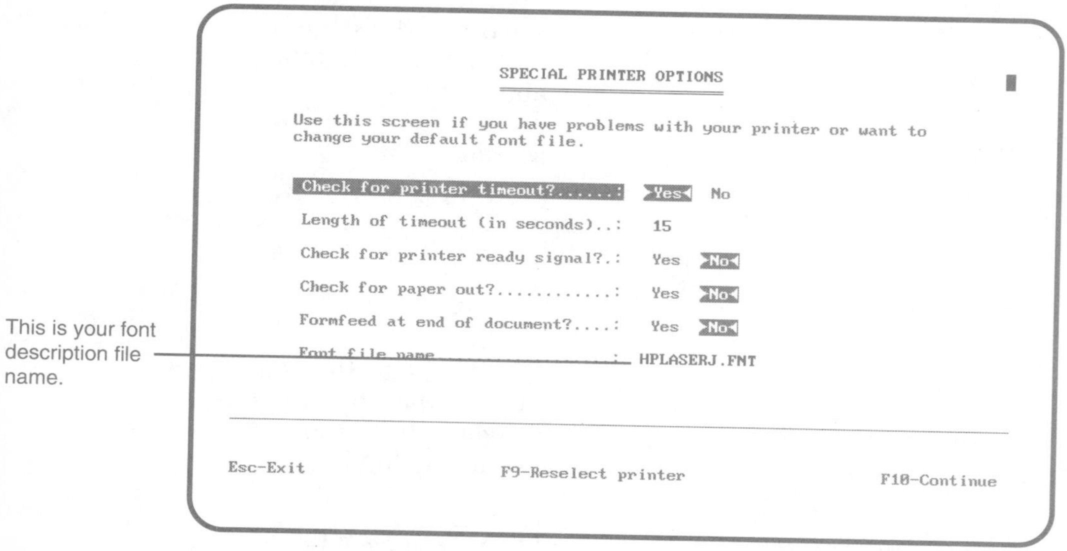

**288**

```
                     SPECIAL PRINTER OPTIONS                    ▌

          Use this screen if you have problems with your printer or want to
          change your default font file.

           Check for printer timeout?......:  ►Yes◄  No

           Length of timeout (in seconds)..:  15

           Check for printer ready signal?.:  Yes  ►No◄

           Check for paper out?............:  Yes  ►No◄

           Formfeed at end of document?....:  Yes  ►No◄

           Font file name                 :  HPLASERJ.FNT


          ─────────────────────────────────────────────────────────

          Esc-Exit              F9-Reselect printer          F10-Continue
```

This is your font description file name.

*Figure 11.6   The Special Printer Options screen allows you to correct a Q&A printer problem or change the default font file (This screen is for a parallel (LPT) printer.)*

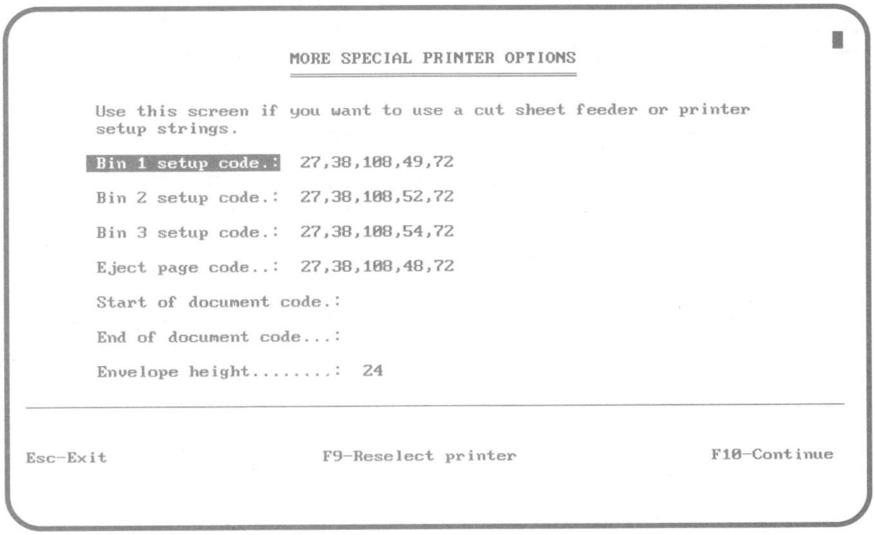

```
┌─────────────────────────────────────────────────────────────────┐
│                                                              ■    │
│              MORE SPECIAL PRINTER OPTIONS                         │
│              ─────────────────────────────                        │
│                                                                   │
│      Use this screen if you want to use a cut sheet feeder or printer │
│      setup strings.                                               │
│                                                                   │
│      ┌─────────────────┐                                          │
│      │ Bin 1 setup code.:│  27,38,108,49,72                       │
│      └─────────────────┘                                          │
│      Bin 2 setup code.:  27,38,108,52,72                          │
│                                                                   │
│      Bin 3 setup code.:  27,38,108,54,72                          │
│                                                                   │
│      Eject page code..:  27,38,108,48,72                          │
│                                                                   │
│      Start of document code.:                                     │
│                                                                   │
│      End of document code...:                                     │
│                                                                   │
│      Envelope height........:  24                                 │
│                                                                   │
│  ─────────────────────────────────────────────────────────────── │
│                                                                   │
│   Esc—Exit              F9—Reselect printer          F10—Continue │
│                                                                   │
└─────────────────────────────────────────────────────────────────┘
```

*Figure 11.7   The More Special Printer Options screen enables
you to use a cut sheet feeder or printer setup strings  (This
screen is for a parallel (LPT) printer.)*

**289**

# Modifying Font Files

Use this Utilities option to add, change, or delete font description
files. Note that font description files only *describe* the fonts; they are
not the fonts themselves.

> ⊘ **Caution:** Modifying Font File is an advanced, and very
> dangerous, option to use. If you decide to proceed, back
> up the font description files that you intend to change. Make a
> copy of the file that you want to modify and then experiment on
> the duplicate file rather than the original font description file.

## **Q** Creating or Modifying a Font Description File

1. From the Main menu, choose Utilities.

   Q&A displays the Utilities menu.

2. Choose Modify Font File.

   Q&A displays the Modifying Fonts screen (Figure 11.8) and asks for the name of the font file.

3. If you want to modify an existing font file, type its name and press Enter. If you can't remember the name of the file that you want to modify, press Enter to see a list of files in the current directory. Select a file and press Enter. If you want to create a new font file, type a new, unique font file name and press Enter.

   Q&A displays the Modify Font Descriptions screen (Figure 11.9).

**290**

4. For all new fonts, fill in the information in the upper portion of the screen. For proportional fonts, type the printer resolution and character width for each font you are defining. Press F10.

   Q&A adds the font you have defined to the current Font Description File.

5. Either press F9 (or F10).

   Q&A displays the previous (or next, if it is available) font in the file.

6. Press Shift-F10.

   Q&A saves all changes you have made to the Font Description File. □

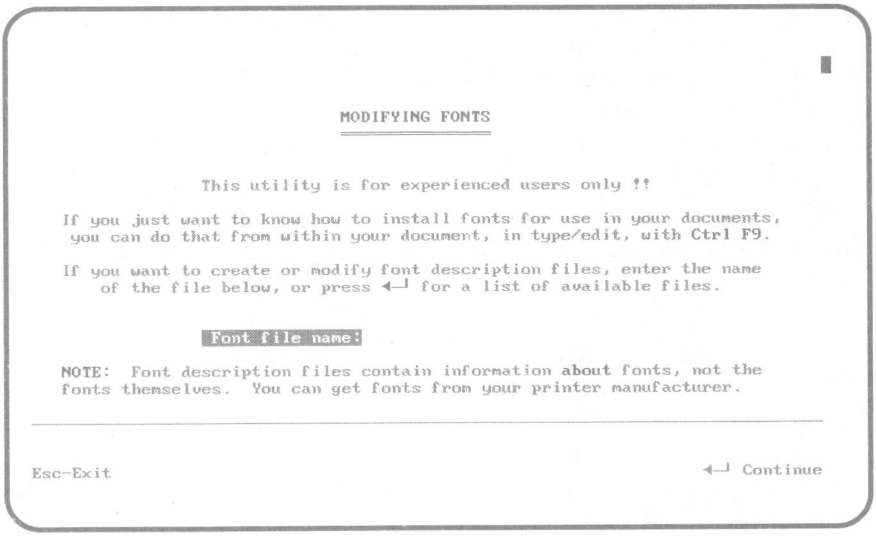

```
┌─────────────────────────────────────────────────────────────────┐
│                                                            ▪      │
│                                                                   │
│                         MODIFYING FONTS                           │
│                         ──────────────                            │
│                                                                   │
│            This utility is for experienced users only !!          │
│                                                                   │
│    If you just want to know how to install fonts for use in your documents,│
│      you can do that from within your document, in type/edit, with Ctrl F9.│
│                                                                   │
│    If you want to create or modify font description files, enter the name  │
│       of the file below, or press ◄┘ for a list of available files.        │
│                                                                   │
│             ▐Font file name:▌                                     │
│                                                                   │
│    NOTE:  Font description files contain information about fonts, not the   │
│    fonts themselves.  You can get fonts from your printer manufacturer.     │
│    ───────────────────────────────────────────────────────────   │
│                                                                   │
│    Esc-Exit                                         ◄┘ Continue   │
│                                                                   │
└─────────────────────────────────────────────────────────────────┘
```

*Figure 11.8    Enter the name of a font description file on the Modifying Fonts screen*

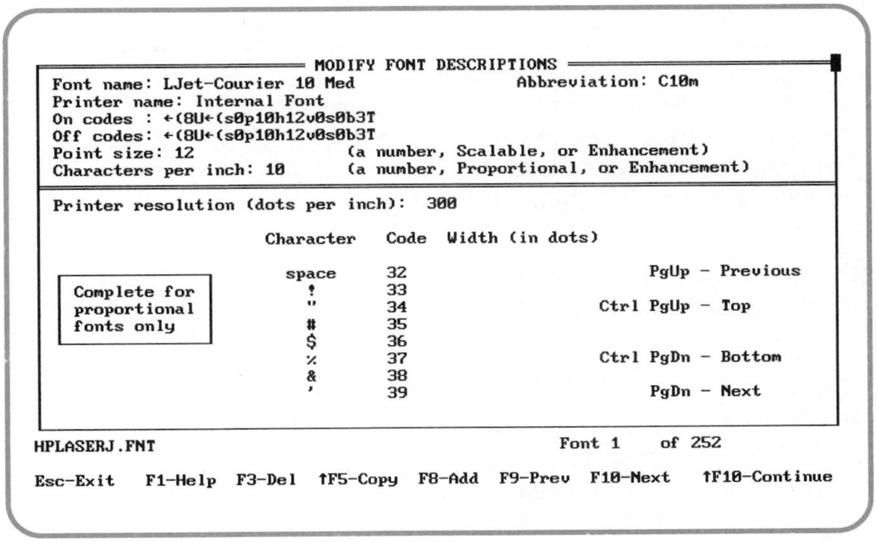

```
┌─────────────────────────────────────────────────────────────────┐
│  ═══════════════ MODIFY FONT DESCRIPTIONS ═══════════════  ▪     │
│  Font name: LJet-Courier 10 Med              Abbreviation: C10m   │
│  Printer name: Internal Font                                      │
│  On codes : ◄(8U◄(s0p10h12v0s0b3T                                 │
│  Off codes: ◄(8U◄(s0p10h12v0s0b3T                                 │
│  Point size: 12         (a number, Scalable, or Enhancement)      │
│  Characters per inch: 10   (a number, Proportional, or Enhancement)│
│  ───────────────────────────────────────────────────────────     │
│  Printer resolution (dots per inch):  300                         │
│                                                                   │
│                  Character   Code  Width (in dots)                │
│                    space      32                  PgUp - Previous │
│   ┌──────────────┐   !        33                                  │
│   │ Complete for │   "        34             Ctrl PgUp - Top      │
│   │ proportional │   #        35                                  │
│   │ fonts only   │   $        36                                  │
│   └──────────────┘   %        37             Ctrl PgDn - Bottom   │
│                      &        38                                  │
│                      '        39                  PgDn - Next     │
│  ───────────────────────────────────────────────────────────     │
│  HPLASERJ.FNT                          Font  1   of  252          │
│                                                                   │
│  Esc-Exit  F1-Help  F3-Del  ↑F5-Copy  F8-Add  F9-Prev  F10-Next  ↑F10-Continue│
└─────────────────────────────────────────────────────────────────┘
```

*Figure 11.9    Create or modify a font description on the Modify Font Descriptions screen*

Q&A supports all Postscript fonts. Because there are so many, you may have to download a specific font to your printer. If you have called for a Postscript font that is not available, your printer tries to load the font that is the most appropriate. Use the Font Assignments screen in the Write module to change Postscript point size, color level, line spacing, and so on.

Table 11.1 lists the keys that are available for the Modify Font Descriptions screen. The following paragraphs describe this screen's fields.

*Table 11.1   Modify Font Descriptions Keys*

| Key | Function |
| --- | --- |
| F3 | Deletes the current font description |
| Shift-F5 | Copies the current font description |
| F8 | Adds this font description to the current font description file |
| F9 | Refers to the previous font description |
| F10 | Refers to the next font description in the file |
| Shift-F10 | Saves the font description and continues |

*Font name* is the name that you give to the font description file. It is one to eight characters long and should have the extension .FNT. Refer to the Modify Font Descriptions help screen for the file-naming conventions that Q&A recommends.

*Abbreviation* is the four-character abbreviation that appears on the Font Assignment screen, the Text Enhancements and Fonts menu, and the status line when the cursor is on text formatted with this font.

*Printer name* is the name of the printer that uses this font description. When Q&A displays the Font Assignments screen, this printer name appears.

*On codes* and *Off codes* are the codes that the printer uses to turn the font on or off. Refer to the Modify Font Descriptions help screen for nonprinting on or off codes. If you are defining a scalable font, the on code must be an asterisk (*). For information about on codes for your printer, refer to the printer's reference manual.

> ⊘ **Caution:** Be especially careful when you enter on and off codes. If they are entered incorrectly, you may have difficulty printing.

*Point size* is either a point size number, E (for enhancement, such as underlined or italicized text), or S (for a scalable font). If you want to enter a number, you must know the point size for this font (from 1 to 999 for proportional fonts). Q&A decides the *leading* (or vertical space between lines of text).

When you enter S (for scalable fonts), you can set the leading by typing a number after the S. For example, s5 indicates that leading is set to 5.

*Characters per inch* is the number of characters that fit in an inch on a printed line. Either enter a number, E (for enhancement, such as underlined or italicized characters), or P (for proportionally spaced).

**293**

If you are creating or modifying a proportionally spaced font description, fill in these fields.

*Printer resolution* is the number of horizontal dots per inch for your printer.

*Width (in dots)* is the number of dots per inch required for each proportional character that is listed under Character on the Modify Font Descriptions screen. For example, you must know the width of these symbols: space, exclamation point (!), double quotes ("), pound sign (#), dollar sign ($), percent sign (%), ampersand (&), and single quote (').

# Using the DOS File Facilities

The DOS File Facilities enable you to

- ▶ Display a file directory
- ▶ Rename a file
- ▶ Delete a file
- ▶ Copy a file

These options are the equivalent of the DOS commands DIR, REN, DEL, and COPY, respectively. This means that you can use some DOS facilities without exiting Q&A.

For example, if you are not sure of the files in a directory (even a directory that is not related to Q&A), you can use the list option to display the files in that directory. If you have just thought of a better name for an existing database, you can rename it without exiting Q&A. If you no longer need a document file, use the Delete a File option. If you like the design of a database and want to use it as a template for a new database, use the Copy a File option.

The following Quick Steps show you how to rename, delete, and copy a file using the DOS File Facilities.

### **Q** Using the DOS File Facilities

| | |
|---|---|
| 1. From the Main menu, choose Utilities. | Q&A displays the Utilities menu. |
| 2. Choose DOS File Facilities. | Q&A displays the DOS File Facilities screen. |
| 3. Choose from the options— List Files, Rename a File, Delete a File, or Copy a File. | Q&A adds a dialog box to the screen with the option you selected and the current directory. If you have worked on a file during this session, the file name is displayed. If the name of an existing file appears in the dialog box and you have selected List Files from the DOS File Facilities, when you press Enter, Q&A does not respond. If the name of an existing file appears in the dialog box and you have selected one of the other options from the DOS File Facilities screen, the dialog box reflects your choice. |

4. If no file name appears in the dialog box, press Enter; or if you want to search another directory, type its name and press Enter.

Q&A displays a listing screen, which shows the files that you specified (Figure 11.10). The List of Files heading displays the last file or wildcard information that you typed.

5. Press Up, Down, Left, Right, or Spacebar to move the highlight to the file name you want.

Q&A changes the name in the prompt line to reflect the movement of the highlight. As the highlight moves, a one- or two-line description for a specific file appears at the bottom of the screen.

6. Use the Search option to narrow the search within the listing screen. Press F7 and then move the cursor to the blank space at the top left of the screen.

The cursor is positioned in the dialog box so that you can enter a file name or a combination of wildcard characters.

7. If you want to rename the file that you have selected or typed, press F8.

Q&A asks for the new file name.

8. Enter the file name; then press F10.

Q&A issues a message stating the new name of the file.

9. If you want to delete the file that you have selected or typed, press F3.

Q&A displays a warning message that the file is to be deleted, and allows you to cancel the deletion. If you delete the file, Q&A issues a message stating that it has been deleted.

10. If you want to copy the file that you have selected or typed, press F5.

Q&A asks for the name of the target file, which is the file to which you want to copy the selected file (Figure 11.11).

11. Enter the file name; then press F10 or Enter.

Q&A issues a message stating that the file is copied. □

295

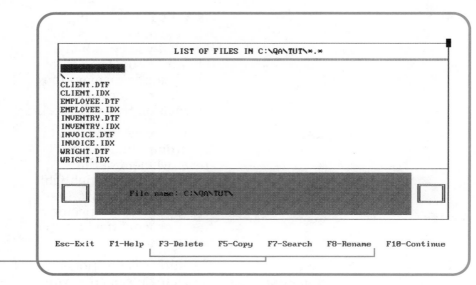

Press any
of these
keys to use
Q&A's DOS
facilities.

**296**

*Figure 11.10   The listing screen shows you all or part of the
files in a directory or subdirectory*

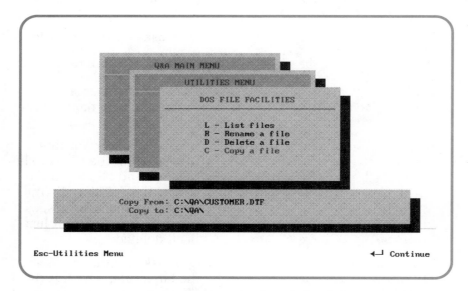

*Figure 11.11   Q&A asks you for the name of the target file or
the name of the copy of the original file*

Use wildcard characters to search for or change a group of files rather than one file. For example, if you want to see a list of all files beginning with a specific character, or ending with a certain extension, use wildcard characters. You also can use them to change the names of every file in a particular group. The two wildcard characters that DOS recognizes are the asterisk (*) and the question mark (?). The asterisk represents all characters and the question mark represents one character. Table 11.2 offers several examples of wildcard usage.

*Table 11.2    Wildcard Characters*

| Wildcard | Function |
| --- | --- |
| *.* | Searches for every file with every extension |
| *.DTF | Searches for every file with the .DTF extension |
| Q*.OVL | Searches for every file beginning with Q and having the extension .OVL |
| *.??? | Searches for every file that has a three-character extension |
| LTR*.DOC | Searches for every file starting with LTR, containing up to five more characters, and having the extension .DOC |
| LTR?????.DOC | Searches for every file starting with LTR, containing five more characters, and having the extension .DOC |
| F????E.* | Searches for every file starting with F, containing four other characters, ending with E, and having any extension |

**297**

# Setting Global Options

The Set Global Options screen allows you to define subdirectories, decrease your use of the Enter key, and identify yourself to the network. However, if you are not using the network facility, Q&A tells you that the network identifier is not set. The Set Global Defaults menu allows you to

▶   Set the path through Q&A directories and subdirectories

▶ Tell Q&A to start a function as soon as you type the first character of a menu choice

▶ Identify yourself as a member of a network, if Q&A is installed as part of a network

For an example of the Set Global Options screen, see Figure 11.12.

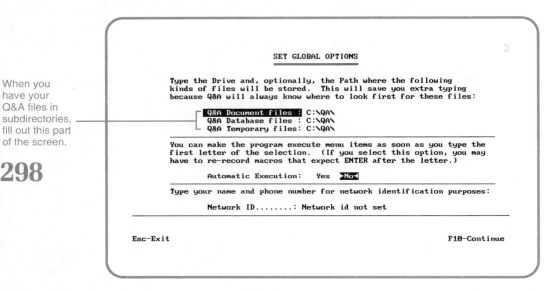

When you have your Q&A files in subdirectories, fill out this part of the screen.

**298**

*Figure 11.12    The Set Global Options screen*

## Setting the Path through Directories and Subdirectories

Q&A automatically knows where to look for three groups of files: database files, document files, and temporary files. When you first use Q&A, it knows that it can find these file groups in a single directory, the one that you defined when you installed Q&A. Later on, when you create subdirectories under the original directory, you can use Set Global Options to tell Q&A the default location of the file groups. Using this option makes Q&A file searches more efficient. Of course, if you store files in other subdirectories that are not defined here, Q&A won't know that; it looks in these subdirectories.

## *Q* **Setting Default Directories**

1. Choose Utilities from the Q&A Main menu.

   Q&A displays the Utilities menu.

2. Choose Set Global Options from the Utilities menu.

   Q&A displays the Set Global Options screen.

3. Enter path names for document files, database files, and temporary files, and press F10.

   You are returned to the Utilities menu.

   □

## *Setting Automatic Execution*

You can tell Q&A to start a function as soon as you type the first character of a menu choice. This saves you many keystrokes.

**299**

> ▶ **Tip:** If you use cursor movement keys to select a menu choice, you have to press Enter; in this case, Automatic Execution does not work.

## *Q* **Setting Automatic Execution**

1. Choose Utilities from the Q&A Main menu.

   Q&A displays the Utilities menu.

2. Choose Set Global Options from the Utilities menu.

   Q&A displays the Set Global Options screen.

3. Choose Yes or No for Automatic Execution.

   If you choose Yes, Q&A executes a menu choice when you type the first character. If you choose No, Q&A executes a menu choice after you type the first character and press Enter.

4. Press F10.

   You are returned to the Utilities menu.

   □

> **Tip:** If you change to Automatic Execution after creating macros (especially those that contain Enter keystrokes), you may have to edit them.

## Identifying Yourself to a Network

If you are a member of a Q&A network, other members should know that you sometimes work on common files. To identify yourself as a member of a network, you have to formally add your name and, optionally, a telephone number.

**300**

### *Q* Identifying Yourself to a Network

| | |
|---|---|
| 1. Choose Utilities from the Q&A Main menu. | Q&A displays the Utilities menu. |
| 2. Choose Set Global Options from the Utilities menu. | Q&A displays the Set Global Options screen. |
| 3. Type your name and, optionally, your telephone number for network ID. Press F10. | You are returned to the Utilities menu. |

□

# Setting Alternate Programs

Q&A allows you to define up to six alternate programs or Q&A macros on the Q&A Main menu.

When you add a program, you can start it without leaving Q&A. For example, if your spreadsheet program is installed as an alternate program, you can import spreadsheet files to Q&A or export Q&A files to the spreadsheet program without exiting Q&A. When you quit an alternate program, you return to the Q&A Main menu, not to the DOS prompt.

If you define often-used macros as alternate programs, you can get to them more easily. Complex menus, which use several modules, are easier to use from (and end at) the Main menu. For more information about macros, see Chapter 12.

> ▶ **Note:** Any macro you install on the Main menu must reside in the macro file that is currently loaded into memory.

## Installing an Alternate Program

1. Choose Utilities from the Q&A Main menu.

   Q&A displays the Utilities menu.

2. Choose Set Alternate Programs.

   Q&A displays the Alternate Programs screen. (For an example of this screen with the spreadsheet program Quattro defined, see Figure 11.13.)

3. Enter the drive, path, file name and extension of an alternate program, and the menu selection number. Press F10.

   Your alternate program is installed, and Q&A returns you to the Utilities menu.

   □

**301**

```
                        ALTERNATE PROGRAMS
                        ═══════════════════

     You can install up to six alternate programs for the Main Menu.
     You can then execute those programs by selecting them at that menu.
     When you exit from these programs, you will return automatically
     to the Main Menu.
                ┌─────────────────────────┐
                │ Alternate program 1:     │                        ■   Fill out the
                  Menu selection.....:                                   complete
                  Alternate program 2:                                   path.
                  Menu selection.....:
                  Alternate program 3:
                  Menu selection.....:
                  Alternate program 4:
                  Menu selection.....:
                  Alternate program 5:
                  Menu selection.....:
                  Alternate program 6:
                  Menu selection.....:

     Esc-Exit                                        F10-Continue
```

*Figure 11.13    This shows the Alternate Programs screen with Quattro Pro defined as an alternate program*

You cannot install an alternate program unless you know the name of the directory in which the program is located and the file name and extension of the main program file.

If you enter a specific word to start the alternate program, that word is most likely the file name. To verify this, look in the directory in which the program is located. Enter the following DOS command:

```
DIR fn.*
```

where fn represents the word that you enter to start the program and the asterisk (*) represents any file extension. If you see a file name with the extension .EXE or .COM, you have verified that this is the program file. If the extension is .BAT, this is probably a file that starts the program.

As an example, let's say you want to start Quattro Pro from Q&A. If the program directory is QPRO and the reference manual tells you to start the program by typing Q, look for the program name, which in this case is Q.EXE. When you want to start an alternate program from Q&A, go to the Main menu, then type the first character. Remember that if you have set Automatic Execution to Yes, you don't have to press Enter.

---

⊘ **Caution:** If an alternate program has the same first letter as a Q&A module (for example Write and Word), either start the alternate program with a different first letter or set Automatic Execution to No. If you forget to do this, use your mouse to move the cursor to the desired name. Then correct the Alternate Programs screen as soon as you can.

---

# What You Have Learned

► Q&A can print to a printer, a disk file, or to an Intel fax board.

► Although Q&A allows you to create or modify font description files, you should be an expert user before you do so.

► You can use some DOS-like facilities to list, rename, delete, or copy files.

► You can customize Q&A so that you can choose a Q&A option by typing one letter.

► Q&A allows you to start as many as six programs or Q&A macros from the Main menu.

**303**

# Using Q&A's Macros and Programming Features

## In This Chapter

▶ *Defining, saving, and running macros*

▶ *Deleting, getting, and clearing macros*

▶ *Creating custom menus*

▶ *Editing macros*

▶ *Programming with Q&A*

▶ *Using programming expressions in merge documents*

If you regularly enter a series of commands to accomplish an operation, you can combine the commands into one command file, a *macro*. For example, every time you add data to a new form, you have to select File and Add Data, and name the database. You can define a macro so that you press a single key combination to issue those steps automatically.

> ⊘ **Caution:** When you are defining macros, don't use a key that Q&A already uses. Refer to the inside back cover of this book for a list of Q&A keys.

From Q&A's Macro menu, you can perform all types of macro functions—run, define, delete, get, save, and clear—and, in addition, create a menu.

# Defining a Macro

You can define a macro and make a recording of it so that you can get it and run it later.

## *Q* Creating and Recording a Macro

1. From any screen, including the Main menu, press Shift-F2.

   Q&A displays the Macro menu (Figure 12.1).

2. Select Define Macro.

   Q&A asks you to assign a key identifier.

3. Press a key combination to uniquely identify the macro.

   If you assign a key combination that is already in use, Q&A informs you. You can select another key combination or overwrite the existing macro. If you do not define a key combination, Q&A defines one for you.

4. Use Q&A menus and keys to perform each step that you want added to the macro.

   Q&A indicates that the macro recorder is turned on with a flashing square at the bottom right of your screen.

5. Press Alt-F2 any time you want to enter text.

   Q&A indicates that it is ready to accept text when the regular cursor on the screen changes shape to a flashing rectangle. At this point, the macro recorder is turned off.

6. Press Alt-F2 to resume recording.

   The cursor changes back to its original shape.

7.  Press Shift-F2 to indicate that you are finished recording the macro.

    Q&A displays the Macro Options dialog box (Figure 12.2).

8.  Enter a macro description—which can be as many as 31 characters, including spaces but excluding a quotation mark—in the Macro name field.

    If you have defined a key combination, it already appears in this field. If you add a description, the key combination defined to run the macro is still in effect.

9.  Select Yes or No for the Show Screen field.

    If you select Yes, the macro displays menus, screens, and all activities as it runs. If you select No, the macro keeps the original screen on display.

10. In the End with Menu field, enter the name of a custom menu.

    Q&A displays this menu when the macro ends.

**307**

11. Optionally, press Alt-F7 for a list of menus and assigned mouse buttons. If you want to enter the name of a custom menu here, you can.

    Small arrows indicate that there are more names than can be displayed at one time.

12. Press F10 to accept the settings in the dialog box. (If you press Esc, you do not save it and can run it only during this session.)

    Q&A adds a dialog box to the bottom of the screen (Figure 12.3). The macro file name, usually `QAMACRO.ASC`, is the default Q&A macro file.

13. Press Enter.

    Q&A saves the macro to the macro file.  ☐

# Saving a Macro

You can save a macro when you define it or you can save it later in the Q&A session.

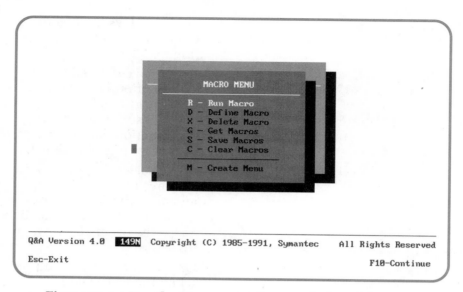

**308**

Figure 12.1   *Use the Macro menu to run, define, delete, get,*
*save, and clear macros*

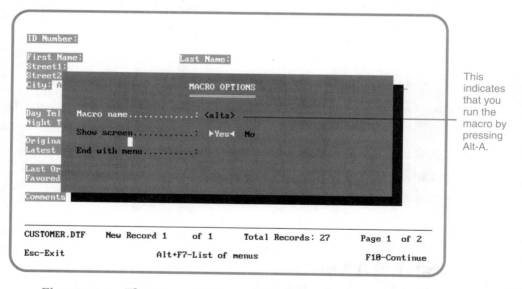

This
indicates
that you
run the
macro by
pressing
Alt-A.

Figure 12.2   *The Macro Options dialog box allows you to*
*specify information for this macro*

```
┌─────────────────────────────────────────────────────────────┐
│  ID Number:                                                   │
│                                                               │
│  First Name:                     Last Name:                   │
│  Street1:                                                     │
│  Street2:                                                     │
│  City: Albany                    State: NY         Zip Code: ─│
│                                                               │
│  Day Telephone:      ··  ··      Fax:      ··  ··             │
│  Night Telephone:    ··  ··                                   │
│                                                               │
│  Original Date:     █            Catalog Numbers:             │
│  Latest Date:                                                 │
│                                                               │
│  Last Order:                     Order:                       │
│  Favored Customer:                                            │
│                                                               │
│  Comm   Save macros to file: C:\QA\QAMACRO.ASC               │
│                                                               │
└─────────────────────────────────────────────────────────────┘
 CUSTOMER.DTF    New Record 1     of 1       Total Records: 27      Page 1  of 2
 If you want to save your macros to disk now, press ENTER. Otherwise, press Esc.
 Esc-Exit                                               ◄─┘ Continue
```

*Figure 12.3    Save the macro to the default macro file*

**309**

## Q Saving a Macro

1. Press Shift-F2.

    Q&A displays the Macro menu.

2. Select Save Macros.

    Q&A displays the Save Macros to File dialog box at the bottom of the screen with the default macro file name in the dialog box.

3. Press Enter.

    Q&A saves the macro to the macro file. If you use the name of an existing macro file, Q&A displays a warning that saving the new macro will overwrite the macros already in the file. □

---

⊘ **Caution:** Never give a macro the same name as a Q&A menu. If you do, Q&A will run the macro rather than the menu.

# Running a Macro

There are three ways to run a macro:

1. By pressing the key combination that you assigned to the macro
2. By choosing Run Macro from the Macro menu
3. By defining a macro as an *autostart macro*

Use an autostart macro at the beginning of every Q&A session. When you define an autostart macro, name it with any key combination ranging from Alt-0 through Alt-9.

To run an autostart macro, type `QA -mn` at the DOS prompt. The letter m in the command indicates that Q&A will run a macro when it starts, and n indicates a number between 0 and 9. For example, if you enter `QA -m5`, Q&A runs the macro associated with the Alt-5 key combination.

**310**

> 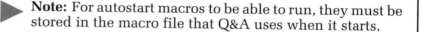 **Note:** For autostart macros to be able to run, they must be stored in the macro file that Q&A uses when it starts.

# Deleting, Getting, and Clearing Macros

The Macro menu also offers quick ways to delete macros, get macros, and clear macros.

To *delete a macro*, select Delete Macro from the Macro menu. Q&A then displays the Macro Names list from which you can select the macro to be deleted.

To *get a macro*, select Get Macros from the Macro menu. Q&A then displays a dialog box containing the name of the current macro file. Press Enter to select this file or enter a macro file name. Q&A puts the macro file into memory, thereby enabling you to use any of the macros in it.

To *clear a macro*, select Clear Macros from the Macro menu. Q&A clears the current macro file, including all its macros, from memory.

# Creating Custom Menus

To fully customize your use of Q&A, you can define custom menus. For example, if you have written several macros to help in data entry for your databases, you can run them from a custom menu. Through the Utilities module, you can even display their names on the Main menu. In addition, you can use custom menus to replace an existing Q&A menu or to fit into a group of custom menus.

You also can create a custom menu to replace a Q&A menu. In this case, give the replacement menu the same name as the original menu that it is replacing.

**311**

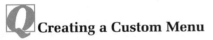 **Creating a Custom Menu**

1. From any screen, press Shift-F2.

   Q&A displays the Macro menu.

2. Select Create Menu.

   Q&A displays the Menu Names list (Figure 12.4). If you haven't designed any custom menus, none are listed.

3. Select New Menu or if other custom menu names are displayed, select a menu name. Press Enter.

   Q&A displays the Macro Menu Options screen (Figure 12.5).                                    □

Another way to define a custom menu is to select File from the Main menu, then Design Menu, Customize Application, and Create Application Menu. You also can use a custom menu to protect a macro file from editing or even viewing.

There are no other macros associated with this database.

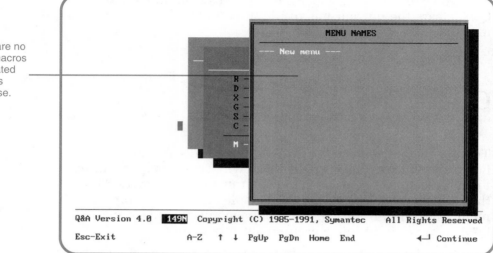

**312**

*Figure 12.4    The Menu Names list displays the names of all the custom menus that you created*

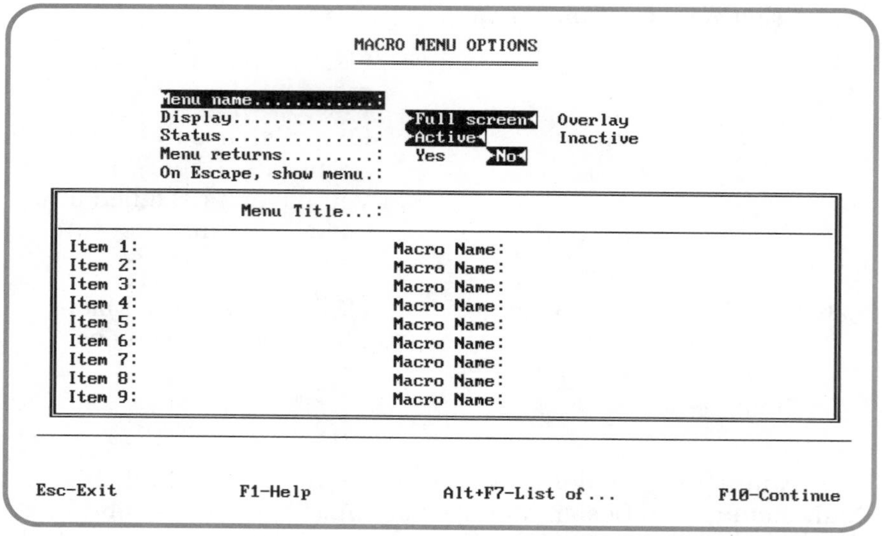

```
                        MACRO MENU OPTIONS


              Menu name............:
              Display..............:   ►Full screen◄   Overlay
              Status...............:   ►Active◄        Inactive
              Menu returns.........:   Yes      ►No◄
              On Escape, show menu.:
          ┌───────────────────────────────────────────────────────┐
          │          Menu Title...:                                │
          │                                                        │
  Item 1:                        Macro Name:
  Item 2:                        Macro Name:
  Item 3:                        Macro Name:
  Item 4:                        Macro Name:
  Item 5:                        Macro Name:
  Item 6:                        Macro Name:
  Item 7:                        Macro Name:
  Item 8:                        Macro Name:
  Item 9:                        Macro Name:



  Esc-Exit          F1-Help            Alt+F7-List of...      F10-Continue
```

*Figure 12.5    Use the Macro Menu Options screen to thoroughly define the custom menu on which you are working*

⊘ **Caution:** If you replace the Q&A Macro menu with a custom menu, the only way you can get to it is by ending your Q&A session and loading another macro file when you start Q&A again. You also can rename the macro file to solve this problem.

# Using the Macro Menu Options Screen

The Macro Menu Options screen offers the following settings for you to fill in.

*Menu name.* When you want a macro to call this menu, this is the name that you enter. Before you assign a name, think of all the implications of using it. If you want to replace a current Q&A menu with this menu, press Alt-F7 to get a list of the menu names.

*Display.* If you specify Full screen, Q&A displays the menu by itself on the screen. If you specify Overlay, Q&A displays this menu over the screen that is currently being displayed.

*Status.* If you specify Active, Q&A displays the menu when it is called by a macro, and can run macros from the menu. Inactive means that the menu is not displayed and Q&A cannot run macros from the menu.

*Menu returns.* If you specify Yes, Q&A displays this menu when the functions performed by the macro end. If you specify No, Q&A returns to a Q&A menu at the end of the macro. At the end of Menu returns, you return to the Q&A Main menu.

⊘ **Caution:** Use Menu Returns with custom menus rather than Q&A menus. You don't want to define a return to the Q&A Main menu when this structure is already built into the Q&A program.

313

*On Escape.* This setting indicates the menu that is displayed if you press the Esc key. You can use this to link several custom menus.

*Menu Title.* Use this area to define the name that is displayed at the top of the menu. The title does not have to be the same name as the Menu Name.

*Item 1 - 9.* Type a brief description of as many as nine options that you want displayed on the menu.

*Macro Name.* For each item, enter the name of the macro that the option will use. If you want to follow the Q&A format, enter a letter, follow it with a space, type a hyphen, follow it with another space, and add a short option name. To get a list of the current macros, highlight this entry and press Alt-F7.

---

 **Caution:** Think carefully before you change the Q&A menus, particularly, the Main menu.

# Creating or Editing a Macro Using Write

You can use Write to edit a macro. Simply select Get from the Write Menu, select the macro, and begin editing. Note that a macro is in ASCII format. Save a macro file by pressing Ctrl-F8.

Follow these rules when using Write to work on a macro:

1. Separate each macro from the next by typing an asterisk (*).
2. Use less than (<) and greater than (>) symbols to define the individual parts of a macro.
3. Don't specify line endings; let Write's word wrap feature work.

Use the order of elements listed in Table 12.1 to create an executable macro.

**Table 12.1   Macro Elements**

| Element | Meaning |
|---|---|
| <begdef> | Beginning of the macro |
| <keystroke ID>\|<nokey> | Key combination naming the macro |
| <name> | Macro name immediately follows |
| "Macro Name" | Macro name |
| <vidon>\|<vidoff> | Q&A does or does not display changes as the macro runs |
| recorded keystrokes | All executable keystrokes, including text |
| "Menu Name" | Menu name when macro ends |
| <wait> | Enter text and press a key (the default is <enter>) |
| <keyname> | Keystroke that ends the <wait> |
| <enddef> | End of the macro |

You also can use Write to edit macros that contain custom menus. Use the order of elements listed in Table 12.2 to define a custom menu.

**Table 12.2   Menu Elements**

| Element | Meaning |
|---|---|
| <begdef> | Beginning of the menu |
| <nokey> | No keystroke |
| <name> | Menu name immediately follows |
| "Menu Name" | Name of the menu |
| <menu> | Menu information immediately follows |
| "Menu Title:FAN: On escape menu/ The item 1, The macro 1/ the item 2, The macro 2/ ...Itemn/Macron" | Menu title, name of On escape menu, menu options, macro names called by each |
| <enddef> | End of the menu |

> ▶ **Tip:** Be sure to enclose all the element from menu title through macro names in quotes. This element can be up to 255 characters and must not include spaces.

When you use Write to edit a macro, there are certain approved keystrokes. When you type the letters A through Z as keys or in combination with Shift, Alt, and Ctrl, approved key codes are, respectively

a through z
A through Z
<alta> through <altz>
<ctrla> through <ctrlz>

When you press F1 through F10 as keys or in combination with Shift, Alt, and Ctrl, approved key codes are, respectively

<f1> through <f10>
<capsf1> through <capsf10>
<altf1> through <altf10>
<ctrlf1> through <ctrlf10>

Table 12.3 lists the remaining macro key codes.

*Table 12.3  Macro Key Codes*

| Key | Shift | Alt | Ctrl |
|-----|-------|-----|------|
| *Shift, Alt, Ctrl Combinations* | | | |
| 1 | ! | <alt1> | |
| 2 | @ | <alt2> | |
| 3 | # | <alt3> | |
| 4 | $ | <alt4> | |
| 5 | % | <alt5> | |
| 6 | ^ | <alt6> | <ctrl6> |

| Key | Shift | Alt | Ctrl |
|---|---|---|---|
| 7 | & | \<alt7> | |
| 8 | * | \<alt8> | |
| 9 | ( | \<alt9> | |
| 0 | ) | \<alt10> | |
| - | _ | | \<ctrl-> |
| = | + | | |
| [ | { | \<esc> | |
| ] | } | | \<ctrl]> |
| ; | : | | |
| ' | " | | |
| ´ | ~ | | |
| \\ | \| | | \<ctrl\\> |
| , | \<caps,> | | |
| . | \<caps.> | | |
| / | ? | | |

| Key | Unshifted | Shift | Ctrl |
|---|---|---|---|

*Unshifted, Shift, Ctrl Combinations*

| Key | Unshifted | Shift | Ctrl |
|---|---|---|---|
| Esc | \<esc> | \<esc> | |
| Tab | \<tab> | \<caps-tab> | |
| Backspace | \<bks> | \<bks> | \<ctrlbks> |
| Enter | \<enter> | \<enter> | \<ctrlent> |
| * | * | * | \<ctrlprt> |
| PrtScr | | | \<ctrlprt> |
| Home | \<home> | | \<ctrlhom> |
| Up | \<up> | | |
| PgUp | \<pgup> | | \<ctrlpgup> |
| Right | \<rgt> | | \<ctrlrgt> |
| Left | \<lft> | | \<ctrllft> |
| End | \<end> | | \<ctrlend> |
| Down | \<dn> | | |
| PgDn | \<pgdn> | | \<ctrlpgdn> |
| Ins | \<ins> | | |
| Del | \<del> | | |

# Programming with Q&A

Q&A provides programming features to use in File and Report. The rest of this chapter is devoted to an overview of Q&A programming.

You can use programming to calculate various formulas, to navigate through a form in your database, and even to look for information outside your database.

## Form Programming

Q&A uses *expressions*, which are formulas or functions that are used to calculate, find, or change a value in a field. There are three types of expressions in Q&A:

1. A *function* is a predefined expression that always starts with the at sign (@).
2. An *expression* is either a mathematical formula or Q&A function.
3. A *statement* is a combination of expressions that also specifies the result of its action.

## Calculating with Field IDs

When you learned about derived columns in Chapter 6, you were introduced to programming. At that time, you identified fields (or columns) by numbers preceded by a pound sign (#). When you use this combination of characters, you are giving a field an ID, or identifier. This is another type of name for a field. A typical programming statement performs a calculation on two values and places the result in a field. In this example,

```
#6 = Order + Last Order
```

#6 is the Field ID into which the sum of Order and Last Order is placed. You can perform many types of calculations using the same sort of format. This example is a *calc* statement. Q&A also has on-entry and on-exit statements.

If you look at the example again, you'll see a plus sign. This is a *mathematical operator*. Table 12.4 is a complete list of Q&A mathematical operators, arranged in the order in which they are executed within a single programming statement. Remember that you can change the order of precedence when you enclose parts of the statement in parentheses.

*Table 12.4  Mathematical Operators*

| Operator | Function |
|----------|----------|
| + | Addition |
| – | Subtraction |
| * | Multiplication |
| / | Division |
| = | Equal to |
| < | Less than |
| > | Greater than |
| <= | Less than or equal to |
| >= | Greater than or equal to |
| <> | Not equal to |
| AND | Both are true |
| OR | One is true |
| NOT | Reverses the values being compared |

The following Quick Steps show you how to enter a form programming statement. When you select a field affected by a programming statement (steps 6 and 7), consider fields referenced by a programming statement or fields that hold programming statements. A typical ID for a field referenced by a programming statement is #5. A typical ID format for a field holding a programming statement is #1 = #6 * .05.

## **Q** Entering a Form Programming Statement

1. From the Main menu, select File.

   Q&A displays the File menu.

2. Select Design File.

   Q&A displays the Design menu.

3. Select Program a File.

   Q&A adds a dialog box to the screen.

4. Enter the name of a database or press Enter for a list of files. After you select a file, press Enter.

   Q&A displays the Programming menu (Figure 12.6).

5. Select Program Form.

   Q&A displays the Program Spec (Figure 12.7).

6. Press any combination of cursor movement keys to move to any field affected by a programming statement. Enter a field ID and, optionally, a programming statement. If the length of the field is too short to hold the statement, press F6.

   Q&A starts the Program Editor, which acts like a small word processor.

7. Optionally, press F8.

   Q&A displays the Entry/Exit Profile box (Figure 12.8).

8. Enter a field number in one or both fields and press F6.

   Q&A saves the information in the Program Editor.

9. Repeat steps 6 through 8 until you have entered the programming statements for the Spec. Then press F10.

   Q&A closes the Program Editor and returns to the Programming menu.

   □

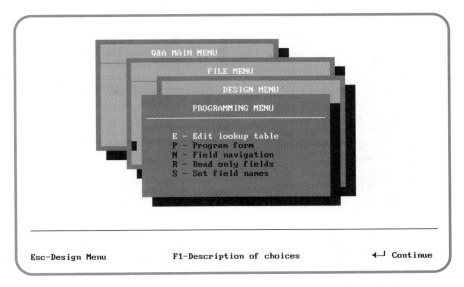

*Figure 12.6   The Programming menu offers several choices*

**321**

> ▶ **Note:** Because the Program Spec and Navigation Spec are independent of each other, you can enter different field IDs for each.

## Using Calc, On-Entry, and On-Exit Programming Statements

Q&A executes calc statements when you press F8 or when you move to the next field in the database. Statements are executed in order of field IDs.

```
ID Number:

First Name:                    Last Name:
Street1:
Street2:
City:                          State:              Zip Code:


Day Telephone:                    Fax:
Night Telephone:

Original Date:      ▮        Catalog Numbers:
Latest Date:

Last Order:                 Order:
Favored Customer:

Comments


CUSTOMER.DTF                Program Spec              Page 1  of 2

Esc-Exit    F1-Help    F2-Print    F3-Clear Spec    F6-Program editor   F10-Continue
```

**Figure 12.7    Enter programming statements into the Program Spec**

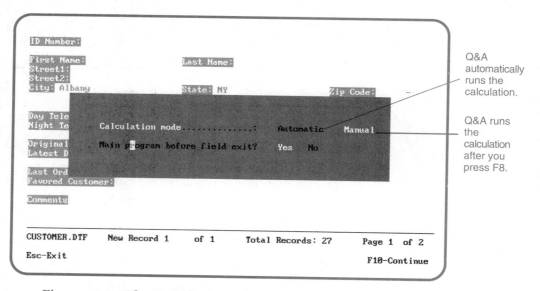

**Figure 12.8    The Entry/Exit Profile box enables you to specify a field in which on-entry or on-exit calculations take place**

On-entry and on-exit statements are executed on entering or exiting a field, respectively. You cannot press F8 to calculate one of these statements. Use them to add or edit information automatically in every field that you add. Unless you add navigation programming statements to a form, these statements are only executed when you move forward from field to field. For example, in the CUSTOMER database, every new customer is not a favored customer. You might want to have a statement that puts an N automatically into that field. Enter

```
Favored Customer:>#170 = "N"
```

to have N automatically placed in the Favored Customer field.

Because calc, on-entry, and on-exit statements are executed at different times, there are occasions when it might be important to change the order of execution (for instance, if one statement depends on the results of another statement). You can only add one on-entry and one on-exit field per record.

**323**

---

Ø **Caution:** If you press Esc to leave a record before completing it, some calculation may have taken place already.

---

## Q Setting Calculation Mode

1. From the Main menu, select File. — Q&A displays the File menu.

2. Select Add Data. — Q&A adds a dialog box to the bottom of the screen.

3. Select a database and press Enter. — Q&A displays a blank record.

4. Press Shift-F8. — Q&A displays a box over the record (Figure 12.9).

5. Select either A (automatic) or M (manual, you must press F8 for calculations to run). Select either Yes or No next to Main Program before Field Exit. — If you select Yes, Q&A sets on-field-exit programming before calc statements. If you select No, Q&A sets on-field-exit programming after calc statements.

6. Press F10. — Q&A saves the changes. □

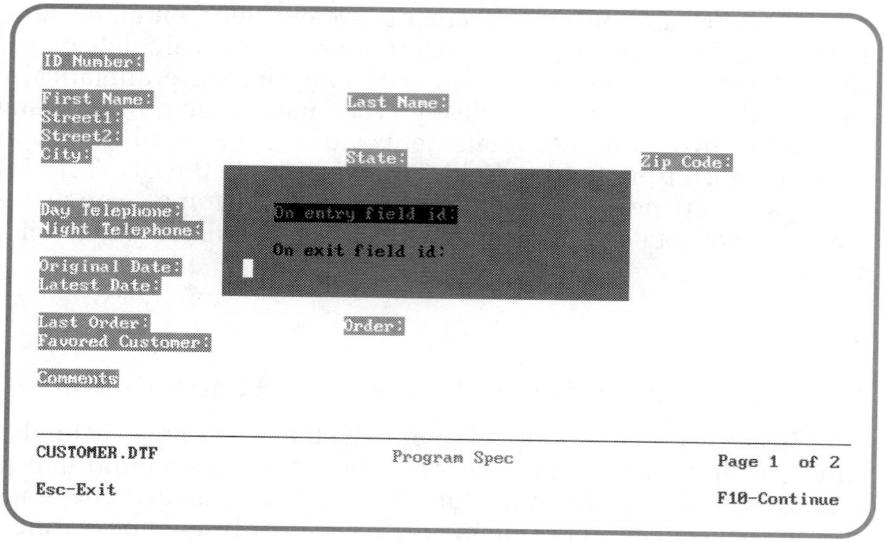

*Figure 12.9   Fill in this box to change the order in which statements are calculated*

## Conditional Statements

Q&A has two conditional statements—IF ... THEN and IF ... THEN ... ELSE.

An IF ... THEN statement tests if a statement is true; if so, another calculation is performed.

An IF ... THEN ... ELSE statement adds a third factor. It tests if a statement is true and if so, a calculation is performed. If not, another calculation is performed.

Either of these statements can test complex formulas.

## Q&A Predefined Functions

Q&A provides a long list of predefined, precalculated programming functions that you can place in a programming statement. For a list of common functions, see Table 12.5.

## Table 12.5  Q&A Programming Functions

| Function | Abbreviation | Description |
| --- | --- | --- |
| @ADD | @AD | Executes the statement only when adding records |
| @AVG(list) | @AV() | Finds the average of the values in the list |
| @DATE | @DA | Return to today's date |
| @DITTO(list) | @DI() | Retrieves the values in the listed fields from the previous record and places them in the same fields of the current record |
| @DOM(n) | @DM(n) | Returns the day of a date n |
| @DOW$(n) | @DW$(n) | Returns the day of the week for a date n |
| @FILENAME | @FN | Returns the name of the current file |
| @GROUP | | Returns the name of the protection group to which the user belongs |
| @HELP(n) | @HP() | Displays the user-defined help screen for field n |
| @LEFT(x,n) | @LT() | Returns the n leftmost characters of the text x |
| @LEN(x) | @LN() | Returns the number of characters in the value in the field x |
| @LOOKUP | | Look up a value in a Lookup Table in this database |
| @MAX(list) | @MX() | Returns the maximum value of the list |
| @MID(x,n,m) | @MD() | Returns m characters from text x starting at n |
| @MIN(list) | @MN() | Returns the minimum value of the list |
| @MONTH$(n) | @MT$(n) | Returns the name of the month for a date n |

**325**

*(continued)*

**Table 12.5    (continued)**

| Function | Abbreviation | Description |
|---|---|---|
| @MONTH(n) | @MT(n) | Returns the month of date n |
| @MSG(x) | | Displays message x on the Message Line |
| @NUM(x) | | Converts the number x to text |
| @Number | @NMB | Returns a unique number that is 1 greater than the last number |
| @Number(n) | @NMB[(n)] | Returns a unique number that is n greater than the last number |
| @RIGHT | @RT | Returns the n rightmost characters of x |
| @ROUND(n,m) | @RND() | Rounds the value of n to m decimal digits |
| @SQRT(n) | @SQ() | Returns the square root of n |
| @STD(list) | | Returns the standard deviation of a list (if a field is blank, it is not considered part of the list) |
| @STR(n) | | Returns the text equivalent of n, to be used in a string expression |
| @SUM(list) | | Adds every value in the list |
| @T(time) | | Interprets the string time as a time |
| @TIME | @TME | Returns the current time |
| @TODATE(x) | @TD() | Converts x to a date |
| @TOMONEY(x) | @TM() | Converts x to money |
| @TONUMBER(x) | @TN() | Converts x to a number |
| @TOTIME(x) | @TT() | Converts x to a time |
| @TOYESNO(x) | @TY() | Converts x to a Yes/No value |
| @UPDATE | @UD | Executes a statement only when updating records |

| Function | Abbreviation | Description |
|---|---|---|
| @USERID | | Returns the value of the User ID of the current user |
| @VAR(list) | | Calculates the variance of the list (if a field is blank, it is not considered part of the list) |
| @WIDTH(n) | @WTH() | Returns an integer, which is the width of the field (not the contents) |
| @XLOOKUP | | Look up a value in an external database |
| @YEAR | @YR(n) | Returns the year of the date n |

Table 12.6 lists examples of programming statements and their meanings.

*Table 12.6   Programming Statement Examples*

| Statement | Meaning |
|---|---|
| #30 = #5/2 | Divide the value in #5 by 2 and put the result into #30. |
| #20 = "nothing" | Put the text "nothing" into #20. |
| #30 = #30 + #20 | Add #30 and #20 and replace the original contents of #30 with the result. |
| #10: #30 = #30 + #20 | The calculation immediately above is taking place in #10, which is probably the first field to be calculated, other than an on-entry statement. |
| #50: IF #10 = "SMITH" AND #20 <= 20000 THEN #60 = #70 * .5 | In field #50, test #10 for a name and #20 to see if the value is less than or equal to a value. If both conditions are true, #70 is multiplied by .5; the results are put in #60. |
| #40: #30 = #30 + #20; #80 = #70 + "APPLE" | Two simple statements in the same field, separated by a semicolon. |

*(continued)*

*Table 12.6   (continued)*

| Statement | Meaning |
|---|---|
| #40: IF NOT #10 < 50 THEN #60 = #30 | If the value in #10 is not less than 50, place the value in #30 into #60. |
| #40 = @DATE + 7 | Today's date and 7 are added; the result is placed in #40. |

## Lookup Commands

Q&A can look up information by using the LOOKUP command for the current database and the XLOOKUP command for an external database.

The LOOKUP statement retrieves information from the Lookup Table and then tells Q&A the field into which the value goes. The format of a LOOKUP statement is

```
LOOKUP (key, column, field)
```

where key is the key information, column is the location on the Lookup Table, and field is the database field that holds the value.

The @LOOKUP function returns information but does not put it into your database. The format of the function is

```
@LOOKUP (key, column)
```

The Lookup Table stores the information that LOOKUP and @LOOKUP need.

The LOOKUPR statement returns the next lower value in the Lookup Table when an exact match isn't found. The format of a LOOKUPR statement is

```
LOOKUPR (key, column, field)
```

This statement must find a match to place a value in the field.

The @LOOKUPR function works in a similar way to the @LOOKUP function, and its format is

```
@LOOKUPR (key, column)
```

You can edit a Lookup Table for any database.

## Editing a Lookup Table

| | | |
|---|---|---|
| 1. | From the Main menu, select File. | Q&A displays the File menu. |
| 2. | Select Design File. | Q&A displays the Design menu. |
| 3. | Select Program a File | Q&A adds a dialog box at the bottom of the screen. |
| 4. | Select a database and press Enter. | Q&A displays the Programming menu. |
| 5. | Select Edit Lookup Table. | Q&A displays the Lookup Table for this database (Figure 12.10). |
| 6. | Fill in a unique key value. Enter values, which do not have to be related, in any of the columns to the right of the key column. If you need more room than the column provides, press F6 to expand the field while you type information. | Q&A returns these values when you use the LOOKUP command. |
| 7. | When you have added all the information that you want to the table, press F10. | Q&A returns you to the Programming menu. |

329

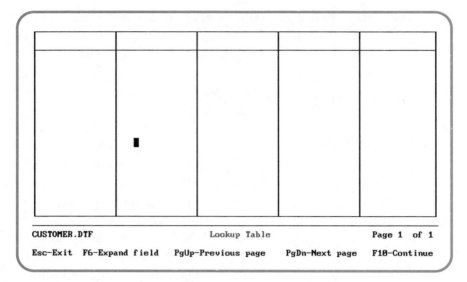

*Figure 12.10   Fill in the Lookup Table so that you can use the LOOKUP command*

The XLOOKUP commands retrieve values from an external Q&A or dBASE database. Q&A matches a key value from the XLOOKUP command with an indexed key field in the external database.

> ▶ **Tip:** To index a field within Q&A, use Speed Up Searches from the Customize menu (see Chapter 3).

The XLOOKUP statement returns a value from an external database and places it in a field in the current database. The format of an XLOOKUP statement is

```
XLOOKUP(fn, key, xkf, lf, df)
```

where fn is the name of the external file, key is the key information, xkf is the key field in the external file, lf is the lookup field in the external file, and df is the destination file in the current database.

If you want to retrieve information from more than one field simultaneously, add pairs of lookup fields and destination fields. For example, if you set up a table containing city, state, and ZIP code (it's best for small cities with one ZIP code), use XLOOKUP to get the information from the external file and place it into your current database. When you are filling in a form, look up the ZIP code in the external file, and Q&A will fill in the form with the city and state information.

The @XLOOKUP function returns information from the external file but does not put it into your database. The format of the function is

```
@XLOOKUP(fn, key, xkf, lf)
```

The XLOOKUPR statement returns the next lower value in the external database when an exact match isn't found. The format of a LOOKUPR statement is

```
XLOOKUPR(fn, key, xkf, lf, df)
```

**331**

## *Navigation Programming*

Navigation commands tell the cursor how to move through a form. You can automate cursor movement, and it does not have to be in the traditional left-to-right, top-to-bottom order. For example, based on a value that you enter in one field, you may want to skip over some fields before you type the next value.

Q&A gives form programming priority over navigation programming. There is one exception to this—if you enter a GOTO command on the Program Spec, Q&A executes it during any form programming.

To enter a navigation programming statement, follow the same Quick Steps given earlier in this chapter for "Entering a Form Programming Statement." There is one difference. In step 5, select Field Navigation. Q&A takes you to the Navigation Spec, and you continue with the rest of the steps.

To execute a navigation statement as the cursor moves into the field, begin the statement with a less than symbol (<). To execute a navigation statement as the cursor moves out of the field, start the statement with a greater than symbol (>). For example, enter `<CHOME` to move the cursor to the first field in the record.

You can use the GOTO command on both the Navigation Spec and the Program Spec. For a complete list of navigation programming commands, see Table 12.7.

Table 12.7   *Navigation Programming Commands*

| Command | Function |
| --- | --- |
| GOTO n | Move to field n, where n is the field ID. |
| CNEXT | Move to next field in order. |
| CPREV | Move to previous field in order. |
| CHOME | Move to first field in the form. |
| CEND | Move to last field in the form. |
| PgDn | Move to first field on the next page of the form. |
| PgUp | Move to last field on the previous page of the form. |

# Using Programming Expressions in Merge Documents

When you use mail merge, you also have the capability of embedding programming expressions in your merge documents in order to further customize the document. The format for using a programming expression is

```
*program { <expression> }*
```

where <expression> is individual or combined functions, field names, and/or field identifiers no longer than 80 characters. Surround the expression with braces ({}), and make sure that an asterisk (*) follows the right brace with no intervening space. Use appropriate functions within a merge document. You cannot use the following Q&A functions within a merge document: @ADD, @DITTO, @HELP (n), @LOOKUP, @MSG (x), @NUMBER, @UPDATE, @XLOOKUP.

# What You Have Learned

▶  Use a macro to combine commands that you regularly use into a single command file.

► As you navigate through the menus, you can have Q&A record your choices and make them into a macro.

► There are three ways to run a macro: by pressing the key combination that you assigned to the macro, by choosing Run Macro from the Macro menu, or by defining a macro as an autostart macro.

► You can define custom menus to enhance Q&A or to replace Q&A menus.

► Q&A provides form programming, which is used to calculate, find, or change values, and navigation programming, which is used to speed your movement through a form.

► Q&A has many predefined functions that you can place in a programming statement.

► Use the LOOKUP commands to find information in the database or in external databases.

**333**

# Installing Q&A

The minimum requirements for installing Q&A are

- ► An IBM PC, PC/XT, PC/AT, PS/2 computer, or 100% compatible personal computer
- ► PC DOS or MS-DOS 2.1 or a more recent version (DOS 3.1 is required for network use and DOS 3.3 is required for PS/2 model computers)
- ► 512K of RAM (640K RAM for DOS 4.0 and for network use)
- ► Expanded memory (EMS) for linking to Structured Query Language (SQL), a standard database-handling language for both mainframes and PCs
- ► Hard disk drive
- ► Floppy disk drive—either 3.5-inch or 5.25-inch, double- or high-density
- ► Monochrome or color monitor

A *kilobyte* is 1,024 bytes; one byte represents one character of information.

*Random access memory* (RAM) is your computer's main memory; your computer uses RAM to run DOS and programs and to store information temporarily. When you turn off your computer, the contents of RAM are deleted.

There are three types of RAM: *conventional*, *extended*, and *expanded*. Conventional memory, which is as much as 1M, is the regular RAM that your computer uses. Extended memory is an extension to conventional memory. Expanded memory requires both a special board and software; it is memory that is separate from conventional and extended memory.

If you plan to use Q&A on a network, each local computer must have 484K.

# Optional Equipment

The following are not required, but are useful additions:

► Most printers, including laser and postscript printers
► Expanded memory
► Microsoft mouse
► Intel Connection Coprocessor and SatisFaxtion fax transmission

**336**

# Protecting Your Software Investment

When you open your Q&A package, you should see either seven 5.25-inch disks or four 3.5-inch disks.

## *Write-Protecting Q&A's Program Disks*

Before you start installation, make sure that all Q&A program disks are *write-protected*, which means that you cannot accidentally copy data onto your installation disks.

To write-protect a 5.25-disk, cover the notch located on the upper right side of the disk with a write-protect tab, a small (approximately $1/4"\times 1/2"$) piece of tape. You can usually find one or two sheets of write-protect tabs in packages of blank disks.

If you don't have any write-protect tabs, you can make them out of masking or electrical tape. Cut a piece of tape just large enough to cover the notch on both sides of the disk. When your computer tries to write to a disk, the disk drive mechanism senses whether the notch is open. If it is open, information can be written; if it is closed, information cannot be written.

On the back of the 3.5-inch disk, there is a small rectangular slot in the corner with a plastic tab that you can slide up and down. To write-protect the disk, slide the plastic tab so that you can see a hole in the rectangular slot. Note that some disks are labeled "Write Protect" and "Write Enable." Make sure that the tab is next to the "Write Protect" label.

# Installing Q&A

The Q&A Installation program is menu-driven and well documented. Simply follow the prompts throughout the installation process. You should not install Q&A on your root directory (\) or the \DOS directory. It is better to put it into its own uniquely named directory.

337

> ▶ **Tip:** If you have an old version of Q&A on your computer, before you start installation you should backup (make copies of) all Q&A data, word processing, and label files.

C: is the most popular, but not universally used, hard drive identifier. For example, if your hard drive is *partitioned*, or subdivided, into three areas, you may have C:, D:, and E: hard drives. If Q&A is on the D: drive, you need to get to D: to use it.

If you have 5.25-inch Q&A program disks, you have to use a 5.25-inch drive for installation; if you have 3.5-inch disks, use a 3.5-inch drive. If your computer has two disk drives, they are probably called A: and B:. If you don't know your disk drive identifiers, insert write-protected disks, which are the appropriate size, in each drive. Then type the DOS command, `DIR A:`, and press Enter. (If a disk drive is empty when you press Enter, DOS displays an error message. Press F to get back to the DOS prompt.) You will see a light on the front of the A: drive. Then type `DIR B:`; this time the light identifies the B: drive. Although Q&A senses your computer's disk drives during installation, you have to identify the source drive (into which you insert the installation disks and from which Q&A is installed) and the destination drive.

**Installing Q&A**

1. Turn on your computer and wait until you see the DOS prompt (usually `C:\`) on the computer screen. If you have Windows or DOS 4.0 (or greater), you have to move through at least one menu to get to the DOS prompt. For more information about this, see Chapter 1. If your computer has more than one hard drive and Q&A is not on the active drive, type the drive name you need.

   The prompt indicates that your hard drive is active.

2. Insert the Q&A Installation Disk into one of your computer's floppy disk drives. If the drive holds a 5.25-inch disk, close the disk drive door. If the drive holds a 3.5-inch disk, there is no door to close. Type `x:INSTALL` (where x represents the source drive name) and press Enter.

   The Install program starts. After the welcome screen, Q&A displays the names of all disk and hard drives found on your computer and asks you to identify your source drive.

3. Move the cursor to the name of the source disk drive and press Enter.

   Q&A asks you to identify your destination drive, the drive on which you are installing Q&A.

4. Move the cursor to the name of the destination hard drive and press Enter.

   The Install program checks your hard drive to make sure that there is enough space to completely install Q&A, and for any version of Q&A on your computer. If the Install program finds a copy of Q&A, you may replace the old copy or put the new version in a different directory whose name Q&A suggests. If the Install program does not find a copy of Q&A, it suggests the name of a directory in which to install Q&A.

5. If you want to accept the suggested directory name, press Enter.

The Install program gives you the chance to use a directory name other than the one that it suggests.

6. If you want to enter a different directory name (either new or any existing directory), press the Spacebar key to erase the suggested name, type in a new name, and then press Enter.

After you have decided where to install Q&A, the Install program asks you what sort of installation you want—Complete or Selective.

**339**

7. If you are installing Q&A for the first time or want to completely reinstall the program, highlight Complete Installation. If you need to reinstall a single file or a group of files, highlight Selective Installation.

When you select Complete Installation, Q&A copies the new program files over the old. Nonprogram files (such as data files or word processing files) in the Q&A directory are not affected.

8. Follow the prompts and insert a new disk every time you are prompted.

The Install program tells you the name of each file as it is installed. It also displays a horizontal bar that shows you the progress it is making in the installation of that file. If you inadvertently insert the wrong disk during installation, Q&A prompts you with the name of the appropriate disk. When installation is successfully

completed, Q&A displays
the message, `Installation
of Program Files
Successfully Completed.`
Before you can start your
first Q&A session, you are
offered some options.

9. If your printer has fonts
   and if you want to use
   fonts with Q&A, install
   font description files.
   Install tutorial files to run
   Q&A and utilize databases
   that Q&A developers
   created.

Q&A installs the files you
choose.

**340**

10. If your computer has
    extended memory, you
    may want to install the
    extended memory driver.
    If your computer printer
    is equipped with fonts,
    you may want to install
    the font conversion utility.
    During installation, if you
    need to go back to a prior
    screen, press the Esc key.
    If you decide to stop the
    installation before it
    finishes, hold down the
    Alt key and then press
    the X key simultaneously.

The message, `!!
Installation Successful !!`
is displayed.

## Installing Printers

Q&A allows you to install as many as five printers. The program not
only supports both parallel and serial printers but also fax boards
(through an Intel Fax Connection Coprocessor). If you don't install
a printer, you are prompted to do so when you start Q&A the first
time. Before you install a printer or fax, you need to know

► The port to which each printer is attached
► The manufacturer of each printer
► The model of each printer

The LPT and COM options refer to the types of printer ports on your computer. Choose an LPT option for a parallel printer; choose a COM option for a serial printer. If you don't know what port to select, try LPT1 first. If you aren't sure if your printer is parallel or serial, refer to its manual, or ask your dealer.

## Installing Printers

1. If you aren't in the Q&A directory, change to it by typing CD \QA (where QA represents the name of the directory in which you installed the program).

   You are now in the Q&A directory.

2. Start Q&A by typing QA.

   The Title screen is displayed, followed by the Main menu.

3. Select Utilities and press Enter.

   The Utilities menu is displayed.

4. Select the Install Printer option by pressing P and then Enter.

   The Printer Selection screen is displayed.

5. Press any combination of Up or Down keys until you highlight the printer port; then press Enter.

   Names of printer manufacturers are displayed.

6. Move the selection bar until the name of your printer's manufacturer is highlighted. Press PgDn if you don't see the name on the first screen. After selecting a name, press Enter. If you don't see the name of your printer's manufacturer, look in your printer's reference guide for names of printers with which it is compatible.

   Names of models for that manufacturer are displayed.

**341**

7. Move the selection bar until the model name is highlighted. Press Enter.

Your first printer is now installed. You are given the choice of whether to install another printer.

8. If your printer has two modes (such as draft quality and near letter quality), it is a good idea to install it as two printers, for example, PtrA and PtrB. Then you can print in both modes by switching between PtrA and PtrB. If you want to install another printer, move the selection bar to Y = Yes and press Enter, and repeat steps 5 through 7. If you don't want to install another printer, move the selection bar to N = No and press Enter.

You are automatically returned to the Utilities menu.

**342**

9. Press Esc.

You are returned to the Main menu.

10. If you want to start working with Q&A, choose a function from the Main menu.

You are now in Q&A.

11. If you want to exit Q&A, press X.

You are now out of Q&A.

☐

During printer installation, you also had the opportunity to display the Special Printer Options screen. For information about the available printer options, refer to Chapter 11.

*Appendix B*

# Q&A Database Security



If you are working for a small company or even for yourself, you should ensure that at least some of your databases are not accessible by others and that all databases are protected from loss of data and other damage. Although you should protect all your databases (for example, by backing up data regularly), plan to protect some databases more stringently. Examples of these types of databases are those that hold confidential information—customer credit card numbers or employee earnings, for example.

In addition, you may not want others to modify your database without your knowledge or permission. When many users can access and/or change the same database, data integrity becomes very important.

Security is the act of keeping data safe. Use Q&A security features to protect your information.

## Locking Files and Records

A database administrator is the individual who manages and maintains the database. When you are the only person creating and maintaining databases, you serve as your own database administrator. In a small department, one person should be placed in charge of

343

security. This person decides who is allowed access to each database by assigning each user ID (unique user identification) the starting password (the secret word by which a user is identified to the database).

If the company is small, the database administrator might have to decide what a user ID looks like—for example, all first names, nicknames, last names, or a combination of letters and numbers.

The database administrator can also delete, copy, or rename a user ID, and decide what access each user can have within databases. For example, the administrator can decide whether an individual is allowed to enter data, redesign databases, or perform mass updates and/or deletions. Table B.1 lists access rights fields.

*Table B.1    Access Rights Fields*

| Field | Extent of Access |
| --- | --- |
| Can assign password rights? | The right to define a user to the security system, thereby allowing the user to obtain a password and to utilize some or all parts of this database; at least one user must have this access (for administrative use only!) |
| Can change design and program? | The right to allow a user to redesign, program, customize, or secure this database (for administrative use only!) |
| Can mass delete? | The right to either remove selected or duplicate records |
| Can delete individual records? | The right to delete a record by pressing F3 when viewing a form |
| Can run mass update? | The right to change more than two forms simultaneously |
| Can design/redesign reports? | The right to design or redesign a report (a user who is denied this right can still print reports and make temporary changes to reports) |
| Can enter/edit data? | The right to enter data or edit a field |

The administrator defines security for one database at a time. One database might be protected in every way possible, but another left totally unprotected. Two secured databases might have two different lists of user IDs and two different levels of protection.

The first user ID defined to the system should be that of the administrator.

## Q Assigning or Changing Access Rights

1. Choose File from the Main menu.

   Q&A displays the File menu.

2. Choose Design File.

   Q&A displays the Design menu.

3. Select Secure a File.

   Q&A adds a dialog box to the screen. If you have worked on a database during this session, its name appears in the dialog box.

4. If you want to secure the file whose name is in the dialog box, press Enter. If there is no file name in the dialog box and you want to see a list of names for the current directory, press Enter. If you want to enter a specific file name, do so and press Enter.

   Q&A displays the Security menu.

5. Choose Assign Access Rights.

   Q&A displays the List of Users/Groups screen.

6. Enter a unique user identification, which can be up to 20 characters long, and press Enter. You can also use this screen to change an existing user ID or identify that user's access rights.

   Q&A recognizes your ID and displays the Access Control screen.

**345**

7. Enter a password, which can be up to 10 characters long, and press Enter. This is the password that the user starts with. During the user's first session using this protected database, he or she should create a new password. You can also accept the initial password that Q&A displays in the Initial Password field—PASSWORD.

If you are the administrator who is accessing information for that user ID, you see a line of asterisks (*) rather than a password for that individual; Q&A does not display that individual's password.

**346**

8. Tab through the access rights fields; for each field, either select Yes to indicate that this person has the right to access this Q&A option or No to deny this person access to this Q&A option. Press F10.

Q&A issues a message that the user ID has been saved and offers you the choice of editing (or adding) another user ID.

9. If you decide to edit (or add) another user ID, answer Yes.

Q&A returns you to the List of Users/Groups.

10. If you decide to stop editing, answer No.

Q&A returns you to the Security menu.         □

Once the user IDs are identified and assigned, the database administrator can delete, copy, or rename them.

## Deleting, Copying, or Renaming a User ID

1. Choose File from the Main menu.

Q&A displays the File menu.

2. Choose Design File.

Q&A displays the Design menu.

3. Select Secure a File.

Q&A adds a dialog box to the screen. If you have worked on a database during this session, its name appears in the dialog box.

4. If you want to secure the file whose name is in the dialog box, press Enter. If there is no file name in the dialog box and you want to see a list of names for the current directory, press Enter. If you want to enter a specific file name, do so and press Enter.

Q&A displays the Security menu.

5. Choose Assign Access Rights.

Q&A displays the List of Users/Groups screen.

6. To delete a user ID, enter the user ID to be deleted or move the highlight to that user ID on the list, and press F3.

Q&A issues a warning that if you continue, the user ID will be deleted; the program allows you to decide whether to continue.

**347**

7. Respond to the prompt and press F10.

Q&A tells you that the user ID is deleted.

8. To copy a user ID, enter the user ID to be copied or move the highlight to that user ID on the list, and press F5.

Q&A prompts you to enter the new user ID.

9. Enter a new user ID and press F10.

Q&A registers the new ID.

10. To rename a user ID, enter the user ID to be renamed or move the highlight to that user ID on the list, and press F8.

Q&A prompts you to enter the new user ID.

11. Enter a new user ID and press F10.

Q&A replaces the old user ID on the list with the new one (the list is arranged in alphabetical order). □

While working in a protected database, a user can change his or her password.

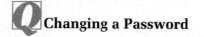

## Changing a Password

1. Start Q&A and access a restricted database.

   Q&A displays a dialog box on the screen before you are allowed to use the database.

2. Enter your user ID. Press F8.

   The dialog box changes and Q&A issues a prompt.

3. Enter your user ID again and press Enter, enter your old password and press Enter, and enter the new password and press Enter. Then press F10 to continue.

   As you type your new password, you can see it on the screen.

4. Check and then correct the new password for any errors. Press F10.

   From now on, if you are the administrator, you will see asterisks in the Initial Password field when you look at the Access Control screen. □

**348**

# Accessing a Secure Database

To access a secured database, a user must type a user ID and password (in either upper- or lowercase) in a dialog box. When the user types the password, it does not appear on the screen.

If the user is denied the right to access this database, the computer issues a beep when the user presses Enter or F10 to continue. The user is allowed to press Esc to return to the previous screen.

If a user wants to enter his or her user ID and password once in a Q&A session, he or she can press F6 at the Main menu.

You can clear out the current user ID and password. This is useful if you want to leave your machine without exiting Q&A and ensure that no one can access your data while you are away. To clear your user ID and password, go to the Main menu and press Shift-F6.

You may forget your password, which means that you no longer have access to your database. If this occurs, the database administrator can give you a new password.

---

⊘ **Caution:** If you are the database administrator and forget your password, you must send your database files to Symantec, so that your password can be reset. This costs $50.00!

---

# Removing Protection from a Database

You can remove the protection from a database by deleting all the users named on the List of Users/Groups screen. This removes the Access Control Form for each user. When the last ID is removed, Q&A displays a message stating that the database is not protected. If you remove a protected database, all user IDs and associated passwords remain.

**349**

# Assigning Security for a Selected Field

You can protect a database on a field-by-field basis. Users who are not assigned to a Field Security Spec can see and edit all the fields in a database. The only users that you can add to the Field Security Spec are those who do not have the right to assign passwords and those who cannot change the database design and program. You can create a maximum of eight Field Security Specs for each database.

*Q* **Creating or Editing a Field Security Spec**

1. Choose File from the Main menu.

   Q&A displays the File menu.

2. Choose Design File.

   Q&A displays the Design menu.

3. Choose Secure a File.

   Q&A adds a dialog box to the Design menu.

**350**

4. If you want to secure the file whose name is in the dialog box, press Enter. If you have secured this file and have not entered your user ID and password, Q&A prompts you to enter a user ID and password. If there is no file name in the dialog box and you want to see a list of names for the current directory, press Enter. If you want to enter a specific file name, do so and press Enter.

After you have entered a valid user ID and password, Q&A displays the Security menu.

5. Select Field Level Security.

Q&A displays the List of Field Security Specs screen.

6. Type a field security spec name, which is up to 31 characters long and describes the type of restrictions—for example, `no credit info`. Press F10.

Q&A displays the User Selection screen.

7. Assign the field security spec, which is named at the bottom of the screen, to one or more users or groups—the same user IDs that you previously defined on the List of Users/Groups screen.

Q&A issues a warning if you try to change access to user IDs already added to the User Selection screen.

8. If you want to see a list of user IDs for this database, press Alt-F7. You can fill in up to five User Selection screens with valid user IDs.

If there are no users identified to this database, Q&A tells you. Any valid user IDs are displayed. Users who have either Password rights or Change Design and Program rights set to Yes are not on this list. If you already have other Field Restriction Specs, users assigned to them are not on the list for the new spec.

9. If you want to edit an existing field security spec, highlight the name, and press Enter or F10 to open the field.

The protection code is displayed next to each field name. (See Table B.2 for protection codes.)

10. Press cursor movement keys to move around the fields to add or change protection codes. Press F3 or Esc.

All protection codes are removed from the Field Security Spec. If you press F3, Q&A clears all codes. If you press Esc, you return to the list of field security specs.

11. When you have finished, press F10.

Q&A displays the User/ Group selection profile for this spec. ☐

**351**

*Table B.2   Protection Codes*

| Code | Meaning | Description |
|------|---------|-------------|
| W | Read and write | The user can read from and write to this field. This is the default. |
| R | Read only | The user can read from this field but cannot write to it. |
| N | No access | The user is not allowed to read from or write to this field. |

# Set XLOOKUP Password

Use the XLOOKUP option to ensure that only those users who know a default password can gain access to protected external databases from the current database. This default password is used if the user's regular password is not valid for the external file.

See Chapter 12 for more information about the XLOOKUP statement and @XLOOKUP function.

## Setting an XLOOKUP Password

1. Choose File from the Main menu.

   Q&A displays the File menu.

2. Choose Design File.

   Q&A displays the Design menu.

3. Choose Secure a File.

   Q&A adds a dialog box to the Design menu.

4. If you want to secure the file whose name is in the dialog box, press Enter. If you have secured this file and have not entered your user ID and password, Q&A prompts you to enter a user ID and password. If there is no file name in the dialog box and you want to see a list of names for the current directory, press Enter. If you want to enter a specific file name, do so and press Enter.

   After you have entered a valid user ID and password, Q&A displays the Security menu.

5. Choose Set XLOOKUP Password.

   Q&A displays the Set XLOOKUP Password screen.

6. Enter your user ID and password, pressing Enter after each entry.

   Both entries appear on the screen.

7. Press F10.

   Q&A returns you to the Security menu.  □

If an XLOOKUP programming statement tries to access an external database field that does not acknowledge the validity of either the user or XLOOKUP password, Q&A displays an error message and does not continue trying to access the field.

*Appendix C*

# Using Q&A on a Network

353

As more people use personal computers, the use of networks is also increasing. Q&A is designed so that you can use it on networks such as 3Com's 3Plus, Novell's NetWare, Torus Tapestry, and IBM's PC Network and Token Ring Lan.

## What Is a Network?

A local area network (LAN) connects two or more personal computers that are located in the same room or building. Many networks have a central server, which is a personal computer, minicomputer, or mainframe; the server may also be connected to one or more printers and other computer peripherals. Each personal computer in a network has a means of connecting to the network—a network board in the PC and cables that run between the PC and the server.

There are three ways of using Q&A on a network:

1. Each user has a copy of Q&A on his or her computer, and there is a single copy of Q&A on the network.
2. Each user has an installed copy of Q&A.
3. The network has Q&A Network Pack.

If each user has an installed copy of Q&A, he or she can use Q&A as a single user but can use the networked equipment for other services—storage or printers, for example.

If Q&A is installed on a network file-server (software that manages the network, stores all the network files, and sends files to be printed to the network printer), only one user at a time can access the program.

If the network has the Q&A Network Pack, which converts your copy of Q&A to a multiuser version, as many as three users can access Q&A simultaneously. You can add more users by adding more Network Packs to the network. This is the only way for several users to access Q&A at the same time.

The Network Pack does not contain the basic Q&A software.

## 354    Locking Databases, Records, and Commands for Multiple Users

Q&A allows specific databases, records, and commands to be secured in various ways. In multiuser systems, only one user at a time has the right to change files, although others can look at the contents of a file. Q&A only allows one authorized person at a time to redesign a database. For more information about database security, refer to Appendix B.

## Accessing a Networked Database

Single-user and multiuser access to Q&A commands for either shared or locked files is categorized as shown in Tables C.1, C.2, and C.3.

Q&A allows more than one user at a time to use any of the commands listed in Table C.1.

*Table C.1    Shared File/Multiuser Commands*

| Module | Command |
|--------|---------|
| File | Search/Update |
|  | Add Data |
|  | Table View |
|  | Form Printing |
| Report | Report Printing |
| IA | Search/Update |
|  | Add Data |
|  | Report Printing |
| Write | Mail Merge |
| Utilities | Import/Export |
| Other | Macros |

The first user to retrieve a record when using Search/Update is the only user who can write to the record; all other users can only read the record.

During the time that a user is writing to a record in Table View, that record is locked to other users.

When there is a print request for reports, forms, mailing labels, or mail merge, Q&A takes a *snapshot* of the file at the time of the request. A snapshot is the exact information in each record at the time of the request; all changes to the file subsequent to the request are not included in the "image" of the file. In other words, users can keep working on the database regardless of the print request.

If two users are trying to write to a record, the first user that started to write is successful; Q&A issues a message to the second user stating that he or she can only read the record at this time.

If you have not set the network ID in the Utilities Set Global Defaults, Q&A advises you that the network ID is not set.

When a database is shared, only one user at a time can use the commands listed in Table C.2.

**355**

*Table C.2    Shared File/Single-User Commands*

| Module | Command |
|--------|---------|
| File   | Design Print Spec |
|        | Assign Password/Rights |
|        | Named Specs |
| Report | Design Report |
| IA     | Teach |

If one user tries to use any of the commands in Table C.2 while another user is using the same command, Q&A issues a message stating that the function is already in use.

When a user issues one of the commands listed in Table C.3, all other users, even those normally granted access, are denied use of the command.

**356**

*Table C.3    Locked File/Single-User Commands*

| Module | Command |
|--------|---------|
| File   | Redesign |
|        | Customize |
|        | Copy/Design Forms |
|        | Mass Update |
|        | Posting |
|        | Remove Records |
|        | Delete Duplicate Records |
| IA     | Teach |
|        | Mass Update |
| Query Guide | Teach |
| Utilities | DOS commands |

# Specifying File-Sharing Mode

Q&A determines whether a database is stored on a remote, dedicated server; if so, Q&A selects the file-sharing mode. You can override the mode.

## Q Declaring a File-Sharing Mode

1. Choose File from the Main menu.

   Q&A displays the File menu.

2. Choose Design File.

   Q&A displays the Design menu.

3. Choose Secure a File.

   Q&A adds a dialog box to the Design menu.

4. If you want to secure the file whose name is in the dialog box, press Enter. If you have secured this file and have not entered your user ID and password, do so. If there is no file name in the dialog box and you want to see a list of names for the current directory, press Enter. If you want to enter a specific file name, do so and press Enter.

   After you have entered a valid user ID and password, Q&A displays the Security menu.

5. Choose Declare Sharing mode.

   Q&A displays these choices: Automatic, Disallow, and Allow.

6. Highlight a mode in order to choose it. Then press F10 to save the setting.

   Q&A saves the setting you selected.                           □

**357**

With *Automatic* mode, Q&A finds whether the database file is stored on a dedicated network file-server, that is, one whose only function is file-server. If it is, Q&A automatically lets multiple users share this file; otherwise, Q&A does not allow simultaneous sharing. This mode is the best choice for most users.

*Disallow* enables only one user at a time to access and use the database, whether or not the file is on a network.

*Allow* enables multiuser access of the database, whether or not the file is on a network. This mode is appropriate for use on a nondedicated or distributed network.

Networks such as TOPS and LANtastic must be running under Allow mode.

A file that accesses multiusers using XLOOKUP operations should be set to Allow; otherwise, the mode can be either Allow or Disallow.

If you set the sharing mode to Allow for a network-based database that is subsequently moved off the network, you cannot access the database until you run the DOS SHARE command. For information about this command, see your DOS reference manual.

**358**

# Index

359

**361**

**362**

**363**

**364**

**365**

**366**

**367**

**369**

**371**

**373**

374

**375**

**S**

**378**

**379**

**380**

# Sams—Covering The Latest In Computer And Technical Topics!

# Sams' Series Puts You "In Business"

The *In Business* books have been specially designed to help business users increase their productivity and efficiency. Each book comes with a companion disk that contains templates for common business tasks, as well as tear-out quick references for common commands. In addition, the books feature Business Shortcuts—boxed notes and tips on how to improve the performance of the software. Regardless of the size of the business or the level of user, these books will teach you how to get the most out of your business applications.

**Quattro Pro In Business**
*Chris Van Buren*
400 pages, 73/8 x 91/4, $29.95 USA
**0-672-22793-2**

**Lotus 1-2-3 In Business**
*Michael Griffin*
400 pages, 73/8 x 91/4, $29.95 USA
**0-672-22803-3**

**Q&A In Business**
*David B. Adams*
400 pages, 73/8 x 91/4, $29.95 USA
**0-672-22801-7**

**WordPerfect In Business**
*Neil Salkind*
400 pages, 73/8 x 91/4, $29.95 USA
**0-672-22795-9**

# Sams' First Books Get You Started Fast!

*"The First Book Series ... is intended to get the novice off to a good start, whether with computers in general or with particular programs ...."*

**The New York Times**

The First Book of WordPerfect 5.1
*Kate Miller Barnes*
275 pages, 7 3/8 x 9 1/4, $16.95 USA
0-672-27307-1

## Look For These Books In Sams' First Book Series

**The First Book of C**
*Charles Ackerman*
300 pages, 7 3/8 x 9 1/4 $16.95 USA
0-672-27354-3

**The First Book of dBASE IV 1.1**
*Steven Currie*
300 pages, 7 3/8 x 9 1/4, $16.95 USA
0-672-27342-X

**The First Book of DeskMate**
*Jack Nimersheim*
315 pages, 7 3/8 x 9 1/4, $16.95 USA
0-672-27314-4

**The First Book of DrawPerfect**
*Susan Baake Kelly & James Kevin Kelly*
340 pages, 7 3/8 x 9 1/4, $16.95 USA
0-672-27315-2

**The First Book of Fastback Plus**
*Jonathan Kamin*
275 pages, 7 3/8 x 9 1/4, $16.95 USA
0-672-27323-3

**The First Book of GW-BASIC**
*Saul Aguiar & The Coriolis Group*
275 ppages, 7 3/8 x 9 1/4, $16.95 USA
0-672-27316-0

**The First Book of Harvard Graphics**
*Jack Purdum*
300 pages, 7 3/8 x 9 1/4, $16.95 USA
0-672-27310-1

**The First Book of Lotus 1-2-3/G**
*Peter Aitken*
350 pages, 7 3/8 x 9 1/4, $16.95 USA
0-672-27293-8

**The First Book of Lotus 1-2-3 Release 2.2**
*Alan Simpson & Paul Lichtman*
275 pages, 7 3/8 x 9 1/4, $16.95 USA
0-672-27301-2

**The First Book of Microsoft Excel for the PC**
*Chris Van Buren*
275 pages, 7 3/8 x 9 1/4, $16.95 USA
0-672-27322-5

**TheFirst Book of Microsoft QuickPascal**
*Elna R. Tymes & Fred Waters*
275 pages, 7 3/8 x 9 1/4, $16.95 USA
0-672-27294-6

**The First Book of Microsoft Windows 3**
*Jack Nimersheim*
275 pages, 7 3/8 x 9 1/4, $16.95 USA
0-672-27334-9

**The First Book of Microsoft Word 5.5, Second Edition**
*Brent Heslop & David Angell*
320 pages, 7 3/8 x 9 1/4, $16.95 USA
0-672-27333-0

**The First Book of Microsoft Word for Windows**
*Brent Heslop & David Angell*
304 pages, 7 3/8 x 9 1/4, $16.95 USA
0-672-27332-2

**The First Book of MS-DOS**
*Jack Nimersheim*
272 pages, 7 3/8 x 9 1/4, $16.95 USA
0-672-27312-8

**The First Book of MS-DOS 5**
*Jack Nimersheim*
275 pages, 7 3/8 x 9 1/4, $16.95 USA
0-672-27341-1

**The First Book of Norton Uttilities**
*Joseph Wikert*
275 pages, 7 3/8 x 9 1/4, $16.95 USA
0-672-27308-X

**The First Book of Paradox 3**
*Jonathan Kamin*
275 pages, 7 3/8 x 9 1/4, $16.95 USA
0-672-27300-4

**The First Book of PC-Write**
*Rebecca Kenyon, Ph.D.*
350 pages, 7 3/8 x 9 1/4, $16.95 USA
0-672-27320-9

**The First Book of PC Paintbrush**
*Deke McClelland*
289 pages, 7 3/8 x 9 1/4, $16.95 USA
0-672-27324-1

**The First Book of PFS: First Publisher**
*Karen Brown & Robert Bixby*
308 pages, 7 3/8 x 9 1/4, $16.95 USA
0-672-27326-8

**The First Book of PC Tools Deluxe, Second Edition**
*Gordon McComb*
304 pages, 7 3/8 x 9 1/4, $16.95 USA
0-672-27329-2

**The First Book of Personal Computing**
*W.E. Wang & Joe Kraynak*
275 pages, 7 3/8 x 9 1/4, $16.95 USA
0-672-27313-6

**The First Book of PROCOMM PLUS**
*Jack Nimersheim*
250 pages, 7 3/8 x 9 1/4, $16.95 USA
0-672-27309-8

**The First Book of PS/1**
*Kate Barnes*
300 pages, 7 3/8 x 9 1/4, $16.95 USA
0-672-27346-2

**The First Book of Q&A**
*Brent Heslop & David Angell*
275 pages, 7 3/8 x 9 1/4, $16.95 USA
0-672-27311-X

**The First Book of Quattro Pro**
*Patrick Burns*
300 pages, 7 3/8 x 9 1/4, $16.95 USA
0-672-27345-4

**The First Book of Quicken in Busines**
*Gordon McComb*
300 pages, 7 3/8 x 9 1/4, $16.95 USA
0-672-27331-4

**The First Book of UNIX**
*Doglas Topham*
300 pages, 7 3/8 x 9 1/4, $16.95 USA
0-672-27299-7

**The First Book of WordPerfect Office**
*Sams*
275 pages, 7 3/8 x 9 1/4, $16.95 USA
0-672-27317-9

**To order books, call 1-800-257-5755.
For More Information, call 1-800-628-7360.**

# Reader Feedback Card

Thank you for purchasing this book from SAMS FIRST BOOK series. Our intent with this series is to bring you timely, authoritative information that you can reference quickly and easily. You can help us by taking a minute to complete and return this card. We appreciate your comments and will use the information to better serve your needs.

1. Where did you purchase this book?

☐ Chain bookstore (Walden, B. Dalton)  ☐ Direct mail
☐ Independent bookstore  ☐ Book club
☐ Computer/Software store  ☐ School bookstore
☐ Other _____

_____

2. Why did you choose this book? (Check as many as apply.)

☐ ·Price  ☐ Appearance of book
☐ Author's reputation  ☐ SAMS' reputation
☐ Quick and easy treatment of subject  ☐ Only book available on subject

3. How do you use this book? (Check as many as apply.)

☐ As a supplement to the product manual  ☐ As a reference
☐ In place of the product manual  ☐ At home
☐ For self-instruction  ☐ At work

4. Please rate this book in the categories below. G = Good; N = Needs improvement; U = Category is unimportant.

☐ Price  ☐ Appearance
☐ Amount of information  ☐ Accuracy
☐ Examples  ☐ Quick Steps
☐ Inside cover reference  ☐ Second color
☐ Table of contents  ☐ Index
☐ Tips and cautions  ☐ Illustrations
☐ Length of book
☐ How can we improve this book?_____
☐ _____

5. How many computer books do you normally buy in a year?

☐ 1–5  ☐ 5–10  ☐ More than 10
☐ I rarely purchase more than one book on a subject.
☐ I may purchase a beginning and an advanced book on the same subject.
☐ I may purchase several books on particular subjects.
☐ (such as _____ )

6. Have your purchased other SAMS or Hayden books in the past year? _____
If yes, how many _____

7. Would you purchase another book in the FIRST BOOK series? _____

8. What are your primary areas of interest in business software? _____

☐ Word processing (particularly _____ )
☐ Spreadsheet (particularly _____ )
☐ Database (particularly _____ )
☐ Graphics (particularly _____ )
☐ Personal finance/accounting (particularly _____ )
☐ Other (please specify _____ )

Other comments on this book or the SAMS' book line: _____
_____

Name _____
Company _____
Address _____
City _____ State _____ Zip_____
Daytime telephone number _____
Title of this book _____

Fold here
- - - - - - - - - - - - - - - - - - - - - - - - - - - - - - - - - - - - - - - - - - - - - - - -